THE LIMITS OF NATIONAL LIBERATION

The Limits of National Liberation

Problems of economic management in the Democratic
Republic of Vietnam, with a Statistical Appendix

ADAM FFORDE and SUZANNE H. PAINE

CROOM HELM
London • New York • Sydney

© 1987 Adam Fforde and Suzanne H. Paine
Croom Helm Ltd, Provident House, Burrell Row,
Beckenham, Kent, BR3 1AT
Croom Helm Australia, 44-50 Waterloo Road,
North Ryde, 2113, New South Wales

British Library Cataloguing in Publication Data
Fforde, Adam
  The limits of national liberation.
  1. North Vietnam — Economic conditions
  I. Title II. Paine, Suzanne H.
  330.9597'04   HC444
  ISBN 0-7099-1036-3

Published in the USA by
Croom Helm
in association with Methuen, Inc.
29 West 35th Street
New York, NY 10001

Library of Congress Cataloging-in-Publication Data
Fforde, Adam.
  The limits of national liberation.

  Bibliography: p.
  1. Vietnam (Democratic Republic) — Economic policy.
2. Vietnam (Democratic Republic) — Economic conditions.
I. Paine, Suzanne. II. Title.
HC444.F46 1987   338.9597   87-8977
ISBN 0-7099-1036-3

Printed and bound in Great Britain
by Billing & Sons Limited, Worcester.

CONTENTS

List of tables
Preface
Acknowledgements
Introduction and Chronology   1

PART I : PROBLEMS OF ECONOMIC MANAGEMENT IN THE DEMOCRATIC
         REPUBLIC OF VIETNAM

1 : THE HISTORICAL INHERITANCE: THE CONSTRAINTS OF   13
    TIME AND PLACE

    1.1 Introduction
    1.2 The pre-modern Vietnamese nation-state
    1.3 The basic socio-economic constraint:
    long-run changes in the balance between pro-
    duction technology and population pressure in
    the Red River Delta
    1.4 The long-run balance between technology
    and population pressure
    1.5 The traditional Vietnamese corporate rur-
    al commune
    1.6 The generation of economic surplus in
    pre-modern Vietnam: the overall picture
    1.7 The colonial impact
    1.8 The Party's Revolutionary Goals: experi-
    ence and norms

2 : THE DRV - IMMEDIATE ORIGINS, PROBLEMS OF THE TRAN-   34
    SITION AND BASIC STRUCTURE. THE AGGRAVATED SHORT-
    TAGE ECONOMY.

    2.1 Introduction; experiences under the pre-
    1954 administration; problems of the politi-
    cal transition; non-Communist attitudes to-
    wards the new government
    2.2 Basic shortcomings of the neo-Stalinist

strategy
2.3 The formal institutions of the DRV and
the principles governing their operation
2.4 The likely macro-economic and structural
consequences of forced industrialisation in
the North Vietnamese context
2.5 Planning in the DRV: some general obser-
vations
2.6 Conclusions

3 : CONSTRAINTS IN OPERATION - THE CREATION OF AN   55
AGGRAVATED SHORTAGE ECONOMY AND THE DETERIORATION
OF DOMESTIC AND FOREIGN BALANCES

3.1 Introduction
3.2 Systemic malfunction and the creation of
an aggravated shortage economy
3.3 The weight of the development programme
3.4 Institutional evidence for the aggravated
shortage economy : the 10th Plenum - 'prices
and markets'
3.5 The state's fiscal deficit - the immediate origins of monetary inflation
3.6 The trade deficit and the shift to import
dependency for current consumption
3.7 Comparison of the DRV economy before and
after the years of US bombing
3.8 Conclusions

4 : POPULATION GROWTH AND STRUCTURAL CHANGE   75

4.1 Introduction
4.2 Population
4.3 Changes in sectoral employment
4.4 Changes in labour productivity
4.5 Sectoral output and the 'sources of
growth'

5 : INDUSTRY   84

5.1 Introduction
5.2 Artisanal and modern industry before
1954-55
5.3 Creation of the mature system and its operation: 1955-75
5.4 The artisanal and collective sectors
5.5 Conclusions: North Vietnamese industrial
development to 1975

6 : AGRICULTURE AND FORCED DEVELOPMENT: THE PEASANTRY   100
    COPES

        6.1 Introduction
        6.2 Overview of agricultural development
        1960-75
        6.3 The basic institutional models: agri-
        cultural producer cooperatives and state
        farms
        6.4 Policy response: towards the New Manage-
        ment System
        6.5 Conclusions: the North Vietnamese 'Agra-
        rian Question' on the eve of National Reunif-
        ication

7 : CONCLUSIONS: THE LIMITS OF NATIONAL LIBERATION   127

                PART II : STATISTICAL APPENDIX

                    Introduction   133
                    Supplementary Table   134
        Translations from 'The Economic and Cultural
        Development of Socialist North Vietnam 1960-
        75'   136

                    Statistical Tables

Section 1 : Natural Conditions and Geography   138
Section 2 : Population and Labour   141
Section 3 : Fixed and Circulating Capital   147
Section 4 : Total Social Product and National Income   150
Section 5 : Finance and Credit   154
Section 6 : Industry A. General Indicators   157
                       B. Enterprises
                       C. Labour
                       D. Output
                       E. Individual Branches
Section 7 : Basic Construction   177
Section 8 : Agriculture   186
Section 9 : Domestic and Foreign Trade   202
Section 10 : Transport and Communications   216
Section 11 : Living standards, culture, education and
             health services   226

Bibliography   237

LIST OF TABLES

Tables in the Text

Chapter 3

3.1 : Share of consumption goods in total imports   68
3.2 : Soviet food exports to the DRV   69
3.3 : Crude balances in domestic trade of the state trading network for some commodities   70

Chapter 4

4.1 : Absorption of the rising labour force, 1960-75   77
4.2 : Comparisons of sectoral gross labour productivity growth   80

Chapter 5

5.1 : Monthly incomes of state employee families   95

Chapter 6

6.1 : Reported levels of staples availability from domestic suppliers   107
6.2 : State procurement expressed as a percentage of reported output   109
6.3 : Machinery and electricity available to agriculture (excluding state farms)   111
Notes : DRV Pig-herd   125

Tables in the Statistical Appendix

Principal ('planned') products at the time of the First Five Year Plan (1961-65)   134-5

Section I : NATURAL RESOURCES AND GEOGRAPHY

1 : Areas and use of land   138
2 : Major deltas   138
3 : Major rivers   139
4 : Peaks of high mountains   139
5 : Average yearly termperatures, C. deg.   139
6 : Average yearly rainfall, mm.   140
7 : Average yearly level of humidity, %   140

Section II : POPULATION AND LABOUR

8 : Average yearly population   141
9 : Population by ethnic group (based upon materials from the 1-4-1974 census)   142

10 : Population of working age   142-3
11 : Social labour in branches of the national
     economy   143
12 : Numbers of workers and functionaries in the
     branches of the national economy   144-5
13 : Numbers of workers and functionaries distributed
     according to the level of management   145
14 : Scientific-technical and economic management
     cadres   146
15 : Technical workers   146

Section III : FIXED AND CIRCULATING CAPITAL

16 : Indicators of the development of fixed and cir-
     culating capital in the sphere of material pro-
     duction   147
17 : Fixed capital in material production by branch   148
18 : Circulating capital in material production by
     branch   148-9

Section IV : TOTAL SOCIAL PRODUCT AND NATIONAL INCOME

19 : Indicators of the development of Total Social
     Product and National Income   150
20 : Distribution of total Social Product   150-1
21 : Distribution of Produced National Income   151
22 : The use of National Income   152
23 : Accumulation   152
24 : Consumption   153

Section V : FINANCE AND CREDIT

25 : Receipts and outlays of the State budget   154
26 : The structure of cash receipts by the banking
     sector   155
27 : The structure of cash outlays by the banking
     sector   155
28 : Long-term loans by the banking sector   156
29 : Short-term loans by the banking sector   156

Section VI : INDUSTRY

30 : Some principal indicators of the development of
     industry   157
31 : Some principal indicators of the development of
     State and Joint State-Private industry   158
32 : Some principal indicators of the development of
     artisanal and light industry   158
33 : Some principal indicators of the development of
     central industry   159
34 : Some principal indicators on the development of

		regional industry	159
35	:	State industrial enterprises, Joint State-Private (JSP) industrial enterprises, and specialised artisanal and light industrial cooperatives	160
36	:	State industrial and Joint State-private (JSP) enterprises according to Group and Branch	160-1
37	:	Industrial labour according to economic branch	161
38	:	Productive industrial employees, production workers in State and JSP enterprises according to level of management	162
39	:	Production employees in State and JSP industry	162-3
40	:	Production workers in State and JSP industry	163
41	:	Specialised labour in small and artisanal industry according to the form of production	164
42	:	Labour in fisheries, salt-making and wood exploitation	164
43	:	The value of total industrial output	165
44	:	Index numbers of the development of the value of Total Industrial Output	166
45	:	The structure of Total Industrial Output	167
46	:	Output of the principle products of industry	168-71
47	:	A number of industrial products, calculated on a per capita basis	171
48	:	Some general indicators of the development of the heavy and energy industries	172
49	:	Some general indicators of the development of manufacturing industry	173
50	:	Some general indicators of the development of the chemical industry	173-4
51	:	Some general indicators of the development of the basic construction, pottery, porcelain, glass, wood, forestry products, cellulose and paper industries	174-5
52	:	Some general indicators of the development of the food and staples industries	175-6
53	:	Some general indicators of the development of the textile, leather, clothing and dyeing industries	176

Section VII : BASIC CONSTRUCTION

54	:	A number of general indicators for the construction branch	177
55	:	Average numbers of officials and workers in the construction branch	178
56	:	Actual volume of capital invested in basic construction distributed according to form of investment	178-9
57	:	The actual volume of capital invested in basic construction distributed according to level of	

	management	179–80
58	: Capital invested in basic construction divided according to economic branch	180–1
59	: Index numbers of the development of investment in basic construction managed by the State in branches of the national economy	182
60	: Investment in basic construction managed by the State divided according to type of investment and economic branch	182
61	: Index numbers of the development of investment in basic construction managed locally in branches of the national economy	183
62	: Investment in basic construction managed locally divided according to type of investment and branch of the national economy	183–4
63	: Capital invested in basic construction in industry	184
64	: Investment in basic construction in agriculture	184
65	: Investment in basic construction in transport	185
66	: Value of new fixed capital according to level of management	185

Section VIII : AGRICULTURE

67	: Land use in agricultural production in 1974	186
68	: Some general indicators of agricultural development	187
69	: Agricultural Cooperativisation	188
70	: Cooperatives and cooperators	188–9
71	: The size of agricultural cooperatives	189
72	: Workers in agriculture (of working age, thousands)	189
73	: The value of the output of agriculture, forestry and other material sectors	190
74	: Capital invested by the State in agriculture and loans by the State to agricultural cooperatives and peasants	191
75	: State agricultural water-works fully brought into use	191–2
76	: Electricity and machines serving agriculture	192–3
77	: Crop areas	193
78	: Staples output in paddy equivalent	194
79	: Sown rice area	194
80	: Rice yields	195
81	: Rice production	195
82	: Area of crops and staples	196
83	: Yields of crops and staples	196
84	: Output of crops and staples	197
85	: Vegetables and beans	197
86	: Jute and Hemp	198
87	: Rushes and sugar cane	198

88 : Peanuts and soybeans   199
89 : Sesame and tobacco   199
90 : Area of perennial industrial crops   200
91 : Output of perennial industrial crops   200
92 : Numbers of livestock and poultry   201
93 : Main agricultural products supplied to the State   201

Section IX : DOMESTIC AND FOREIGN TRADE

94 : A number of general indicators on the develop-
     ment of State trade   202
95 : The State retail trade network   203
96 : Average number of registered employees in trade
     belonging to the systems of the Ministries of
     Domestic Trade and Staples and Food   203-4
97 : Numbers in petty trade and service activities   204-5
98 : Value of merchandise received by the trading
     branch in the country   205
99 : Index numbers of the development and structure
     of the total value of goods received by the
     trading branch in the country   206
100 : Principal industrial goods received in the coun-
      try by the trading branch   206-7
101 : Principal agricultural goods received in the
      country by the trading branch   207
102 : Total retail sales of social trade divided acco-
      rding to economic branch   208
103 : Indicators of the development and structure of
      total retail sales of the social trading sector
      divided according to economic branch   208-9
104 : Total sales of the pure trading sector divided
      according to economic branch   209
105 : Indicators of the development and structure of
      total retail sales of the pure trading sector
      divided according to economic branch   210
106 : Total retail sales of the public restaurant
      sector divided according to economic branch   210-11
107 : Indicators of the development and structure of
      total retail sales of the public restaurant
      sector divided according to economic branch   211
108 : A number of principle commodities sold by State
      trading organisations and purchase/sale coopera-
      tives   212
109 : Price indices for commodity retail sales of the
      social trading branch   212-13
110 : Price indices for retail sales of State trade   213
111 : Price indices of commodities in the unorganised
      market   213
112 : Total value of exports   214
113 : Total value of imports   214-15

Section X : TRANSPORT AND COMMUNICATIONS

114 : Some general indicators of the development of transport and communications — 216
115 : Average registered number of employees in the transport branch divided according to level of management — 217
116 : Surface communications — 217
117 : Types of roads — 218
118 : Means of transport — 218
119 : Volume of merchandise transported — 219
120 : Indicators of the development of the volume of merchandise transported — 219
121 : The structure of the volume of merchandise transported — 220
122 : Merchandise transport volume — 220
123 : Indicators of the volume of merchandise transport activity — 221
124 : The structure of the volume of merchandise transport activity — 221
125 : Passengers carried — 222
126 : Indicators of the development and structure of passenger transport — 222-3
127 : The volume of passenger transport activity — 223
128 : Indicators of the development and structure of the volume of passenger transport activity — 223-4
129 : Some general indicators of the development of the postal and telegraphic services — 224
130 : Telephone lines and equipment — 225
131 : Output and receipts of the postal and telegraphic services — 225

Section XI : LIVING STANDARDS, CULTURE, EDUCATION AND HEALTH SERVICES

132 : Indicators of the development of the average monthly pay of employees in different economic branches — 226
133 : Indicators of the development and structure of the average per capita income in employee households — 227
134 : Indicators of the development and structure of average monthly per capita expenses of employee households — 227
135 : The proportion of total employee household expenditures supplied by the State — 228
136 : Indicators of the cost of living for employees — 228
137 : Indicators of the development and structure of the average monthly income of cooperator households in agricultural producer cooperatives — 229
138 : Indicators of the development and structure of

average per capita monthly expenses of cooperators households in agricultural producer cooperatives   229

139 : Average yearly purchases of merchandise and sales of products by cooperators in agricultural producer cooperatives, per family   230

140 : Books published   230

141 : Public libraries   230

142 : Domestic film production   231

143 : Cinematography   231

144 : Theatrical Art   231

145 : Student and pupil numbers   232

146 : Numbers studying per 10,000 head of population   232

147 : The general schools - schools, classes, teachers and pupils according to level   232-3

148 : Specialised middle and tertiary schools in the country - numbers, teachers and students   233-4

149 : Teachers and students at tertiary establishments during the academic year 1975-76   234-5

150 : Preventative and curative installations   236

151 : Health Service Staff   236

152 : Numbers of doctors, medical assistants and sickbeds per 10,000 head of population   236

PREFACE

This study has limited aims. It does not seek to provide a complete historical analysis of the Democratic Republic of Vietnam's evolving political economy. Instead, it concentrates upon three interrelated areas in order to provide an introduction both to the subject and the statistical collection of Part II. These are as follows:

1) The fundamental domestic constraints facing North Vietnamese socio-economic development. These would have confronted any Vietnamese government that came to power in the North during the period after World War II.

2) The basic system of socio-economic organisation adopted in the Democratic Republic of Vietnam (DRV) - the various property-forms introduced into industry, agriculture and trade, and the associated mechanisms of economic planning and social control.

3) A priori arguments for the likely consequences of the use of such organisational forms in the North Vietnamese context, and an exploration of the actual results of that use as the main means to attaining - or so it was hoped - planned social and economic development. We base this investigation upon both the Statistical Tables of Part II and selected readings from the extensive North Vietnamese literature.

We hope both to stimulate further study of Vietnamese attempts at socialist development and to highlight the constraints that face such policies. Vietnamese Communism is extremely under-researched. A particular area of difficulty remains the relative absence of political studies [but see Turner 1975]. Recent work has started to explore the substantial primary sources available for the period [Vickerman 1984; Spoor 1985; Fforde 1982]. Although this has extended the results of earlier studies [White 1981; Moise 1977; Elliott 1976; Woodside 1970] which concentrated upon rural affairs, the volume of Vietnamese materials still unutilised remains very large.

Quite apart from a substantial output of books and pamphlets, the specialised Research Institutes (Vien) in Hanoi produce their own journals, which are of great value. In addition, there are the more widely disseminated publications such as Nhan Dan (The People), Quan Doi Nhan Dan (People's Army), Hoc Tap (Study) and others. Most of these are available in the West, so it would be untrue to suggest that a lack of research materials is responsible for the limited development of Vietnamese studies. The chief reasons for this are lack of academic interest and difficulties in obtaining direct access. But the situation is nevertheless improving. The substantial refugee community now provides an additional source of information to supplement on-the-spot investigation, whilst Vietnamese with valuable inside knowledge are starting to publish openly [Truong Nhu Tang 1985; Vo Nhan Tri 1985; Tran van Tra 1982]. Statistical sources, such as the one upon which Part II is based, have also begun to show improvements in the data available to Western researchers. This is of particular value to economists.

Better academic understanding of Vietnam is and should be attainable; this work is intended to move towards that goal by setting out a rigorous analysis of what we see as the main trends in the DRV's economic development. We ourselves now take a generally critical view of DRV socio-economic policies, concluding that they were on the whole both inappropriate and deeply wasteful of resources. Furthermore, they created acute systemic difficulties which became deeply entrenched in the social institutions of the North and had severely adverse effects upon national economic development in the reunified Socialist Republic of Vietnam (SRV) after 1975. The limits of national liberation can be found in the nature of the post-reunification economic crisis. In a forthcoming study of Vietnamese industrial organisation one of us examines the cathartic events of 1979-80 and the resulting policy changes [see also Fforde forthcoming:ch.12]. These shifts were deeply marked by the top leaders' experiences of economic management in the DRV.

We hope that the present study will provoke thorough and appropriate criticism which will lead to better research in the future. We believe that a clearer understanding of the difficulties facing the DRV economy is valuable both to the analysis of contemporary problems of socialist development in other countries and to an appreciation of the principles governing the operation of the Vietnamese economy in the late 1980s and beyond.

ACKNOWLEDGEMENTS

This work owes much to many people, most of whom would probably find in it something with which they disagreed. In particular, we would like to express our gratitude to Professor Peter Wiles of the London School of Economics, who was instrumental in encouraging publication of the statistics in Part II. In Hanoi, the Vietnamese Language Faculty and the Faculties of Economics and History of Hanoi University, the Economics Research Institute, the National Economics University and other institutions have all provided valuable assistance during our stays in Vietnam (one or other of the authors visited Vietnam in 1978-79, 1980 and 1985-86). In England, we have benefited from discusions with many people, including in particular Dr. Andy Vickerman and Dr. Peter Nolan as well as many members of the Department of Economics, Cambridge, and the Department of Economics, Birkbeck College, London. David Fleming, Hugh Davies, Irene Norlund and Melanie Beresford kindly read various drafts of the text. Cressida Fforde undertook the tedious task of checking the Statistical Tables. Jane Maurice and Nigel Foster kindly helped produce the final manuscript. The study has been supported financially by the Economic and Social Research Council under their Studentship and Post-Doctoral Research Fellowship Schemes. The Nuffield Foundation provided funding for Suzanne Paine's 1980 visit. In particular, we both owe much to the spirit of liberal academic enquiry that both permits and encourages - if not requires - independent research into such highly contentious and emotionally charged areas as the contemporary history of that unhappy country, Vietnam.

This book was completed after the death of Suzy Paine in November 1985, and she was unfortunately unable to read the final manuscript. The surviving co-author must therefore take sole responsibility for the contents.

London and Cambridge, 1985 and 1986

To Crispin

INTRODUCTION

The DRV provides a valuable example of the adverse consequences of attempting to implement 'forced' development with
Soviet institutional models. We call this a 'neo-Stalinist'
development strategy. Such a strategy has the following characteristics (1.):

1. The prior and basic assumption, that the main constraint upon economic development is the lack of modern industry, and that the main constraint upon development of industry
is the lack of industrial capacity - i.e. inadequate past
investment in that sector's fixed assets.

2. The secondary but also basic assumption, that the
institutional models developed by the Soviet Union during the
1920s are the most suitable means for overcoming this constraint.

3. The use of these institutional models, first to secure
direct central control over mobilisable economic surpluses and
then to concentrate those resources into a program of rapid
and 'forced' (in Vietnamese - 'cap bach') expansion of the
fixed capital stock in industry. This involves reliance upon
administrative measures (taxation, procurement, direct allocation of materials and labour etc) since the immediate incentives acting upon economic agents often lead them to do things
that impede central control and implementation of the plan.

The DRV was an area of extremely low economic surplus, and
relied heavily upon a program of aid-financed investment in
State industry. The economic consequences of the neo-Stalinist
development effort were particularly extreme, and macro-economic tensions rapidly manifest themselves in a combination of
severe macro-imbalances and horrendous micro-level inefficiencies in resource use.

1

Macro-economic tensions revealed themselves in many ways. Before heavy US bombing started in 1965 the area was already exhibiting strong tendencies towards chronic dependency upon imports of both consumer goods and current industrial inputs. Domestic inflationary pressures had begun to push up free market prices, creating the forum for endemic distributional conflicts between the administratively-supplied Socialist sectors and the rest of the economy. An extensive development of free-market and quasi-free-market distributional relations became a distinctive feature of the economy. Sharply rising incremental capital-output ratios in modern industry showed how these problems were leading to its growing isolation from producers and consumers in the rest of the domestic economy, who were unable and/or unwilling to supply the labour and other current inputs needed to operate much of the new machinery.

The area's deep poverty was of overriding importance in explaining these unfavourable outcomes, for this meant that consumption goods were in relatively inelastic supply. Other factors exacerbated the situation, of which some of the most important were:

- the delta peasantry's historical familiarity with collective rural institutions and tactics of tax avoidance;

- the continuing rapid rate of population growth;

- the Vietnamese Communist Party's lack of the rigid internal discipline needed to override immediate material incentives and concentrate scarce resources upon priority areas.

Wartime economic aid masked these deep systemic problems, however, and limited renovation of the economic management system in the early 1970s did not confront fundamental issues. Two reasons for this were, first, the political immobilities associated with the top leadership's commitment to neo-Stalinist methods, and, second, wartime hyper-nationalism, which sought to fuse Nationalism with Socialism as integral parts of the Vietnamese Revolution. Thus defined, the neo-Stalinist model became politically almost impossible to challenge despite its evident shortcomings.

As an extreme example of Statist development, DRV experience is of some comparative value. Problems that are masked by more favourable conditions in other Socialist countries come strikingly to the fore in the DRV. Of great interest is the manifestation of macro-economic imbalances and micro-economic inefficiencies in a systemic 'aggravated shortage economy'. Here conventional and well-known micro-level problems of simultaneous shortage and slack (**dong thoi thua, thieu**) for the same good in the administered sectors co-

2

existed with extensive free-market relations in the so-called 'outside economy' ('**kinh te ngoai**'). Unlike the developed Socialist economies of Eastern Europe, in the DRV the free market played an extensive role in revealing to economic agents the comparative value of the economic choices they faced. Under North Vietnamese conditions, market and quasi-market relations grew up as the necessary counterpoint to the orthodox Soviet material supply system in conditions where the authorities did not use administrative methods - i.e. the security forces - to curb them. One can therefore observe systemic competition to control economic resources in the importance to economic agents of the complex pattern of incentives marking the boundary region between the Socialist and non-Socialist sectors. This interface rapidly came to dominate socio-economic behaviour in North Vietnam as people adapted to an environment dominated by the need to make choices based upon the comparative costs and benefits offered by the two sectors: even for the 'Reddest' State industrial enterprise, 'everything had a price'.

This institutionalised social competition created considerable ideological and moral problems. The new government was dominated by people with characteristically Vietnamese respect for literary discussion, and much of their self-legitimisation depended upon popular acceptance of the ethical and logical validity of Marxism-Leninism ('**Mac Le-nin**'). From this point of view, a certain social harmony should have followed from the neo-Stalinist adoption of Soviet models and development policies. For some, the social tensions that actually resulted were dismissable as part of the necessary costs of the nation's historical tasks; social harmony was essentially contradictory. For others, they were a source of considerable economic inefficiency, delaying sought-after industrialisation and true national independence. And for yet others they revealed the shortcomings of Marxism-Leninism itself. Although these views are detectable from very early on, they did not come into full prominence until the profound 'atmosphere change' induced by the 6th Plenum of August 1979 at the height of the economic crisis that built up in the late 1970s after national re-unification in 1975-76.

The present study concentrates upon the period 1960-75. We consider that this is best seen as a period of Socialist Construction rather than one of transition [Le Chau 1966], primarily because of the predominance of the new Socialist property-forms throughout the DRV by the end of 1960 (2.). Clearly, the underlying reality behind these forms was still fluid; indeed, we argue that the processes accompanying the rising importance of the aggravated shortage economy during the First Five Year Plan (1961-65) were instrumental in defining these social relations. After the 1954 Geneva Conference the French departure meant that the Vietnamese Communist leadership, already in firm control of the nationalist Vietminh,

had a largely free hand in setting up the institutional framework of the Democratic Republic. There is little evidence of
any real political threat to their position after 1954, and
this supports the assertion that the period after 1960 is best
not seen as one of transition. Crucially, by the start of the
First Five Year Plan in 1961, collectivisation of the deltas
had basically finished, with over 90% of peasant families in
producer cooperatives.

The First Five Year Plan heralded a period during which,
it was hoped, the DRV could embark upon rapid industrialisation based upon the substantial programme of aid from the
Soviet bloc and China. This was to be Socialist Construction.
In the event, US intervention in South Vietnam and the severe
bombings that began in 1965 forced policy changes that had
effectively to abandon the system of Five Year Plans. The
second Five Year Plan did not start until 1976. But from 1965
a second massive aid program began that enabled the DRV to
maintain gross industrial output at rather high levels throughout this first period of US bombing, which ended temporarily
with US President Johnson's 'unconditional bombing halt' in
1968. The infamous Christmas bombings ordered in 1972 to force
the DRV leadership to sign the Paris Agreements (1973) were
unable to reduce industrial output below the 1965 level. By
1973 industrial output was over 25% above that at the end of
the First Five Year Plan (1965) [Table:31]. It is not true to
say that US bombing destroyed DRV industrial capability.

During the short period of peace between the Paris Agreements and the fall of the South in 1975 the DRV economy showed
clearly the limits imposed upon it by previous policies and
its economic management system. Modern industry was
precociously over-developed. The levels of fixed capacity
installed by the aid program and grimly defended by the administrative supply system far exceeded the economy's ability to
supply the requisite complementary inputs. It was therefore
isolated from the rest of the domestic economy. Ending that
isolation posed policy-makers with enormous problems because
of economic agents' by then long-established facility with
tactics designed to prevent resource extraction on unfavourable terms. Large food imports had begun in the late 1960s as
domestic availability fell well below subsistence, and they
continued at around 10-15% of domestic production. Modern
industry therefore tended to rely upon imports both for food
and other supplies needed by its workforce, as well as for
much of its current inputs. Dominated by cadres whose ideology
taught them that under-development meant an absolute capital
shortage, the North Vietnamese economy was in fact over-
supplied with fixed industrial capital. This fact flagrantly
contradicted the first basic assumption of the entire neo-
Stalinist strategy, which was that an absolute capital shortage was the binding constraint upon development.

4

Methodology

The basic methodology of the study is an examination of the interrelations between technological and institutional changes. By the latter we mean actual socio-economic processes rather than formal structures (e.g. of the neo-Stalinist model). These interrelations are viewed as dynamic and changing over time, so the study necessarily takes a long-run perspective. Neither institutions nor technology are taken as fixed. These arguments have implications for other areas, such as the Socialist Republic of Vietnam (SRV) in the late 1970s, or the early processes of State-formation in the Red River Delta.

The study starts with an examination of the Inheritance: the constraints time and place imposed upon the area and upon policy-makers. Crucial to this was the combination of the particular rural institutions that had evolved under the centralised dynastic State and the precise form French colonial rule took. This meant that the area was not only extremely undeveloped, with almost no modern industry at all, but that peasants placed great value upon collective rural institutions as a protection against risk and State interference. Within this framework orthodox Communist intentions and desires had little room to express themselves freely. Communists therefore had to seek major changes in Vietnamese society. Thus whilst colonial rule effectively broke the link between rural institutions and the requirements of national development, the post-Independence Communist government confronted the task of re-establishing that link. It did so, however, with a strong set of preconceptions that proved in practice to be misleading and inappropriate guides to policy. The second half of chapter 1 examines these subjective constraints.

Chapter 2 looks at the logic of social and economic development in the DRV. It shows how the real content of neo-Stalinist institutional models operating under North Vietnamese conditions could rapidly come to differ sharply from that intended. The development of institutionalised behaviour patterns within these fora would allow re-establishment of a degree of institutional endogeneity, albeit constrained by the immobility of central policy. Chapter 3 examines the practical operation of social and economic constraints during 1960-75, and especially the deterioration in fiscal and foreign macro-balances. This shows how central policy makers' continuing commitment to the neo-Stalinist model was supported materially by the central State organs' effective monopoly of foreign trade and aid, and spiritually by the widespread popular support for war-time mobilisation.

Chapter 4 looks at the changing inter-sectoral balance of the DRV economy and shows how continued rapid population growth interacted with slow growth of consumption goods output in the Socialist sectors, exacerbating macro-economic tensions and ensuring 'diversion' of labour effort and other mobile resources into alternative lines of production. Chapters 5 and 6 examine industry and agriculture respectively in greater detail. This helps to bring out the institutional adaptations of the neo-Stalinist models that took place in response to North Vietnamese conditions and the pervasive effects upon them of the combination of administratively induced shortage with pervasive market-type relations. These chapters concentrate upon the models implemented in the late 1950s and early 1960s, mentioning the largely abortive reform attempts of the early 1970s in passing. These are examined in other studies (3.).

Chapter 7 concludes the essay, drawing together the most important lessons learnt from the DRV and pointing towards the major problems likely to be encountered after reunification. It also makes some suggestions regarding more appropriate Socialist economic policies in areas of low economic surplus.

CHRONOLOGY

939 Recovery of independence after more than 1,000 years of Chinese rule.

11th and 12th centuries: Under Ly dynasty (1009-1225) Buddhist monks gradually lose positions of influence at court, replaced by Confucian scholars.

1407-28 Chinese occupation of country: 'kulturkampf' destroys many historical sources.

1428 Accession of Le Loi, founder of Le dynasty (1428-1786), who implements a State-regulated system of land distribution. Systematic attempts to use Confucian-based Chinese administrative system.

1527-92 First period of national division: Nguyen lords in South, Mac Imperial interregnum in North.

1592 Mac defeated by alliance between Trinh and Nguyen families. Second period of national division - intermittent civil wars continue; Le emperors rule in name only in North, dominated by Trinh.

1774 Tay-Son revolt - after rapidly acquiring popular support, movement deposes Le (1786) and defeats invading Chinese army (1789).

1802 Final defeat of Tay-Son by member of Nguyen family with Western assistance; takes name Gia-Long to found Nguyen dynasty (1802-1945).

1858 Tourane expedition heralds imminent French conquest of South Vietnam.

1862 Treaty cedes 3 provinces around Saigon to France.

1874 Treaty confirms French title to Cochinchina.

1879 Civilian government established in Cochinchina followed by rapid development of Mekong delta.

1882 Hanoi seized by large French expedition. Hue captured 1883.

1884 China recognises Franco-Vietnamese Treaties, ending her claim to suzerainty.

1885-87 French consolidate their rule in Tonkin and Annam, setting up a puppet emperor and establishing the Indochinese Union of Vietnam, Cambodia and Laos (1887).

1897-1902 Paul Doumer (Governor-General) establishes centralised control over Indochina from his capital in Hanoi. Colonial State apparatus consolidated - Hanoi University founded 1902.

1915 Last Confucian exams held in Tonkin - abolished in Annam in 1918.

1929 Founding of Indochinese Communist Party in Hong Kong.

1930 Rising by Vietnamese Nationalist Party (**Viet Nam Quoc Dan Dang** - founded 1927-28) leads to capture of its leadership.

1930-31 Nghe An and other peasant risings spurred by effects of Depression lead to violent French reprisals and near-elimination of Communist leadership.

1940 Japanese occupy Indochina but leave French in control of administration. General rising of Communists in South put down and Party network almost obliterated.

1941 Founding of Vietminh and establishment of guerilla bases in Northern highlands.

1942 Nationalist Chinese finance both Communists and Nationalists in Vietnam. Partial re-establishment of Communist network.

1944-45 Famine in North Vietnam kills approximately 1 million.

1945 March Japanese disarm French, creating power vacuum.
Aug. Emperor Bao Dai abdicates.
Sept. Declaration of Independence in Hanoi by Ho Chi Minh.
Creation of Democratic Republic of Vietnam. Chinese Natio-
nalists move into North to accept Japanese surrender.
British troops in South accept French re-armament and use
Japanese soldiers to crush Vietminh.
Nov. Disbandment of Indochinese Communist Party - replaced
by 'study group' within Vietminh.

1946 March Preliminary Franco-Vietnamese agreement.
Nov. Haiphong shelled by French ships after breakdown of
talks - Vietminh retreat to mountains.

1949 Victory of Chinese Communists; Canton taken in October.

1950 French forced out of border areas allowing Vietminh easy
access to Chinese materiel. DRV recognised by Communist
bloc (January).

1951 Inauguration of Vietnam Workers' Party, founding of Party
daily **Nhan** **Dan** (Feb.). Promulgation of unified agricultural tax, founding of National Bank (May).

1953 Jan. 4th Plenum of Politburo passes provisional outline
of Party's Land Reform policy.
Autumn French set up advanced base at Dien Bien Phu.
Dec. Land Reform law passed.

1954 May Fall of Dien Bien Phu on eve of Geneva Conference -
French agree to leave North Vietnam (July). Early stages
of Land Reform.
June First meeting of Central Land Reform Committee.

1955 Final departure of French from North Vietnam - country
divided at 17th parallel. Elections prior to re-unification never held. March - formalisation of Land Reform:
'People's Tribunals' replace 'Peasant struggle meetings'.
Land Reform extended to newly-liberated areas.

1956 Aug. Official end of Land Reform: Ho Chi Minh publicly
admits to 'errors'.
Sept. 10th Plenum admits to Land Reform 'errors'.
Nov. Resignation of Truong Chinh (Party General Secretary)
in wake of Land Reform.

Late 1956-57 **'Nhan Van'** affair parallels 'Hundred Flowers' in
China. Repression of intellectuals critical of the new
government ends with Party hegemony over public intellec-

tual expression. 'Correction of Errors' in the country-side sees pre-Land Reform local leadership partly recover its position.

1957 12th Plenum sets goal of ending 'reconstruction' and moving on to 'planned development'.

1958 14th Plenum examines 3 Year Plan (1958-1960).

1959 Monetary reform (1:1,000). 15th Plenum formally decides upon a return to armed struggle in the South. 16th Plenum and speech by Truong Chinh to National Assembly herald rapid implementation of agricultural cooperativisation.

1960 Aug. Movement to establish joint State-private enter-prises basically complete, with 97% of both family-units and capital.
Sept. IIIrd Congress approves First Five Year Plan (1961-1965). Movement to establish 'lower-level' cooperatives in agriculture basically completed.
Oct. Movement to set up 'lower-level' artisanal coopera-tives basically completed, with approx. 80% of family-units.

1961 Jan. Incoming President Kennedy told by Eisenhower that Laos (not S. Vietnam) 'the key to S.E. Asia'.
April U.S. troop numbers in South Vietnam exceed limits agreed at Geneva.
July 5th Plenum affirms 'reforming and improving the man-agement of cooperatives is the most important element in developing (agricultural) production'.

1963 March Politburo issues directives on cooperatives for the period 1963-65, focusing upon management methods and the role of the Party.
April 8th Plenum discusses progress of Five Year Plan. Rising macro-economic tensions resulting from over-ambi-tious development targets manifest themselves in growing import dependency and domestic inflationary pressures.
June Beginning of Stage 1 of campaign to 'improve cooper-ative management'.
Oct. Great Buddhist opposition to Ngo Dinh Diem in South - Diem assassinated Nov. 1. President Kennedy assassinated Nov. 22.
Nov. Vice-President Johnson takes office pledged to con-tinue US commitment.

1964 Tonkin Gulf incident (Aug) allows US administration to pass legislation allowing overt use of force in Vietnam.

1965 US commences 'Rolling Thunder' bombings of North Vietnam.

Crisis measures taken by Hanoi include decentralisation of State organs and industry and a general mobilisation. Beginning (October) of Stage 2 of campaign to 'improve cooperative management'.

1966 Heavy US bombing in attempt to prevent continuing support from Hanoi for guerilla and mainforce units in South Vietnam. Culminates in the events of 1968, the 'Tet' offensive' (January, showing the apparent strength of anti-government forces in the South), the refusal of President Johnson to stand for a second term (because of domestic opposition to the war) and the announcement of 'unconditional' bombing halt (March) and the first meeting in Paris of US and Vietnamese negotiators (May).

1968 Shift from 'lower-level' to 'higher-level' agricultural cooperatives basically finished. Reported staples availability from domestic production falls below 13 kg. milled rice equivalent per month for the first time. Soviet food aid rises sharply. So-called 'III contracts controversy' between Le Duan (First Secretary) and Truong Chinh over validity of household-based farming apparently resolved in favour of policies emphasising the collective. Decree (August) expands State management of trade, reinforces regulations against speculation and theft of State property.

1969 Death of Ho Chi Minh (Sept.). Report of Central Agricultural Committee (July) reveals declining collectively-farmed area in many Northern provinces.

1969-71 Extensive diplomatic activity. Nixon doctrine allows for steady withdrawal of US troops from South Vietnam.

1971 19th Plenum (October) advocates reinforcement of local administrative and Party organisations in face of difficulties with Northern agriculture. Beginnings of 'experiments' with the centralised and detailed methods of cooperative management that became the so-called 'New Management System'.

1972 Feb. Visit of President Nixon to Peking.
March Escalation of activities in South Vietnam by North Vietnamese Army. US responds by heavy bombing of Hanoi/Haiphong (April) and harbour mining (May). Central Committee makes 'general appeal' to population.
April 20th Plenum advocates need for economy to 'advance from small-scale to large-scale-production' and attacks 'dispersed small-scale and artisanal methods'.
May Presidential decree on the maintenance of law and order and the management of trade in wartime.

Dec. 'All-out' bombing attacks on Hanoi and Haiphong ordered in order to accelerate North Vietnamese agreement to compromise.

1973 Jan. Paris agreements initialled: US bombing finally to cease for good.
Oct. Census of State property.

1974 National Census. Government Council decides to 'abolish the free market in staples' - decision inoperative. 22nd Plenum (April) re-asserts Party hostility to small-scale production and confirms commitment to centralised management methods in agricultural cooperatives. Thai Binh Conference (August) announces 'Towards a large-scale socialist agriculture' and affirms support for the New Management System.

1975 Retreat from Central Highlands by South Vietnamese Army (March) heralds rapid collapse of South. Embroiled in the aftermath of Watergate, the US refuses to provide increased military support. Saigon falls in May.

1976 Fourth Congress of Vietnam Workers' Party. Name of Party changed to Vietnamese Communist Party. Formal re-unification of country under name of Socialist Republic of Vietnam. 24th Plenum analyses situation in the South, criticises it for import dependency and predominantly small-scale production. Decree 61-CP (April) - 'Towards large-scale socialist agricultural production' re-affirms official commitment to the New Management System. Plans laid for extension of North's collectivised agrarian system to the South and Centre.

Footnotes

1. This characterisation is necessarily simplistic. We use the term neo-Stalinist in order to avoid confusion between the specific historical origins of the Soviet planning system and its underlying ahistorical characteristics. For full discussion of the Soviet planning model see Ellman (1979), Nove (1977) and Wiles (1962). See also Stalin (1952).
2. This particular approach views the main problem of the transition as the establishment of a politically secure government with relatively stable institutions - in this case those of the Democratic Republic. See amongst others Bettelheim (1975), Sweezy and Bettelheim (1971), Griffith-Jones (1981, especially ch.1) in the extensive literature.
3. Two detailed studies by one of the authors provide a major part of the background to the present work. Fforde

(1982) covered the Northern collectivised agriculture of the mid 1970s and was based upon a collection of micro-studies obtained from Hanoi University in 1979. This is published as Fforde (forthcoming) with the addition of a chapter that discusses the post 1979 policy changes. A major piece of work used as a basis for Fforde (1982) was a study of the histori- cal background to agricultural collectivisation, which is available as Fforde (1983). Fforde is currently engaged in finishing a study of Vietnamese Industrial Organisation. The excessive self-reference that will be found in the present study is both regrettable and regretted.

Chapter One

THE HISTORICAL INHERITANCE: THE CONSTRAINTS OF TIME AND PLACE

Pre-revolutionary Vietnam

1.1 Introduction

In this chapter we discuss the objective and subjective constraints that the past imposed upon the rulers of the DRV. Under the former heading lies the basic framework of pre-modern Vietnamese society, which may be summarised as a structural combination of a centralised neo-Confucian state with quasi-autonomous and corporate rural communes. The latter derive from the particular position of the post-1954 Communist leaders as Vietnamese nationalists strongly rooted within the complicated currents of world socialism.

Analytically, two broad themes run through this study. First, that North Vietnam's relatively low levels of both actual and potential economic surplus would have strongly constrained any national government coming to power as the European colonial Empires were disbanded in the period after World War II. The DRV leadership could not escape this. Second, that they nevertheless attempted, by using apparently proven neo-Stalinist institutions, to extract resources from the economy and implement rapid and 'forced' development. This strategy encountered major difficulties.

These themes derive from consideration of two historical issues: first, the long-run dynamics of socio-economic change in the Red River Delta. Here the direction taken by institutional evolution depended greatly upon a long-run tendency towards approximate balance between population pressure and the available production methods. This helped maintain the area at or near a state of demographic saturation. Second, the way in which the colonial impact broke this effective endogenous link between technology, demography and institutional change. Here the analysis must take account of the contradictory effects of the French presence, which simultaneously raised potential per capita output whilst constraining actual per capita output. This fracture of the relationship between rural institutions and changing production methods prevented full realisation of the potential for increased output.

I: Objective constraints: 'state and commune' - the basic social structures of pre-modern North Vietnam, their context and rationality.

1.2 The pre-modern Vietnamese nation-state

The Vietnamese are a homogeneous linguistic group that has probably occupied the delta areas of North Vietnam since well before the time of Christ. From the Red River Delta in the North they and their culture spread slowly southwards down through the coastal region of what is now Central Vietnam before arriving during the mid 19th century in the Mekong Delta situated in the southernmost part of Indochina [Cotter 1968]. Their culture has long depended upon wet-rice cultivation, and they have tended not to settle outside the low-lying regions (1.).

For obvious propaganda reasons, the nature of the Vietnamese nation, as well as its membership and definition, has been and remains highly charged and deeply contentious. These questions have served to stimulate archaeological and historical research, some of which is of great value although much is often premature and over-assertive (2.). The Vietnamese nation, like many others, is a historical nation, and has not resulted from some European Imperialist exercise in colonial map-making.

Unlike many other developing nations, the Vietnamese have also had long experience with centralised administrative systems and over the centuries these have played a major role in organising the Vietnamese nation-state. Vietnam has not, however, avoided the deep influence of foreign cultural contacts as well as intermittent periods of foreign domination. The Chinese ruled Vietnam for most of the first millenium. Expelled violently in 939, Chinese armies successfully occupied Vietnam for over 20 years in the early 15th century. From the closing stages of the Ly dynasty (1009-1225) the Emperors, although Vietnamese, governed the area according to their scholars' interpretations of Chinese neo-Confucian orthodoxy (3.). French colonialism was imposed in the late nineteenth century, replacing the Imperial dynasties by the 'Union indo-chinois'. In modern times, Ho Chi Minh's famous September 1945 Declaration of Independence in Hanoi's Ba Dinh Square was the first formal step towards the re-establishment of an independent and sovereign Vietnamese state [Patti 1980:248]. Viewed historically, it is clear that Vietnamese nationalism is not the modern creation of a struggle to overthrow Western colonial rule. Thus, unlike the rulers of many other developing countries, those of the newly-independent DRV did not confront the problems involved in creating a nation-state ab ovo. Instead, Vietnamese nationalism had long shown its vitality in generating popular support for armed struggle against foreign domination.

Like Western Europeans, the Vietnamese have the nation-state deeply etched into their popular consciousness. The nature of this nation is not, however, an immutable concept. The colonial scholar Paul Mus's comment about the French loss of the 'mandate of heaven' after the 1945 August Revolution referred to Vietnamese concepts of the state that were rooted in the dynastic past, but operated in the contemporary conflict between colonialism and nationalism. The basic issues then were those of neo-Confucianism, of French colonialism, of nationalism and of socialism. But the fundamental questions behind such issues remain valid today, for they are closely bound up with problems to do with the relationship between individuals and their social context, ultimately bounded by the Vietnamese nation-state (4.).

The success of the anti-French nationalist movement of the late 1940s largely depended upon this long-established sense of nation. But, particularly as the movement subsequently developed in the early 1950s, this accompanied sectional pressures for a better society, most especially from many peasants. Land reform ending the landlordism that had grown up sharply under colonial rule was attractive to many. National economic development became an essential part of any political platform. Later, once the Vietnam Workers' Party (VWP) had become the dominant force in North Vietnamese politics through its control of the institutions of the DRV, the attempt at full-scale implementation of the Socialist Revolution accentuated the contrast between nationalism as a state of opposition to other nations and as a focus for debates about social organisation. Since the DRV was both the main tool by which the proletariat was to exercise its dictatorship and the base area for the continuing struggle to liberate the South, it was intended to play both nationalist and socialist roles: the National Liberation struggle and the drive to liberate the South cannot be isolated from the social change experienced in North Vietnam. However, the general unsuitability in North Vietnamese conditions of the DRV's institutional forms meant that their impact was limited. The massive increase in output potential offered by new technology could not be fully utilised.

1.3 The basic socio-economic constraint: long-run changes in the balance between production technology and population pressure in the Red River Delta

The pre-modern North Vietnamese economy was dominated by wet-rice cultivation, and in the particular conditions facing farmers in the Red River Delta this had certain important

15

implications. The delta consists of over one million hectares; farmers' lives were dominated by the risk of catastrophic river flood and by rain [Table:2](5.).

The economy was basically static, and there is little evidence for significant technological change in the centuries immediately prior to the French conquest. From at least the 16th and 17th centuries the agro-economic culture of the Red River Delta confronted buoyant demographic pressure on a fixed land area. The river's violent and unpredictable nature itself determined the key large-scale hydraulic problem. With existing technology this had to be flood-prevention rather than irrigation aimed at water supply to the fields. At the local level, work to improve water supplies was possible, but with pre-modern hydrology this tended not to go beyond moving rainwater over rather short distances. Here the local pattern of topographical relief was of great importance.

These two considerations argued for the importance of stable and reproducable institutions at two quite separate levels. These were essentially the 'macro' or national level and the 'micro' or local 'village' level.

For the macro-system of the entire Red River Delta only a single integrated system of dikes could cope adequately with flood control [Le Thanh Khoi 1981:32-9; Phan Khanh 1981]. Large dikes had to be built on either side of the Red River from the mountains to the sea. They had then to be extended in both directions along the sea-shore away from the river mouth in order to prevent back-flooding. Such a vast social good generated incentives for the creation of a way of organising those who stood to benefit from it in order to allocate costs. This was one function of a centralised nation-state. Thus a largely technical problem could be solved, so long as other conditions for the reproduction of the nation-state were satisfied. These were: stable resource flows to finance it (i.e. some form of tax base); ways and means of maintaining the state's independent existence in competition with others (i.e. some form of military potential); and some method of controlling imbalances between technology and population. Yet once the Red River was diked-in to prevent flood, scope for further investment in economically valuable works at the national level was rather limited. This was perhaps the greatest constraint pre-modern technology placed upon the economic role played by the dynastic state.

At the local level, social organisation confronted different problems. Water control was certainly important, and maintenance of the efficacy of local infrastructural investments clearly a stimulus to the creation of local organisation. But this does not really provide a satisfactory explanation for the evolution of villages ('villagisation'). One of the most basic facts of life in the North Vietnamese delta areas is the concentrated rather than dispersed settlement pattern. In the frontier regions of the Mekong Delta the initial settlement pattern was, if not (like many Celtic farmers) scattered, at least far less concentrated [Rambo 1973 et passim:42-9]. Unfortunately, the historical origins of the Northern system are unclear. On the other hand, however, once local corporate organisations were established various plausible hypotheses suggest their stability under conditions of population saturation. Such institutions helped provide important insurance against the uncertainty arising from both the sharply unpredictable weather and the wide variation in household labour supply. The violence of the Red River itself and the unreliability of precipitation accentuated the need for methods of providing insurance against risk. Once the delta population was settled in villages, such institutions would provide a social forum for dealing with such issues as local water-control and disputes over water with other villages. Again, once a centralised state existed, such corporate organisations could, by facilitating cooperation amongst their members, help defend local interests, for example by organising tax-avoidance. This might be seen as a form of inter-village competition. A concentrated population could more easily be made to deliver resources to the state.

Further arguments might be made, but it seems reasonably clear that corporate villages provided institutions suited to the socio-economic conditions of pre-modern North Vietnam (6.). In practice the absence of foreign domination throughout most of the second millenium created considerable scope for the creation of appropriate institutional forms. These apparently responded to the basic rationality of the situation, most especially the static technology and long-run tendency to population saturation. At both national ('macro') and local ('micro') levels, appropriate and reproducible institutions developed.

Thus from the simple technological questions associated with problems of water-control at different levels comes an argument for a fundamentally dualistic and hierarchical social organisation articulating centralised state and local village. In North Vietnam this basic framework was provided by a structural combination of the neo-Confucian state administration adopted by the dynasties and the rural corporate 'commune' (xa). Since this framework had long historical roots, it is not at all surprising that deep cultural practices linked these two levels, of which the most important were the integrated religious practices. A key element of the latter were each commune's tutelary spirits, which, conferred directly by the Emperor, provided a focus for ritual. The dynastic state's role in military mobilisation against foreign competitors becomes more striking when it is realised that these tutelary spirits were often those of famous wartime leaders.

1.4 The long-run balance between technology and population pressure

Until modern times population saturation in the regions of long-established settlement in the North has been a major stimulus to Vietnamese territorial expansion. This has pushed migrants towards the relatively empty but fertile areas suitable for them. In practice this has always meant southwards (the so-called 'March to the South'): first into the area of Central Vietnam then occupied by the Indianised kingdom of Champa and then into the Mekong Delta of South Vietnam to which, although largely unpopulated, the Khmer had previously claimed sovereignty. Once established, the Vietnamese dynastic state therefore tended to exist in violent competition with others, if not the Chinese Empire to the North then those athwart the southern border. During the seventeenth and eighteenth centuries, however, this competition turned its focus inwards, and civil war divided the country. The secessionist lords who ruled the Centre continued the southern expansion but largely limited it to people from their own areas. Eventual reunification was only attained around the end of the 18th century. The Tay-Son movement, despite defeating other contenders for power as well as a Chinese invasion, could not consolidate its rule. It fell eventually to the Nguyen who established the last Vietnamese dynasty in 1802.

In the early 19th century the immediate background of the new rulers' policies was the recent experience of bloody and protracted civil war. To strengthen their administration the Nguyen reverted to familiar neo-Confucian authoritarian policies that probably seemed the best principles of government to hand [Woodside 1971]. However, their quest for legitimacy often failed and they faced frequent peasant uprisings. They appeared largely unaware of the gathering threat from expansionary Western powers equipped with far superior military technology. Especially under Minh-Mang (1820-1841), xenophobic policies sought to minimise contacts with the West and preserve the country's isolation. These policies point, not to their naivety and stupidity, but rather to the overriding importance to them of their own immediate problems - establishment of a secure and dependable administrative system that would meet the requirements of pre-modern Vietnamese society and perpetuate their own rule. The combination of centralised neo-Confucian state and rural commune apparently met these conditions, as it had for centuries. Its main short-coming, however, was the inability to generate the economic growth required for national survival in a world increasingly dominated by the industrialising countries of Western Europe.

Although the imported Chinese model provided the basic framework for meeting these goals, the Court did not adopt Chinese methods of government without question. In the crucial

area of rural administration the Nguyen decided to preserve
and support the indigenous Vietnamese commune in preference to
the Chinese system of group responsibility [Woodside 1971:158-
68]. In so doing, they recognised the greater suitability of
the Vietnamese commune. They accepted that it was derived from
a long period of historical evolution, suggesting that it
would be inadvisable to impose a foreign model derived from
different conditions. In hindsight this confirms the Court's
respect for the communal system, and the lack of any real need
to alter it since it continued to provide an effective basis
for the regime. As Chapter 6 argues, it was in precisely the
rural areas that the problems encountered with neo-Stalinist
institutional models - in this case the producer cooperative -
were most striking.

The Population Question

The relative military strength of the Vietnamese state was
a vital element in maintaining an open southern frontier for
out-migration into areas of low population density. This meant
that in the Northern heartlands a strong but long-run tendency
existed towards an overall balance between the land's productive capacity and the requirements of its residents. The
latter included historical subsistence for cultivators as well
as additional amounts payable to the state and to local
'interests'. Population was kept near saturation levels by the
open southern frontier that acted as a vent for surplus numbers. With a basically static technology and little scope for
investment once the dikes had been built the demographic
capacity of the Red River Delta was limited. As population
reached that limit the substantial harvest variations brought
about by the vagaries of the climate made life increasingly
difficult for poorer members of the rural population. As the
expected per capita food supply fell, migration rather than
death was the vehicle of adjustment.

This is a description of long-term trends, and at different times and places population pressure would have departed
substantially from the long-run equilibrium. A cut in the
intensive subsistence margin could arise if difficulties at
the southern border inhibited out-migration; alternatively, it
could result from increased surplus extraction during wartime.

We argue that the beginning of the 19th century was a
period of departure below the long-run equilibrium associated
with pre-modern technology and social organisation. This is of
some importance to explaining the problems that faced the DRV.
Although reliable data is unavailable (7.), two a priori
arguments support this: first, the fact that the period was
one of recovery from the long and costly civil wars; second,
the beneficial effects of the now fully open southern border
upon population pressure and therefore population growth.

If true, this argument suggests that it was a sharp dip

19

below the then long-run equilibrium population level in the North during the early 19th century that initiated, not only the subsequent rapid increase, but also the momentum behind that growth which continued into the modern period with such devastating effects upon the DRV's food balance. This population growth started to re-encounter constraints in the 1920s and 1930s, but by then the long-run equilibrium had altered. Changes in the rural structure brought about by the colonial presence had reduced the rural population's ability to resist famine (see below). This offset marginal output gains resulting from improved production methods and colonial investment in hydraulic works. Thus whilst technical improvements had raised actual output, which nevertheless remained well below potential, erosion of subsistence entitlement had greatly increased the risks of famine. This perspective helps towards a better appreciation of the effects upon the demographic balance in the Red River Delta of the almost hermetic closure of the southern border to migrants after 1954-55.

The advent of the Nguyen dynasty in 1802 certainly heralded a period of peace during which inter-regional migration was not only far easier but strongly encouraged by the new government. Evidence of wartime depopulation exists in reports that the civil wars had left over 10% of the communes in the Red River Delta classified as 'empty' and without population [UKX 1971:321]. The combination of Northern depopulation and easier out-migration would have encouraged faster population growth and therefore a corresponding change in the demographic structure as population levels moved back towards the long-run equilibrium. If, as is likely, the dip below trend was rather large, then the changes in demographic structure appropriate to rapid growth would have contributed to a considerable momentum of population growth that would ensure that population would 'overshoot' before attaining a new long-run equilibrium. These changes in demographic structure would have occurred most obviously as a result of a shift in the age structure of the population towards the greater proportion of younger people characteristic of rapidly growing populations (8.).

Various social practices helped maintain the high growth potential of the Vietnamese population. One important element was the strong role played by the corporate rural commune in reducing risk (see below). Here the somewhat independent role played by Vietnamese women is also of great interest. Their rights of inheritance and customary participation in trade suggest a social role far less subservient than, for example, in China. This would suggest that the proportion of sexually active women in the population could be higher, partly as a result of the lower degree of female infanticide, and partly as a result of the relative absence of the 'maiden aunts' and un-remarried widows characteristic of deeply patriarchal societies. This meant that the Vietnamese population was capable of relatively rapid demographic expansion, given the means to feed the growing population. The demographic momentum created by the particular circumstances of the early 19th century was probably considerable. The population of the Mekong delta grew extremely rapidly in the late 19th and early 20th centuries as the French encouraged in-migration by farmers in order to generate profitable rice exports [Sansom 1971:18-53; Rambo 1973:177-218].

1.5 The traditional Vietnamese corporate rural commune

The traditional Vietnamese commune (xa) is of abiding historical interest (9.) and some detailed understanding of it is extremely valuable. Vietnam was and remains a predominantly rural society, and the dynastic commune was not only deeply linked to the historical past but is still part of living memory. In South-Central Vietnam its pre-modern forms were only finally removed by collectivisation after the 1975/76 re-unification. Some communes in the Red River Delta seem to have histories going back to the first millenium. This long-run durability suggests that interaction between changes in methods of production and the evolution of its social institutions had led to their general suitability and acceptability. The commune showed remarkable stability in the face of violent social change, so long as that change did not take the form of a sharp alteration in the attitude of the state. In its ideal form it was clearly very attractive to many Vietnamese peasants, and therefore greatly valued. Unfortunately these ideal characteristics were not always realised.

The traditional commune was in principle a corporate body, liable to the state for rural taxes and supplies of corvee labour and military conscripts. In the early 19th century the commune possessed a high degree of day-to-day autonomy from the dynastic state, and its officers were usually appointed by its Council of Notables (Hoi dong Ky muc). The Council provided a clear and unambiguous focus for local status battles although little is known in detail about the social processes that determined their outcomes. The Council's meetings were held in and around the dinh the commune's central building, and therefore close to the shrines of the commune's tutelary spirit. Seating at communal feasts centred upon the dinh and conferred recognition of rank (10.).

The Council of Notables set taxes and labour duties whilst gaining still further power by its right to allocate the communal lands (ruong cong, cong dien). These were a substantial proportion (on average over 25%) of the paddy area, and were meant to be distributed to those in need, and at least 'fairly'. It appears that extensive private landholdings were quite rare, and economic rivalry, as well as social struggles, focused upon the commune's formal organs, of which the Council of Notables was probably the most important. The Vietnamese peasant tended not to be a tenant, but a farmer of land held either as private land (**tu dien**) or as of right, in the form of communal land. Since communal institutions legally enforced access to land, it was correspondingly difficult to hold land in more than one commune. The system placed considerable constraints upon land concentration and the largest landholder in any given commune was usually the commune itself. The social system placed reasonably effective constraints upon the growth of large private landholdings outside the influence of the commune.

Vietnamese peasants were well versed in the concepts of group liability for taxes and labour duties, and therefore with the corresponding avoidance strategies when they saw these claims from higher levels as excessive. Dynastic land records, for instance, were at root used for tax bargaining, and doctored accordingly. The commune kept good control of its agent responsible for contacts with the lowest levels of the state apparatus (usually known as the **ly truong**, or mayor).

Yet communes were far from uniform. In some the communal land extended over almost all the area farmed by the population, whilst in others it was almost negligible. Internal organisation also varied, for instance in the relative importance of large kinship groups (**ho**) and the villages (**thon**, sometimes **lang**) of the commune (11.). This variation emphasises the endogeneity of the communal form, for such wide differences within the unchanging basic framework allowed local issues - such as water-control, use of river-banks for cultivation, extensive artisanal activity, religious variation etc. - to influence precise organisational content. What was universal, however, was the cultural importance of the commune to its members and the corresponding focus of attention upon it as the centre of their social existence.

1.6 The generation of economic surplus in pre-modern Vietnam: the overall picture

Vietnam's overall level of economic development in the mid 19th century was not very high. Foreign travellers commented upon the general poverty of North and Central Vietnam which, as the areas near to population saturation, did not generate large economic surpluses (12.).

The reproducability of commune and state relied upon three main forms of surplus mobilisation and extraction. First, the archetypal peasant-cultivator family, whether farming communal or private land (or both), used the major part of any output that was surplus to the needs of simple reproduction for an extension of the family - extra wives, wives for sons, adopting children etc. This did not tend to involve any great increase in the size of the production unit. Furthermore, in bad times it was all too easily reversed if conditions deteriorated. Second, part of any surplus supported the exploita-

tive superstructure of the commune - bribes to notables, religious ceremonials etc., while a third part went to the state
as tax payments, principally in kind, supplemented by compul-
sory labour services.

Urbanisation was strictly limited, and heavily dependent
upon the resource flows appropriated by the state. Both petty
commodity production and artisanal activities were widespread.
Trade was mainly over relatively short distances, and women
(as mentioned above) played an important role in its organisation. A well-established long-distance trading network flouri-
shed by sea along the coast, and sea trade also took place
with China and the Malay archipelago. Whilst Vietnamese historians have found some evidence for capitalist growth in pre-
modern Vietnam (the so-called 'germs of capitalism'), this was
very weak (13.). There is no real evidence for the buoyant
merchant-capitalist expansion seen, for instance, in late
Tokugawa Japan [Smith 1959]. Technological dynamism based upon
imported innovations was extremely limited; the fertile and
largely empty Mekong delta in the South was only on the thre-
shold of systematic extensive development when the French took
over in the 1860s.

Conclusions

Before the French conquest North Vietnamese society was
relatively well-developed and had evolved institutions over
the centuries that appear appropriate. The area was characterised by broadly static technology and a high-risk agriculture subject to a strong tendency towards population saturation usually offset by out-migration across an open border.
The society was approaching a crisis of intensive stagnation;
with existing technology, any closure of the open frontier
would precipitate a downward adjustment of population as the
prevailing methods of production and surplus mobilisation
showed themselves unable to advance further. The population
losses of the civil wars had delayed the time when this point
would be reached, but had subsequently generated high population growth that would ensure a considerable 'over-shoot' if
and when the moment finally did come. By the late 19th
century, however, expansion at the extensive margin was once
again becoming the sole source of a growth that the momentum
of population growth now demanded with added urgency. The
basic framework of commune and state continued successfully to
generate the relatively low levels of economic surplus required by the technologically static economy; this framework
was aptly suited for takeover by foreign or domestic rulers
who might have quite different aims from those of the neo-
Confucian Vietnamese Emperors.

1.7 The colonial impact

The economic impact of European colonialism differed throughout the various regions of Indochina. The static account was fairly straightforward (as measured by, say, the net resource outflow) but the dynamic effects were much more complex. The French presence induced deep changes in Northern rural society (14.).

With some adaptation, the French were able to use the tax system of the Vietnamese Emperors to extract resources from the predominantly peasant populations in North, Central and South Vietnam (respectively Tonkin, Annam and Cochinchina). This largely financial flow provided the budgetary receipts needed to ensure that their Indochinese Union was 'self-financing', or, in other words, to pay for the top-heavy French colonial administration.

In addition, trade was developed so that profits accrued to French domestic or colonial companies. Such colonial profits derived principally from the following: exports of rice from the low population density regions of the South (the Mekong Delta); exports of plantation products - rubber, tea and coffee - primarily from the red earth lands in the uplands of South-Central and North Vietnam; exports of minerals - coal, tin and other items - predominantly from certain limited areas in North Vietnam and Laos. In the Northern heartlands of the Red River Delta, the most important and profitable areas of colonial economic activity were the plantations, which were far less extensive than those in the South, and the mines, of which those in the Hong Gay coal basin near Haiphong were the largest. Industrialisation was minimal and almost negligible (15.).

Most Vietnamese still lived in their communes and experienced the direct economic impact of the French presence above all in the increased and now monetised tax load. Initially heedless of the likely consequences, the new state lacked the dynastic Court's commitment to the rural commune. The imposition of high taxes payable in cash had profound effects upon rural society (16.). Rising demographic pressure exacerbated the tendency for land to become the object of strategies of private accumulation based upon financial exploitation via usury or commerce. This ran quite against the strongly corporate nature of the ideal traditional commune; the commune's important social functions, especially in such areas as risk insurance, fell into decline. Popular sentiments were strongly opposed to such trends. However, despite a rising incidence of migrant labour, most of the rural economically active population remained in their communes. Some had the unpleasant experience of working in the mines or on the plantations, but employment there was never particularly large compared with the total labour force.

The counterpart of the increased financial outflow from

rural areas to pay taxes was not a rise in peasants' commodity sales. The basic reasons for this were the rising demographic pressure in the already densely populated North and Centre, and the limited capacity of producers there to increase output and the export of food surpluses from the Mekong. Instead the money was re-channelled into the countryside, usually as consumption loans to peasants against the security of land. Loss of land, whether communal or private, and the fear of it, was a major fact of life for peasants in the 1920s and 1930s. As a result, 'individualised' mechanisms such as landlordism, usury and manipulation of trade started to replace the traditional 'corporate' sources of social and economic power [Fforde 1983:52-60]. The new and rising social groups did not fit easily into the communal system, which began to fall into decline. Councils of Notables came to be dominated and manipulated by a rising landlord-usurer group, prompting great hostility from ordinary peasants. Communal lands were no longer 'fairly' distributed, and peasants thereby lost a vital insurance against the vagaries of childbirth and the weather. Making this process of increasing rural differentiation even more distressing, however, was the continued rapid population growth that eroded the aggregate subsistence margin. It is abundantly clear that the outcome for most peasants was an increasingly unpleasant life [Ngo Vinh Long 1973].

Social institutions were now open to radical criticism that could attract peasant support for revolutionary change. Furthermore, the economic potential of the area had increased enormously. Western technology meant that both agricultural and non-agricultural output could rise sharply, given appropriate methods of social organisation (whatever that meant) and adequate resources. French colonialism had not realised this potential, and agricultural technology remained little changed from the pre-modern period. The link between institutions and available production methods had broken, and for many peasants open rebellion offered the only means of securing basic subsistence (17.). Re-establishing this link and realising the opportunities offered by new technology meant placing economic development amongst the highest priorities, and was therefore crucial to discussion of the state's proper role. Any future Vietnamese government would therefore differ sharply from those of the past in its necessary focus upon the dynamics and modalities of 'national economic development'.

An acute problem was the effect of population saturation in the North and Centre upon the regional pattern of the existing economic surplus. Crude colonial calculations suggested the following: after a 10% rise in mass living-standards and a complete levelling-down of all incomes to that of the poor peasants, the North would still have had an aggregate savings potential of only 22%. Maintaining the above-average but still low incomes of the 'middle' peasantry would have cut the savings potential to 5%. For the South, on the other hand, the savings potential was far higher (18.). Thus for the North alone a strategy of reliance upon extraction of domestic surpluses would have implied great pressure upon a 'middle' peasantry that was, by any standards, extremely poor.

Conclusions

This survey of socio-economic developments in the pre-modern period has necessarily been rapid. The effects of the French colonial presence upon Vietnamese society had a number of important implications for the future economic development of the area that the DRV would occupy. First, by making the existing situation intolerable the French made peasants in the North and Centre all too aware of the need for change in rural institutions. The French also provided a new focus against which to revive traditional nationalist sentiments.

Second, whilst the French clearly demonstrated the power and scope of modern production technology, the colonial system revealed an inability to realise this potential in the form of significant gains in per capita output and incomes in the important population saturation areas. Industrial development was almost non-existent. In the meantime, gathering demographic pressures resulting from the population growth momentum built up since the early 19th century could only be absorbed at the extensive frontier - the Mekong Delta. Whilst the potential long-run population equilibrium in the high-density areas had risen, the widespread breakdown of the communal system was increasing risk sharply whilst population growth eroded the intensive subsistence margin.

Third, by retaining the basic forms of the dynastic state at both macro and micro level the French helped to perpetuate the traditional definition of the roles of local institutions in terms of their ability to establish relationships with higher levels that were satisfactory to local interests. Peasants - with good reason - still saw corporate institutions as suitable ways of carrying out valued social functions. Erosion of that role in high-risk areas by the processes of landloss and the shift to more private sources of economic power only heightened the perceived value of collective organisation.

This suggests the following brief summary of the main objective constraints facing socio-economic development in North Vietnam. Viewed statically, the area was extremely poor, without any significant development of modern industry and dominated by subsistence wet-rice cultivation. The basic social structure of centralised state and corporate rural commune had coped well with the technical and military needs of the pre-modern state, but was being radically altered by the French colonial impact. Viewed dynamically, so long as the increased production potential offered by Western technology remained untapped, rapid population growth was only offset by expansion at the extensive margin permitted of the open Southern border. This meant that closure of the frontier would precipitate, sooner or later, a subsistence crisis in the North unless economic resources could be found to finance economic development and the investment needed to raise agricultural output. These resources were not easily available from within the Northern economy. Furthermore, the Northern peasantry valued and was familiar with the roles of corporate rural institutions as sources of insurance against risk and protective intermediaries against unwanted surplus extraction. They would, therefore, probably meet a gathering subsistence crisis by shoring up those institutions and strengthening their collective power.

II: Subjective constraints: the origins of post-independence social structures - Party and Proletarian state.

1.8 The Party's revolutionary goals: experience and norms.

The particular attitudes and perceptions of the nationalist leaders who took power after the departure of the French may fairly be viewed as part of the DRV's historical inheritance. These men were those Communists who had managed to secure effective control over the nationalist movement - the Vietminh - by the early 1950s if not earlier. They were the builders - but not the architects - of the DRV state and its social institutions (19.).

Their struggles against both the French and other elements within the Vietminh culminated in the simultaneous successes of Land Reform and the battle of Dien Bien Phu in 1953-54. The latter effectively gave them the internationally recognised sovereign state of the Democratic Republic, for the 1954 Geneva Conference agreed that the French were finally to leave, although only the northern half of the country. The former, whilst establishing beyond doubt the regime's radical thrust and the political hegemony of the Communist leadership, effectively destroyed the internal unity of the nationalist movement.

After 1954-55 the post-independence DRV government adopted essentially foreign institutional forms [Elliott 1976]. The framework created in the Soviet Union during the 1920s and 1930s provided both the basic principles of organisation and their fine detail. The apparently clear-cut neo-Stalinist framework did not, in practice, provide a strict guide to the realities of Vietnamese socialism, for those controlling the DRV's leading institutions naturally operated both in and through the existing society and economy of North Vietnam. Strong constraints operated to limit the possibilities for Socialist Transformation and Socialist Construction along the lines prescribed, which stressed the extraction of surplus from agriculture and the rapid creation of an industrial base. Consequently, local interests routinely adapted Socialist

27

institutions. This meant that for many years the Party's public pronouncements about social and economic development could not begin to reflect day-to-day reality, and Party theoreticians had to cope with the massive non-implementability of the Party Line, which was, on the contrary, deemed to be both correct and realisable [Fforde 1986]. This resulted in a characteristic combination of pragmatism and idealism [White 1982].

The history of the Party and its leadership throws light upon these and other aspects of the DRV's subsequent development. Precisely because of the existence of an apparently clearly defined 'model' of socialism, Party policy towards the precise nature and content of the Vietnamese Socialist Revolution often appears weakly defined. Clearly the Party itself, based upon the leadership of a nationalist movement, was not primarily or initially the articulation of profound radical forces. During the 1930s the urban proletariat was extremely small (20.). Much of the Party's dynamism derived from the mentality of the top leadership, whose formal thinking on developmental matters was essentially foreign. The Party had avoided the dramatic purges suffered by others and the central group's cohesion greatly depended upon the continuing vitality and high status of the new knowledge : 'Mac Le-nin' (Marxism-Leninism). This reinforced any tendency to persist with inappropriate policies after their shortcomings had become apparent.

The history of the Party prior to 1945 has been well studied although research into the post-war period is surprisingly weak (21.). Here there are a number of important basic points. Whilst nationalism was always a powerful force, there were close historical ties between the Party leadership and the international Communist movement. Ho Chi Minh was a founder member of the French Communist Party, and active in Moscow-dominated international Communist organisations. He survived the Moscow purges of the 1930s, and had taught at the Lenin Institute. He had seen the effects of the close ties with Moscow upon the Chinese Communists' struggle during the 1920s, and had experienced such problems himself in the late 1940s, when the DRV had remained unrecognised by the Communist world whilst Moscow's attention was focused upon the prospects of the French Communist Party.

Material support from the Chinese Communists after they occupied Guangdung in 1949 was a sine qua non for the final French defeat at Dien Bien Phu (22.). As Ho himself had written, it was the international Communist movement's potential for providing a means to attain Vietnamese National Liberation that had first attracted him to Leninism [Ho Chi Minh 1977:250-2]. This suggests that Vietnamese Communists would tend on the whole towards an ambiguous approach to the international Communist movement. This would entail attempting to balance the drive for Vietnamese independence with the global tenets of Socialist Revolution.

A second major factor was the important social role traditionally played by Vietnamese intellectuals. This was historically conditioned by the deep cultural roots of the society
and especially the religious and administrative practices of
the dynastic state. Neo-Confucian mandarins, Buddhist monks
and the **nom** literary tradition, for all their differences, all
placed a high premium upon those who worked with their 'grey
matter' ('**chat xam**'). Whilst A.B.Woodside's statement to the
effect that the country was 'one of the most intensely literary on the planet' is perhaps hard to accept, it should not
be forgotten that, for all its poverty and lack of economic
development, Vietnamese culture had (and has) a deep respect
for intellectual endeavour. This shows up particularly clearly
in the extent and character of the DRV leadership's own published work.

It has often been argued that, by the 1940s, the Chinese
intelligentsia had largely embraced Marxism as a fount of
truth and a new way forward (23.). Even if this is true, it is
doubtful whether this was ever the case in Vietnam. The Party
was far less important in educated circles in the 1930s than
it was in China, and was a much lower percentage of the population in 1945 (24.). For these reasons alone, it appears
certain that Communism was rather less of a force in Vietnamese intellectual life than in China (25.). As the New Society
arose in the 1950s, the Communist Party (then still called the
Vietnam Workers' Party (VWP)) was more deeply influenced by
sources outside Marxism-Leninism. In the end, national characteristics and traditions probably had greater weight and durability than Socialist thought. At the very least, though, new
tenets had to compete, more or less overtly, with other ideas
if they were to retain their power.

The precise international context and the point reached in
the evolution of world Communism in the 1950s was also of
great importance. At that time the international Communist
movement was still dominated by the Soviet Union, and presented a formula for Socialist Revolution far more fixed than it
has since become. North Vietnam's new leaders inevitably found
themselves under pressure to adopt development strategies and
institutions said to be of universal validity. This pressure
was increased by the DRV's dependency on the Communist bloc
for resources to finance the two objectives of economic construction and national reunification. The country's poverty
meant that, at least for much of its early stages, foreign aid
would have to finance the development program. The DRV would
lave to import almost all modern means of production. At the
same time armed struggle against whatever regime had come to
rule the South would, like the success at Dien Bien Phu,
depend upon large supplies of military materiel that the DRV
could not produce for itself.

These considerations meant, in the end, that policy was

reliance on Soviet model

somewhat inflexible. Explicit and overt adaptation of received models was hemmed in by both external pressures and the Communist leadership's perceived need to defend Marxism-Leninism. This is not to deny that ultimate responsibility for social and economic policy in a sovereign state rests with the government. But the strength of the inherited objective constraints and the neo-Stalinist models' inappropriateness argued for a highly flexible approach that was lacking, although in practice local interests saw to it that such modifications were implemented as far as was possible. By the mid 1960s, therefore, the Communist leadership found itself committed to an economic system that experience had shown to be ill-suited to Vietnamese conditions. Furthermore, escalation of the war was occurring in a situation where mass propaganda had already linked popular mobilisation for the nationalist struggle closely to the extant DRV Socialist Revolution. This made policy changes even more difficult as wartime hyper-nationalism ratcheted up psychological pressures to resist US bombing and continue the struggle.

Conclusions

In refering to the above as subjective problems the authors do not wish to treat 'subjectivity' as anything much more than a convenient label for the desires and perceptions of the post-1954 DRV leaders. The value they attached to the neo-Stalinist model was clearly one major constraint on the possible pattern of socio-economic development in the DRV and therefore one source of the limits of national liberation. The other major constraints arose from the objective conditions discussed above - the nature of the society within which the DRV's institutions had to operate and which largely determined how things would go in practice. These constraints had two main characteristics: first, the relatively low level of mobilisable economic surplus - this was exacerbated by the legacy of a strong momentum in population growth previously relieved by extensive expansion across the southern border which was now shut tight; second, the familiarity of the peasantry with methods of coping with the extractive strategies of centralised nation-states. This meant that any attempt, however desirable, to extract resources forcibly from the impoverished rural areas would be met by the tactical responses of people well-experienced in avoiding such strategies.

Footnotes

1. The non-delta areas are referred to as the midlands (trung du) and mountains (mien nui), and have historically been occupied by ethnic minorities [Hickey 1982]. The country is conventionally divided into three regions - the North, Centre and South. In modern Vietnamese, these are mien bac,

mien trung and **mien nam** respectively. This broadly corresponds
to the colonial division of the country into Tonkin, Annam and
Cochinchina. Modern Western usage typically refers to the DRV
as 'the North' and the now-defunct Republic of Vietnam as 'the
South'. The following discussion uses the latter convention
except where the context makes it obvious that the Vietnamese
sense is intended.

2. This is not simply the blast and counter-blast of
ideological conflict (e.g. Chesneaux 1961 and 1966; Honey
1961); see for example Pham van Kinh's review of Dang Phong
(1970) in NCLS 136 1971. Accessible works in Western languages
are Thomas Hodgkin (1981) and Le Thanh Khoi (1981). Fforde
(1983) provides, inter alia, a survey of some of the available
writings in Vietnamese. See Norlund (1986) for a brief introduction to the Western literature. See also Nguyen Khac Vien
(1974) and Taylor's review [Taylor 1974] of a major North
Vietnamese historical study [UKX 1971]. Note that Cotter
(1968) argues that population pressure was less important than
political instability in explaining the March to the South.

3. Woodside (1971) is still the standard work on the neo-
Confucian state of the 19th century. See Taylor (1976) for a
study of state-formation in the 10th century.

4. See Woodside (1976), also Huynh Kim Khanh (1982). For
studies of Vietnamese nationalism see Marr (1971 and 1981),
White (1979) and Duiker (1976). For an explicit comparison of
Vietnam and the West see Smith (1968). The present authors are
not unaware of their own cultural myopia, and are conscious of
the fact that for many Vietnamese the present work most likely
misses the point by focusing upon a rationalist - if not
mechanistic - analysis of socio-economic interaction rather
than the lasting vitalities of Vietnamese culture; they lack
the 'cultural point of view' - **'quan diem van hoa'**. Like
others, however, they try to be consistent.

5. By far the best and most accessible study of the geography of the Red River Delta and the interaction between it
and agriculture remains Chassigneux (1912); see also Rambo
(1973).

6. It is far easier to understand state-formation in pre-
modern Vietnam than it is to understand the evolution of
villages. Yet the latter is probably the more important process. For a discussion of the role of corporate villages in
reducing risk see Scott (1976).

7. Population data prior to the French conquest is unreliable [Rambo 1973:170 et seq.]. The rapid increase in
population just before the Second World War is reasonably
certain but extremely hard to quantify [Fforde 1983:111, 113].
The two best sources on the subject are Ng Shui Meng (1974)
and Smolsky (1937). After a thorough survey of the available
information the former will not attempt any conclusion for
population growth in North Vietnam, but thought that for the
Union as a whole it probably rose from around 1-1.5% annually

31

to around 3% in 1936-45 [Ng Shui Meng 1974:23-24]. Rambo (1973) assembles data from a number of French sources suggesting that the Red River Delta population rose from 5.5 m. in 1906-07 to 6.5 m. in 1931, implying an annual growth rate of around 0.6% [op.cit.:176] that is most unlikely to be accurate. It has to be accepted that population data for North Vietnam is extremely unreliable.

8. For a discussion of somewhat similar processes in 19th century Ireland, with equally tragic result, see Crotty (1966) pp.28-66.

9. For a reasonably full discussion based upon a survey of the extensive North Vietnamese literature, and a bibliography see Fforde (1983). One of the most interesting items in the North Vietnamese literature is Nguyen Huu Nghinh and Bui Huy Lo (1978). For Western language sources, see also Le van Hao (1962), Mus (1949), Ngo Vinh Long (1973), Nguyen Huu Khang (1946) and Nguyen van Khoan (1930), as well as various articles in the series 'Vietnamese Studies'. Since they are rarely footnoted and intended for foreign consumption the latter should be read with caution.

10. These buildings survive today, sometimes in use, sometimes abandoned. They are almost unique amongst Vietnamese architecture in that they are built upon piles, and they sometimes convey an atmosphere of long use for religious and social activity reminiscent perhaps of Norman parish churches. They are largely constructed, though, of wood.

11. Although this is the convention for translation of these terms that is used throughout the present text. Other conventions exist, most commonly the translation of **xa** as village. For an extremely interesting discussion of the traditional commune's internal organisation (in English) severely marred by the almost total absence of sourcing see Nguyen Tu Chi (n/d). Note that **ho** here is a different word from that translated below (chapter 6, fn. 5) as 'family'.

12. See Ngo Vinh Long (1973), Crawfurd (1830) pp.:338-9 and Nguyen The Anh (1967).

13. E.g. Van Tan (1970) and the early interchange between Nguyen Viet, To Minh Trung and Dang Viet Thanh during 1963. An interesting article by Pham van Kinh (1971) argues that better-off peasants tended to avoid diversifying out of agriculture into artisanal activities because of their relative unprofitability.

14. Here it is vital to distinguish the North and Centre, where population densities were near saturation levels, from the South (the Mekong delta) where, on the frontier region, it was possible to mobilise large economic surpluses. Robequain (1944) remains a most informative work, as is Bernard (1934); Fforde (1983) ch.2 explores the ideas presented below in greater detail and lists relevant sources in the bibliography. Murray (1980) places far too much stress upon the integration of Vietnamese agriculture into the world capitalist system; in

the North and Centre this was extremely limited, not least because of the region's poverty (e.g. op.cit. p.315 - 'Colonial rule entailed the metropolitan domination of the processes of production and distribution').

15. Employment in modern industry in the late 1930s totalled some 85,000 [Fforde 1983:62-63; George 1954].

16. See Scott (1976), Popkin (1979) and Ngo Vinh Long (1973).

17. Apart from Scott (1976) and Popkin (1979), the 1930s rebellions have also been studied by John Kleinen, whose preliminary results can be found in Kleinen (1982).

18. Fforde (1983) pp.64-8 based upon Bernard (1934). It should be stressed that these are extremely simple ex post calculations based upon crude data estimating the distribution of personal incomes. They aim only at indicating the poverty of the North and the importance of the South's economic surplus to the mobilisation of resources for any development strategy.

19. By far the best history of the Vietnamese Communist movement is Huynh Kim Khanh (1982). For a biography of Ho Chi Minh see Lacouture (1968).

20. Modern industry employed around 90,000 in the entire Indochinese Union in 1939 [George 1954:50-57]. See also Woodside (1976) pp.205-6.

21. Here the authors follow Huynh Kim Khanh (1982). Mention should be made of the work of Douglas Pike (1978) and R.F.Turner (1975). The offical Party documents in 'Lich su Dang Cong san Viet nam' VBS 1978 and 1979 are also of great interest.

22. According to Tanham (1961) the monthly tonnage transported across the Sino-Vietnamese border rose from 10-20 tonnes in 1951 to 250 tonnes by the end of 1952 and by the beginning of the battle of Dien Bien Phu was averaging over 1,000 tonnes [op.cit.:9].

23. See Pickowicz (1981) and Bianco (1971) chapter 2. Compare Woodside (1976) ch.6.

24. Communist Party membership in 1945 totalled around 5,000, compared with 1.2 m. for the Chinese Communist Party [Woodside 1976:234 et seq.]. 25. For a somewhat contrary view that stresses the important guiding role played by Marxism-Leninism in Vietnam, see Marr (1981) pp.363 et seq. See also Sachs (1959).

Chapter Two

THE DRV - IMMEDIATE ORIGINS, PROBLEMS OF THE POLITICAL TRANSI-
TION AND BASIC STRUCTURE. THE AGGRAVATED SHORTAGE ECONOMY.

2.1 Introduction

This chapter aims to present, in a schematic and general
way, the underlying logic of the pattern of economic and
social development in the DRV. It focuses upon factors leading
to the creation of what we term an 'aggravated shortage
economy'.

Experiences under the pre-1954 administration

For the incoming government in 1954-55 the change from
nationalist struggle to peacetime administration was not as
substantial as might have been expected, for the Vietminh had
controlled substantial areas of North Vietnam since the late
1940s.

The small size of the Communist Party in 1945 meant that
the Party's power largely derived from its position within the
nationalist movement - the Vietminh. Within the Party leadership, the overall effect of French purges during the 1930s had
been to make the top organisation basically an alliance of
individuals. The Vietminh Army was of great importance, made
up, in essence, of 'the Party plus the children of the peasantry'. Many peasants were open to nationalist calls and their
basic demands were for changes in rural organisation to end
the landloss of the colonial period, eviction of the French
and education and social advancement for their children. The
more radical ideas of the Communist leadership were somewhat
foreign to these wishes. Before 1954 the Communist leadership
had three primary aims in its policies towards the administration of the liberated areas. These were, first, the establishment of an effective military opposition to French colonial
rule; second, the creation of a reliable base for those activities; and third, ensuring that their own position within the
nationalist movement was both secure and capable of giving
them control when the French left. The evolution of these
policies paralleled changes in the international context as

34

well as in the armed struggle against the French and their
allies (1.).

One major source of nationalist strength was the Vietminh's successful use of its own local administrative system
to avoid or confront the agents of the colonial state as and
when desired. In principle, each commune in the liberated
areas possessed a 'Resistance Committee' that coordinated
Vietminh activities. This provided taxes both in cash and in
kind, supplied labour for the military and the corvee, and
maintained law and order. The use of Front organisations - the
Peasants' Association, the Women's Union etc, also helped to
mobilise popular support (2.).

These groups sought to provide the Communist leadership
with a method of social control based upon vertical links to
the Centre of the anti-French movement - the so-called
Parallel Hierarchies - and they were therefore an important
mechanism both for coordinating the struggle and for allowing
the Communist leadership to secure its position. French contemporary sources stress the importance of competition between
the existing state apparatus and that of the Vietminh for
control of the population.

Problems of the political transition

By the time that the French left in 1954-55 central authority had greatly weakened. Like the Nguyen dynasty the incoming government needed to exert and extend its influence by
creating an effective mechanism for the use of state power:
the Dictatorship of the Proletariat - chuyen chinh vo san. The
remnants of the French system did not have any great effect
upon the new government, for many Vietnamese who had worked
closely with the colonial power either went to the South or
left for France; competition between the old and incoming
state officials was not an important political problem. The
key conflict at the time of the handover of power (1954-55)
was instead that within the Vietminh that arose as a result of
the second stage of Land Reform.

The official Party history quite correctly divides Land
Reform into two separate stages (3.). During the first, of
'partial reforms under the democratic administration', Communist ideas did not play an overt role. The land reallocation
sought by the great mass of the peasantry was the responsibility of local authority and therefore often outside direct
Communist control. Most of the land reallocated during Land
Reform was given out during this period, which ended in late
1953 [Tran Phuong 1968:Table 7 and p.167]. One implication of
this was that the land available for further redistribution
was extremely limited. But the second stage that followed
immediately upon the first took a far more radical direction.
It aimed ultimately at the creation of a collectivised agriculture and systematically attacked those in the rural areas

35

whom the Party deemed to be exploiters of the 'working peasantry'. This stage was not only avowedly classist, but was also centrally organised and aimed, by 'purifying' the Vietminh, to remove rural opposition to the Communist Party. As such, it inevitably created strong tensions between the great mass of non-Communist Vietminh local leaders, many of whom came from better-off backgrounds, and the zealous teams of young Land Reform cadres who came into villages in order to purge them of anti-Revolutionary elements [Moise 1977; White 1981]. These tensions soon erupted into open conflict that effectively destroyed the unity of the nationalist movement.

The difficulties presented to the Party leadership by Land Reform show rather convincingly the nature of the Vietminh as a somewhat diffuse movement focused predominantly upon nationalist rather than Communist aims. The Party naturally viewed these problems with great concern, and this is shown by the political consequences. Amongst the more notable of these were: the resignation of then Party First Secretary Truong Chinh in 1955; the disbanding of the independent Land Reform structure and its integration into pre-existing channels; and the Correction of Errors campaign of 1956-57 which saw the rehabilitation of many labelled as 'counter-revolutionaries' whose views of the Party must have generated deep suspicion. These rehabilitations appear to have had lasting results, for unlike China and other countries, in Vietnam class affiliation based upon family categorisation during Land Reform does not appear to have had great and lasting social consequences.

The Party's public admission of errors thus occurred on the eve of agrarian collectivisation (1959-60) when local administration was still largely unreconstructed after the turmoil of the closing stage of Land Reform. This suggests, that despite its firm control over the central organs of Party and state, the Communist leadership finished Land Reform without the hoped-for strong and loyal grass-roots apparatus. Such machinery was a prerequisite to enforcing the high procurement levels needed to overcome possible future difficulties in implementing a policy of forced development. The basic structural dichotomy of state and commune persisted, and the centre, as ever, could not fully control the periphery. In addition, the arbitrary and frightening way in which Land Reform was carried out probably made many peasants less willing to place great confidence in the new government.

Non-Communist attitudes towards the new government

We argue, then, that the DRV was from the very beginning a 'weak' state. An important factor here is the general level of support for the new government. Information is limited. Once eviction of the French was no longer the focus of political activity, and Land Reform - for all its problems - finally over, two important sources of Communist popular support had gone. Like any other newly independent government, success or failure in guiding socio-economic development was a major criteria by which the general population would judge the regime. Opposition from the peasantry was likely if they saw threats to their newly acquired landholdings.

It seems likely that the very early 1960s marked a watershed in peacetime support for the Communist government. Economic conditions were still relatively good, and opportunities for social advance plentiful for some in a growing bureaucratic system. By then too the Party had reined-in the excesses of ideological control and 'class-struggle' of Land Reform and the period before de-Stalinisation, whilst the personal and psychological pressures of wartime hyper-mobilisation after 1965 were still absent. Towards the end of the Five Year Plan (1961-65), however, recognition of the shortcomings of the DRV's economic system in the face of worsening economic difficulties and the gathering implications of North Vietnam's international dependency upon the Communist bloc probably started to have adverse effects. At the same time the massive increase in educational and other opportunites for state employment since 1955 had helped to create a quite new 'red bourgeoisie' (4.). This was in practice almost completely excluded from political power and the DRV's central organs, which remained dominated by the top Communist leadership assembled by Ho Chi Minh. The increasing economic difficulties of the First Five Year Plan culminated in the gathering crisis of 1963-64, when the Party's popular position probably started to deteriorate rapidly (see below).

The return to armed struggle in the South and the onset of heavy US bombing in 1965 marked the Party's return to the use of nationalism as the main means to social mobilisation and its own legitimation. The hyper-nationalistic lengths to which this was taken are visible from the reports of many foreign visitors [e.g. Bernal 1971]. Viewed from a longer time perspective, however, this meant that domestic political opposition remained extremely underdeveloped. External threats and the corresponding need and opportunity to mobilise nationalistic sentiments helped stifle the development of both Party and non-Party political institutions in North Vietnam.

Although the DRV was dependent upon foreign aid, its donors cannot be held entirely responsible for the decision in the late 1950s not to modify the neo-Stalinist development model in the run-up to the First Five Year Plan. Abundant evidence existed to encourage misgivings about its applicability in North Vietnam. Quite apart from the Soviet Union itself, the experiences of Poland and other countries in Eastern Europe had already shown the costs involved in imposing extractive policies upon agricultures that possessed higher potential and actual mobilisable surpluses, as well as security forces backed up by the Soviet Army (a 'strong state' lacking in the DRV). Furthermore, by the late 1950s the Chinese had had sufficient experience with the neo-Stalinist model for well-informed policy-makers to be well aware of its shortcomings. The impossibility of a quantum leap to a new level of technology was rammed home by the experiences of the Great Leap itself in 1958. [The DRV leaders' continued commitment to the neo-Stalinist model despite such evidence was ultimately responsible for what was to follow.]

2.2 Basic shortcomings of the neo-Stalinist strategy

The primary duty of the entire transitional period in the North is Socialist industrialisation, of which the key is the development of heavy industry.

IIIrd Congress of the Vietnam Workers' Party,
Sept. 1960, quoted in EPU 1975:28.

Once they had attained power, the Vietnamese Communist leadership consciously sought to implement the process of social and economic development that would constitute their hoped-for Socialist Revolution. The main means to this end had to be the power granted by the Party's control over the apparatus of the DRV state. They believed in the neo-Stalinist assumption that the most fundamental, and therefore most important, constraint upon national economic development was the availability of industrial fixed capital. Implicit in this notion is the idea that production coefficients are so inflexible that a given increase in the capital stock will necessarily result in some more-or-less proportionate rise in output [Nove 1977:37]. Furthermore, since the level of complementary input supplies never - according to this view - constrains output, it follows that questions regarding material incentives are seen as secondary, and not vital to the development of the economy. Efforts must therefore focus upon the overriding goal of investment in modern industry. The strategy assumes that the complementary inputs needed to utilise that capacity will be available.

Certain prerequisites have to be met if there is to be economic growth based upon the new industrial capital. In an area of extremely low economic surplus any substantial initial investment program will necessarily be aid-financed in its early stages. If the decision is taken to allocate priority to modern industry then simply installing the new assets does not pose any great difficulties: they merely come 'off the boat'. The issue is rather how to obtain the resources needed to operate them, and this is, in essence, the complementary inputs problem. Where are these inputs to come from? The implicit assumption behind the neo-Stalinist strategy is that they can be acquired administratively by the state and directed into those key sectors to which the state has given investment priority. This presupposes that the use of such basically extractive policies does not have too adverse an effect, either directly, upon the supply of these complementary inputs, or indirectly, upon factors of production influencing complementary inputs supply. An obvious example is that of the food needed to secure the effective cooperation of the new industrial labour force. In a low-surplus economy such as that of the DRV these prerequisites are absent.

In themselves, extractive policies aimed at securing complementary inputs through administrative methods inevitably depress output levels in agriculture and elsewhere below what they would otherwise have been. These adverse effects act directly in two ways. First, they reduce producer incentives in so far as the state uses administrative power to override direct incentives and ensure its own access to resources. If the direct incentives were favourable then those in a position to supply these resources would be willing to supply them without such coercion. The use of administrative methods therefore of itself means that the incentives encouraging voluntary supply are weak, and so, other things being equal, output will be lower. Second, by using administrative methods the state imposes allocative inefficiencies. This happens because of the shift away from distributional relations that provide incentives for producers to note input costs towards more bureaucratic methods that typically do not. It goes without saying that the output from new industries may partly or completely offset these two types of loss; the point is that they exist. In particular, extraction of surplus from agriculture must reduce real farmer incomes and therefore producer incentives unless there are (contrary to the neo-Stalinist strategy) counteracting increases in supplies to agriculture from industry.

In the DRV foreign aid rather than the domestic economy financed initial industrial investment. Despite this, however, the state's inability to secure the complementary inputs needed by the priority sectors was a major constraint upon growth, as it could be in any developing economy where the state takes responsibility for such supplies. This is conditioned by the alternatives available to whoever supplies such inputs: foreign aid donors, domestic labour, non-socialist sector producers etc. As the 'universal input', labour is of particular importance. In the absence of terror, workers almost always retain some freedom to seek out alternative income-sources. And as and if labour and other incentives move unfavourably, considerable potential is created for the whole-scale diversion of economic resources into other areas, most especially onto some form of 'free market'.

This restriction of complementary input supplies, especially through market effects, may then reinforce the poor incentives both to input suppliers and to efficient resource use in industry, further depressing output below its potential. Modern industry will neither obtain effective and re-

foreign aid financed

39

liable inputs nor, since its inputs will be heavily subsidised, respond properly to the costs of producing them. Any
state cash deficit will, by pushing up free market prices,
assist this process. The state's economic and social policies
will then have created the macro and microeconomic conditions
for an 'aggravated shortage economy'. Within the administratively supplied sectors low levels of capacity utilisation and severe micro-inefficiencies will help constrain output to levels consistent with the state's ability to extract
resources from the rest of the domestic economy and its monopoly control over foreign trade. Over the longer term both the
nature of the accumulation process and the pattern of short-
term resource allocation cut the output potential of the
system. If these losses become sufficiently large, Socialist
sector output may actually begin to fall despite continued
increases in the fixed capital stock. This apparently para-
doxical result is more easily visualised if the reader ima-
gines a situation where, because of acute food shortages
within the state sector, industrial workers start refusing to
turn up for work because they have to seek sources of cash
incomes in order to buy food from peasants with which to feed
their families.

In such situations both macro and micro economic policies
become subject to considerable pressure. Plans become unreal-
isable, not least because of the unpredictability of input-
output and capital-output ratios in practice. In North Vietnamese conditions where the existing economic surplus was low
and widespread terror in rural areas politically impossible
the state could never, in effect, implement such policies.
Thus central directives rarely determined the actual day-to-
day content of the DRV's various micro-level institutional
forms - most importantly the state industrial enterprises,
agricultural producer cooperatives and the combination of
state-controlled trade and petty-producers. Instead these
forms were locally adapted to exploit the most advantageous
opportunities open to those people who lived and worked in
them. The balance of incentives became increasingly less favourable to the Socialist sector as the attempt to implement
neo-Stalinist policies continued.

Some modification in the macro strategy occurred relatively early during the First Five Year Plan but there was no
real shift in the overall stance. The basic issue of the
static and dynamic inefficiency inherent in the overall combination of neo-Stalinist institutions and macro-economic
policies aimed at forced development was never really resolved
before the onset of full-scale US bombing in 1965. From then
on the rapid growth of aid imports from China and the Soviet
bloc pushed these fundamental economic problems to one side.
Foreign assistance sharply increased the state's supplies of
complementary inputs, enabling it to increase gross industrial
output and raise levels of capacity utilisation. Instead of

carrying out a radical rethink the Party leadership committed
itself to an increasingly dogmatic presentation of this
overall development policy as an integral part of the hyper-
nationalist wartime ideology. The Party's Line on the Vietnamese Socialist Revolution reiterated the assertion that the
neo-Stalinist model was both correct and immutable. In practice, however, the Party learnt to live with the day-to-day
consequences.

2.3 The formal institutions of the DRV and the principles governing their operation

The formal institutional changes brought in by the new
government after 1954-55 were based upon then Communist orthodoxy, differing little in broad outlines from those adopted in
the People's Republic of China and elsewhere. It is convenient
to see these as taking three major interlinked directions:

1. Broad socio-political changes.

2. The drive to control production.

3. The drive to control patterns of distribution.

By the late 1950s the period of political transition was
coming to an end and the central authorities had made their
political position as secure as it was likely to get. They
could then move on to the collectivisation of agriculture,
petty-trade and non-agricultural petty-production, coupled
with the nationalisation of industry and further development
of state industry based upon aid from fraternal Socialist
countries. In order to secure resources to maintain the
development programme they attempted to control distribution.
The institutional evolution here has to be understood somewhat
separately from the first two, because under North Vietnamese
conditions it was in distribution that the neo-Stalinist model
most quickly ran into difficulties. Initially, however,
developments under all three headings ran approximately parallel.

In the social field, Party control over the mass media,
education and culture could rely upon the effective co-opera-
tion of the central and local bureaucracies as well as the
security forces. The state managed the output of the radio,
press, journals, books and other mass media. Education was
centrally controlled, with overt political content and close
attention paid to teachers' attitudes to the new regime. The
substantial resources committed to these areas had profound
effects upon a population that had only attained high average
literacy levels in the previous decade.

General political hegemony was ensured by the orthodox
apparatus of Socialist democracy - the use of a National

Assembly dominated by the Party, with election of delegates
from minor Parties being subject to the approval of the Vietnam Fatherland Front, an umbrella organisation of the various
mass Front organisations. The National Assembly and its
Standing Committee provided one source of legislation, supplemented by Decrees issued by such bodies as the Prime Minister's Office, the Council of Ministers and the Presidency.
Close control of the general population was helped by
'Socialisation' of distribution and production, as well as by
use of the police.

Party influence over open intellectual life - crucial to
the value attached to the leadership's possession of the New
Knowledge - was inevitably challenged, in keeping with Vietnamese traditions. The **Nhan Van** affair of 1956-57 centred upon
an independent magazine of that name that was acting as a
forum for criticism. It paralleled the Hundred Flowers episode
in China, and ended with the magazine's closure in 1957 (5.).
The way was then clear for the Party leadership to continue
with the major transformations in the economic sphere prescribed by contemporary orthodoxy without public criticism of
either their appropriateness to North Vietnamese conditions or
their actual consequences.

The mechanism for Socialist transformation of the economy
necessarily took a rather legalistic form. This was because of
the use of the state apparatus to implement transformation in
a top-down manner, coupled with the major role played by
foreign models. Yet in a country with no real experience of
the operation of a uniform system of economic management, this
was a radically novel step. The new government had little
prior experience of the complex framework of precedent and due
process required to operate the bureaucratic systems needed
for large-scale economic organisation. French colonial law,
although steeped with the notion of the Rule of Law that
applied in France, had in practice functioned primarily as a
means for the expression of French interests, whether economic
or racial. Dynastic neo-Confucian legal tenets had in principle sought to maintain social harmony by reliance upon the
virtue and learning of mandarins.

For any newly independent Vietnamese government, development of a modern legal system could not draw easily upon
either colonial or dynastic precedent. In addition, novel
problems arose from the quite different economic conflicts
present in growing economic systems. In neither of the two
historical experiences was there the explicit recognition of a
need to resolve conflicts of material interest which did not
always imply the immorality or inferior nature of one of the
parties, and which reflected economic choices that bore upon
the wider interests of the community. The need for effective
contract law rises as economic specialisation develops and
relations between economic units become more remote and de-
personalised. This requires a disinterested enforcement of

42

clearly-defined economic rights. Such conceptions are somewhat
foreign both to the Soviet and neo-Confucian systems, where
the state has an interest in utilising the legal system to
enforce its own access to resources (6.). In the Soviet system
these are then used as a means to economic development through
their concentration upon priority sectors. In practice the
apparently clear legal distinctions of the DRV's various property-forms became extremely blurred (7.).

Basic administrative principles were also extremely under-
developed, especially those associated with the Ministries'
areas of authority. The use of foreign models tended to give
an impression of surface order whilst day-to-day practice
reflected quite different ways of getting things done. In
particular, de facto property-rights were usually comprehensible only in terms of the rights and duties pertaining in
the particular case. These of their nature were extra-legal.
This was a necessary result of the systematic inability to
enforce formal property-rights and implement the Plan.

Property-forms in the neo-Stalinist model

The basic system of property in the DRV was that established in the Soviet Union during the late 1920s which formed
the basis for the rush industrialisation of the early Five
Year Plans (8.). The fundamental distinction made in the DRV
was that between the so-called 'economic components' ('thanh
phan kinh te'). This was based upon the Party's derivative
theory of post-Revolutionary class structure. It provides the
theoretical underpinning for the statistics given in Part II. *(as a Fn ?)*

This theory defines total social product in an area or
country where Socialist Transformation has occurred. It is
made up of the sum of social product from two distinct socio-
economic categories - the 'individual' ('ca the') or 'private'
('tu nhan') sector and the 'Socialist' ('xa hoi chu nghia')
sectors. This particular way of viewing the economy has important implications even before it is developed further and
given operational meaning. These severely limit its analytical
value. First, it defines socially valuable activity strictly
in terms of physical output. Second, the categorisation uses
the sphere of production as a basis for creating an essen- *(critique)*
tially dualistic division into Socialist and non-Socialist
sectors. This follows Marx's view of the primacy of the sphere
of production in the analysis of capitalism (9.). It suggested
that control over means of production was the key to control
of the DRV economy. This is at least consistent with the first
basic assumption of the neo-Stalinist model, which stresses
the importance of fixed industrial capital. It is also an
effective part of a transition strategy, aimed at securing
political power, that focuses upon the take-over of assets
from exploiting classes; this is consistent with the (inter
alia) Leninist notion that political power derives ultimately

from social class based upon asset ownership.

The theory maintains that there are two Socialist sectors - 'collective' ('tap the') and non-collective. The collective sector uses cooperative forms and, whilst predominant in collectivised agriculture, is also important in the socialist transformation of artisanal industry. The non-collective Socialist sector, made up of the (hopefully) commanding heights of the economy, includes the state sector - most importantly the state industrial enterprises - and the minor and essentially temporary 'joint state-private' (JSP) ('cong tu hop doanh') sector. There are therefore three basic property-forms: 'individual/private', 'collective' and 'state'.

Although extremely simple, this basic triad became deeply integrated into official DRV social theory and so laden with values and expectations (10.). Thus the use of the term state property, or sometimes property of the 'whole people' ('toan dan'), to refer to a state industrial enterprise's legal position signified its importance to the task of national development and the Vietnamese Socialist Revolution. State property was deemed 'good' on the basis of its supposed strongly positive role in national development. The legal terminology naturally presumed the validity of the Party's development model, according to which the priority given to such enterprises should have resulted in rapid economic development.

On the other hand, the use of the term individual or private accompanied perjorative overtones. These implied that such particular and limited units could not contribute effectively - or at least not in any profound way - to the Revolution. This was consistent with the notion that only the state was capable of the vision and identification with the national interest needed for socio-economic advance. In between these two stood the collective form - avowedly Socialist, but not quite so advanced as the state's own property, and therefore of less significance to the Socialist Revolution.

Accordingly, and in keeping with this set of priorities, the basic structure of the economy was to be as follows. The key to the development of the productive forces was the 'expanded reproduction of means of production' (11.): in other words, expansion of the so-called 'heavy goods industries' ('cong nghiep nang'). It should be stressed, however, that the term heavy goods here refers to the so-called Group A industries, which are those producing means of production. They are distinct from those of Group B that produce means of consumption. From this it follows that heavy industry is understood to include production of means of production used in agriculture - most especially electricity, fertiliser and small-scale machinery. Concentration upon heavy industry, even in the North Vietnamese context, does not therefore necessarily mean ignoring the needs of agriculture. But in practice 'expanded reproduction of means of production' was usually understood to mean increased output of means of production used in industry: produced complementary inputs plus fixed capital goods.

The implications of this simple view of economic development were twofold. First, the state should take responsibility for physically directing the resources available to it - aid and domestic surpluses - into industry; within industry, it should give priority to those areas that produced means of production. Second, this should then result in a rapid and sustainable increase in aggregate output. There is little room for a number of problems that have come to be viewed as having major importance in the devising of effective development programs. Some examples would be : the optimal choice of technology, the role of foreign trade, the inter-sectoral and macro-economic balance of the national economy, and the trade-off between freely operating markets and the dynamic and/or scale gains from monopoly.

As the period of transition came to an end in the late 1950s these conceptions became closely integrated with the view taken of the DRV's triadic property system. There were strong arguments that state industry had to be managed responsibly if it was to be the priority recipient of the limited investable resources available to a very poor area. The close direct control over both enterprises and material supply promised by the neo-Stalinist model allowed the central Party leadership to take a close interest and intervene directly as and when they wished [Nove 1977:19 et seq.]. Control of the state apparatus and mass organisations - above all the Trade Unions - apparently assured the Party of a very strong position in the DRV's economic management system. Here human nature surely operated to help convince those in authority that the shining new equipment delivered from overseas had to be subject to the close control of those best qualified to do so. With a proclaimed superior knowledge of the world based upon 'Mac Le-nin' the Party leadership could not show itself as anything other than fully confident in its own abilities. A development model that promised integration of industrial activity and the distribution of industrial output into a single 'planned' entity was therefore welcome.

State industry, then, was the priority core. It had to [& was party controlled] receive the bulk of available investable resources and the closest possible attention from the central authorities. Where, though, were these resources to come from? Both theory and practice recognised two sources: assistance from fraternal Socialist countries, and the domestic economy. The former was constrained by the generosity of the world Socialist community. The latter depended in part upon the development of the state sector itself, but, especially in the early stages before that sector had shown much development, domestic resources obtained from other sectors had to play a major role. In theory, most of these resources were to come from the

45

collective sector. This saw the private sector essentially as a residual - a temporary remnant of the Old Society in the Socialist Revolution. As such it should not be relied upon, and since accumulation was to take place in the priority Socialist sectors its relative weight in the DRV economy was in any case set to decline. A moral state could not allocate essential national tasks to unprogressive sectors of society. Note, though, that the important economic task of labour supply was not the responsibility of the private sector, viewed in these terms, for labour was not owned in the same way as other means of production.

Within the collective sector the agricultural cooperatives bore the main brunt of the intended burden. Whilst staples remained a high proportion of household consumption agricultural production had to play a crucial role. And so long as the rural areas had not moved on from full collectivisation to an expansion of state farms the agricultural cooperatives had to be the main domestic source of means of consumption. Thus the Worker-Peasant Alliance (**Lien minh cong nong**), one of the most important elements of Communist political theory in the DRV, asserted the vital historical role of the collective peasantry in supplying resources to industry (12.).

The set of property-forms outlined above was formally predominant throughout the DRV by the beginning of the 1960s. In agriculture, 86% of all peasant families (ho) were in cooperatives (admittedly of the so-called 'lower' type) by 1960. Throughout the 1960s there was a steady growth in both the size and extent of cooperatives, and by 1968 over 90% were of the so-called 'higher' type [Table:70]. All modern industry was brought under the state enterprise form before the end of the 1950s. The government rapidly took over the extremely limited number of large-scale modern colonial plants that were still outside state control when the French left, and made sure that all new installations were state property from the start. This meant that the only area where Socialist Transformation was still an issue was the artisanal and small-scale sectors. 80% of registered artisans were in collectives by 1960 [VSH 1975:191].

Distribution and exchange

The basic administrative mechanism for establishing state control over distribution was the state monopolies. Covering both domestic and foreign trade, these extended over all goods considered even minimally important to the national economy (e.g. staples, meats, sugars, cloth and most industrial inputs). A list can be found at the beginning of Part II. The monopolies covered both means of production and consumer goods, and were intended to allow the authorities to regulate directly both the terms and quantities of exchange relations. Calling the state organs that operated them 'monopolies' is, however, somewhat misleading because they were expected to act more as taxation agents and rationing houses than as traders. Producers were required to dispose of output to them (i.e. the state's trading organs - co quan thuong nghiep); this is, however, also usefully seen as the imposition of 'duties to supply', so that producers in effect acted as units for the appropriation of output in the name of the state. A state industrial enterprise was to be supplied directly by the state with certain current inputs, which it was to use in production and then supply to the state the resulting output. Agricultural producer cooperatives were subject to a duty to supply rice and other products to the state, partly as tax and partly as 'duty-sales' at low prices.

The conventional Soviet distinction was made between 'inside' (or 'passive') money and cash. Transactions within the overall system of state monopoly were meant to be accounted for by direct clearing between accounts held at the single State Bank. This system covered a state enterprise's sales to and purchases from the state's trading organs as well as inter-enterprise transactions. Inside money paid for inputs or received for duty-sales could not therefore be used to support effective demand for goods available outside the state distributional system. Such detailed control was one of the many areas where lack of administrative experience could lead to great confusion.

State employees were still paid in cash and supplied with consumer goods through the state retailing system as well as the free market. This could lead to difficulties insofar as these and other cash-based transactions created, through a growing fiscal deficit, a mass of funds in the hands of the public available to finance free-market activities outside the direct control of the state. Here the solution implicit in the neo-Stalinist model was to use the security forces to enforce the state's trading monopolies: trade in goods on the list reserved for the state was to be stopped by deeming it illegal and having recourse to the police to impose penalties. The state therefore expected to be able to enforce its monopoly in many goods without having to compete economically, for instance by undercutting smaller producers. In this way the state isolated its own priority sectors from economic competition.

Production, at least in principle, was in many ways easier to control than distribution. At low levels of real income where workers spend a high proportion of their incomes on food it is very difficult to restrain spontaneous expansion of the free market in food during and after price rises during the inevitable bad harvest years. At the same time the minimal levels of capital needed to finance trade, coupled with the persistence of direct off-farm marketing (via the private-plots in the case of neo-Stalinist collectivised agriculture - see Chapter 6), encourage petty-trade. In the DRV large-scale commerce was nationalised early on, helped by its dependence upon imports and the state's effective control over foreign trade. Small-scale trade was far more difficult to manage, and although Socialist property-forms were well established in production throughout most of the economy by the beginning of the First Five Year Plan (1961), it was not until 1962 that the authorities could report success in the Socialist Transformation of private trade with nearly 80% of small traders in some form of state-controlled organisation [VSH 1975:217].

2.4 The likely macro-economic and structural consequences of forced industrialisation in the North Vietnamese context

With hindsight there are considerable grounds for pessimism about the likely outcome of an attempt at accelerated industrialisation along the lines sketched above. High levels of investment in modern industry were realisable, but the need for complementary inputs would place great pressure upon the state to extract resources that were simply not there to any great extent. Incompetent administration would exacerbate the situation, most especially by leading to over-optimism regarding the state's cash ('active money') deficit. This would probably be large, thus helping to push up free market prices and support the creation of aggravated shortage (see below). The state would then settle into systemic conflict with 'unplanned agents' for control over the complementary inputs needed to operate installed state industrial capacity, most importantly labour. State employees would be faced with an erosion of the value of their wages by rising free-market prices, offset by supplies of rationed goods at low subsidised prices. Moonlighting would become widespread.

It is comparatively easy to set out the likely consequences of an attempt to implement the neo-Stalinist system in an environment such as that of North Vietnam. Here it is important to establish the mechanisms that determine the actual operational content of its institutions; in practice such micro-level units as agricultural cooperatives, state industrial enterprises and state trading companies will behave quite differently from planners' intentions. A clear understanding of the processes that divorce prescribed form from actual content is needed in order to appreciate the systemic functions of the striking differences between their practical operational behaviour and the principles laid down in planners' manuals. And it is only when there is such an understanding of the way in which economic agents actually go about acquiring, using and disposing of resources that the trajectory of the macro-economy can be fully explained.

This occurs as a result of two analytically separate but closely inter-related processes. The first is the creation of the systemic 'shortage economy' characteristic of the neo-Stalinist economic system [Kornai 1980 and 1982]. Confronted

48

with quantity output targets and without effective budgetary
constraints state sector production units tend to maximise
their demand for inputs almost regardless of cost. Quasi-
guaranteed output disposal reinforces this behaviour but, by
reducing incentives to satisfy demand, forces customers to
adopt strategies designed to reduce the real cost of input
shortages. The administratively supplied priority sectors
place pressure upon the state to mobilise resources from the
rest of economy, and from foreign suppliers if possible; this
behaviour ultimately depends upon the state's ability to enforce trade monopolies.

The second mechanism is the operation of the variety of
economic activities outside the formal scope of the plan that
are usually described somewhat misleadingly as 'free market'
activities. This description is adequate if refering to activities such as petty-production for the market using minimal
capital inputs and means of production also acquired on a
market. But they include a great variety of activities that
are not so isolated from the administratively-supplied sectors. They shade off into such 'semi-socialist' activities as
(illegal) horizontal links between state enterprises aimed
frequently at securing resources for plan implementation, but
which operate outside the formal control of the system of
planned material supply. Crucial to such activities (known in
the North Vietnamese vernacular as 'outside' - thus 'kinh te
ngoai' - the 'outside economy') is the possibility at some
stage of relatively free exchange of goods or services for
money. But elements of an interrelated set (or 'circuit' -
'vong') of these activities may be based upon swops, favours
and even manipulation of the pattern of resource allocation
within the shortage economy. Thus the two processes are capable of quite complex interactions. From this point, therefore, we will use the term 'outside' to refer to such activities, understanding that it refers to economic processes
that depend at some stage upon the use of cash to acquire or
dispose of resources.

A supply of cash in the hands of the population is therefore the essential prerequisite for such 'outside' relationships (13.). By creating a simple basis for calculating the
relative local economic benefits of alternatives, it provides
a way in which those who control economic resources can select
the most profitable use of them. This means that any percep-
tion by economic agents that the plan does not serve their own
immediate interests can prevent plan implementation by encouraging them not to follow plan directives. Furthermore,
such perceptions of themselves show ways and means of
realising advantageous alternatives to going along with
planners' intentions. Conversely, they also show how going
'outside' can enable a Socialist economic unit operating
within the shortage economy of the administratively-supplied
sectors to fulfil its plan more easily. In both cases the

49

actual behaviour patterns of economic agents will demonstrate considerable autonomy and independence from central control. The deterministic model behind the neo-Stalinist system will not therefore operate. A simple example is agricultural co-operators' likely unwillingness to work for their cooperatives if the value to them of freely marketable output from their private plots has risen sharply above net returns to delivery to state trading organs. Under conditions of forced development inflationary pressures acting on the pattern of resource allocation are an important mechanism by which plan non-implementability will come about in practice.

The origins of the tensions between plan-based and 'outside' activities are certainly primarily to do with the role of money, but other processes accentuate these effects. In a developing economy there are many reasons to expect shortages similar to those characteristic of the neo-Stalinist 'shortage economy' but quite different in origin. Many goods will be unavailable simply because the economy is under-developed. Furthermore, if industrialisation is occuring from a very low base then capital investment will necessarily be 'lumpy', so that there will be few substitutes for domestically produced output.

The relationship between 'outside' activities and the Socialist sector is not a simple zero-sum antagonism. Their interaction will help reduce the static allocative inefficiencies of the system of direct material supply since units in the Socialist sector will be able to go 'outside' in order to seek out and acquire resources that might otherwise remain unused. Furthermore, it is likely that in the early stages of forced development 'outside' activities will play an important role in maintaining the real incomes of the rising numbers in state employment, who will be able to spend cash incomes paid to them by the state on securing food and other supplies on the free market. On the whole, however, and especially if high free market prices start to divert means of production away from the priority sectors, the relationship is best viewed as antagonistic (14.). It should be stressed, however, that the development of 'outside' activities is a consequence of the inappropriate nature of the policies adopted, and cannot therefore be blamed for their failure.

It is the neo-Stalinist model and the forced pace of development that are at fault, for they create the combination of the 'shortage economy' and buoyant 'outside' activities which often appears to planners to prevent fuller utilisation of newly-installed fixed industrial capital by limiting complementary input supplies. The authorities can recognise increasing competition with 'outside' activities as an indicator of macro-economic tensions, reduce the rate of investment and shift the pattern of imports towards consumption goods. Conversely, they can view such difficulties as a reason for increasing the pace of development ('try harder') and raise further the level of investment goods imports. As we argue, however, that this will place a still higher burden on domestic resource mobilisation in order to satisfy the need for complementary inputs it will most likely exacerbate the situation. Put more simply, increases in foreign aid can mask fundamental imbalances in the domestic economy created by the development effort and manifest in the effects of inflationary pressures on the overall pattern of resource allocation and competition for factor and non-factor inputs; they cannot remove them.

2.5 Planning in the DRV: some general observations.

Viewed from the perspective of the mid 1980s, when the practical limitations and realities of planning are far better understood in both Eastern and Western Europe, the DRV's attempt to implement the neo-Stalinist model and thereby determine the overall pattern of economic resource allocation and of economic growth appears almost quixotic. Both main schools in the contemporary debate would surely agree that the low-surplus North Vietnamese economy was extremely unlikely to provide an environment suitable for the creation of a planned economy.

Those who follow a 'Keynesian' current tend to believe that plans can work, even if they often do not, so long as planners are sufficiently realistic in limiting the scope of the activities they try to control. In the 1960s, this perspective led to such notions as the indicative planning fashionable in France and (later) in the UK and elsewhere [Shonfield 1965]. It suggests that the constraints discussed above - the basic poverty of the region, the North Vietnamese peasantry's familiarity with strategies designed to cope with extractive state policies, the rigidity and inexperience of the top Party leadership - would give few grounds for optimism. In addition, the DRV was trying to utilise perhaps the most ambitious planning model yet adopted, with its stress upon direct administrative controls. There is a close relationship between such a position and those theorists who emphasise the likelihood of inflationary macro-economic tensions as a result of problems in financing the development program [Kalecki 1957 and 1972]. By stressing the necessary but uncontrollable consequences of forced development, these latter arguments point to the limits of such planning methods. This supports the view that planning is only possible if it accepts that the socio-economic system, being indeterminate, cannot be entirely planned.

The more advanced - or at least more modern - position typified by the followers of Lucas asserts that planning cannot work, because agents subject to it act so as to falsify the model upon which any plan is based [Lucas 1976]. Here the unpredictability of capital-output ratios in the simple neo-

Stalinist model becomes a clear confirmation of such problems.
The analytical difficulty here lies in the reasoning behind
the notion that agents always act so as to falsify the
planners' models. Whilst it is clear why this could easily
happen it is not immediately obvious why it should always be
true. In North Vietnam, however, such a 'competition between
rationalities' is a useful and informative insight into some
of the problems the authorities faced. One example is the
striking difficulties encountered when the government tried to
learn enough about what was actually going on at the local
level for it to balance material supplies for the DRV economy.
'Breaking the autarky of the cooperatives' had become a major
policy goal by the mid 1970s as many cooperatives refused to
permit higher administrative levels to control their economic
activity [White 1982:16].

Both of these positions accept the limitations of human
knowledge and the consequent inherent difficulties in creating
'planned development' in almost any field of human endeavour.
Common sense might suggest that such difficulties are likely
to increase pari passu with the strength of the idealistic
conviction behind and commitment to 'planned development', and
conversely to decrease as planners become more realistic. In
practice too, both 'Keynesians' and others can more easily
support some form of parametric planning, or market socialism,
where the classical but now outdated deterministic rationality
of Soviet planning methodology no longer pertains (15.). For
'Keynesians', such activities perhaps seek to substitute for
the Keynesian state; for the supporters of Lucas, a 'minimal
state' might ensure the operation of social mechanisms that
provide part of the means for obtaining desired results. But
of course such notions are a great distance away from the
thinking behind the DRV's economic planning methodology, which
stressed the ultimate and universal correctness of the neo-
Stalinist planning model in both scientific and doctrinal-
socialist terms.

2.6 Conclusions

There are strong a priori reasons for supposing that any
attempt to implement planned economic development in North
Vietnam would have been highly problematic in the presence of
the fundamental constraints discussed above. There are two
obvious ways of trying to avoid the consequences of nevertheless making the attempt. These are, first, a hopefully temporary dependence upon consumption goods imports to override
the basic constraint of the low level of mobilisable domestic
economic surplus as industrialisation proceeds; and, second,
dependence upon the security forces to prevent economic agents
from responding to the material incentives offered by non-plan
- 'outside' - activities. The latter course essentially relies
upon extra-economic ways of forcing people to ignore economic

realities.

In the absence of the latter conditions the development plan would become unimplementable at both the macro and micro levels as constraints started to bind. At the macro-economic level the plan would be destroyed by inflationary pressures and chronic shortages of complementary inputs (especially of consumer goods) and/or a growing dependency upon imports, coupled with continued tensions between planned activities and production and trade in the 'outside' economy. At the micro level the plan's non-implementability would result in situations where institutional content differed widely from that intended; the major thrust of these modifications would respond to the desires of local interests to avoid the undesirable consequences of strict obedience to plan directives. Many of them would be quasi or strictly illegal.

Footnotes

1. See Tanham (1961) on military aspects of the Vietminh movement. Standard sources on the Vietminh are Devillers (1952) and Fall (1956).
2. See Fall (1956) pp.25 et seq. for a discussion of the Vietminh's local administrative system, and Fall (1963) pp.133 et seq for details of the 'parallel hierarchies'. See also 'Revue militaire d'information' (1957) pp.30 et seq.
3. The most important Party history of Land Reform is that edited by Tran Phuong (1968); reliable Western studies are Moise (1977) and White (1981).
4. See Elliott (1982) and Woodside (1983) for discussions of Vietnamese attitudes to education and technology.
5. For revealing but unsubstantiated comments on the long-term effects of this affair upon one leading Vietnamese intellectual (the philosopher Tran Duc Thao) see Truong Nhu Tang (1986) pp.299-300.
6. Thus 'Among the significant innovations introduced into Civil Law by the 1922 Code (of the Soviet Union was) ... the view that private rights acknowledged by the Code were conditional upon not being exercised contrary to their socio-economic purpose' [Butler 1983:165-6]
7. See Woodside (1971) pp.713 et seq. for a discussion of the lack of respect for written laws in North Vietnam. See Butler (1983) for a scholarly discussion of the Soviet legal system.
8. See Butler (1983) passim and Nove (1977) especially ch.12.
9. Marx did not, of course, analyse such systems as that of the DRV.
10. It is impossible to read such important textbooks as EPU (1975) without getting a strong impression of the importance of such ideas, not least in supporting various economic arguments, such as the need for priority investment in state

industry.

11. In Vietnamese - 'tai san xuat mo rong cua nhung tu lieu san xuat'. See Ellman (1979) pp.119-128 for a discussion of the sectoral allocation of investment in planned economies.

12. See the Resolution of the important 1961 5th Plenum [TWD 1963] discussed in Chapter 6 below.

13. Here one can see the logic behind such extreme radical positions as that of Pol Pot, which sought to avoid such problems by abolishing money altogether. See Vickery (1984), Kiernan (1985).

14. It is not difficult to imagine examples where diversion of means of production to the 'outside' economy would benefit 'inside' output. For instance, consider the use of a state enterprise's electricity to run pig-feed preparation machines in an enterprise's (illegal) pig-sty, the proceeds of which allow workers to keep working for the factory. For a fascinating anecdotal account of such interactions in a developed country (Hungary) see Kenedi (n/d).

15. For writers who stress the theoretical and ideological problems involved, see Conyngham (1982), Ellman (1979) ch.3, Nolan and Paine (1986(A)) and Wiles (1977) ch.9.

Chapter Three

CONSTRAINTS IN OPERATION - THE CREATION OF AN AGGRAVATED
SHORTAGE ECONOMY AND THE DETERIORATION OF DOMESTIC AND FOREIGN
BALANCES

3.1 Introduction

This chapter starts our empirical discussion of socio-
economic development in the DRV. It is primarily concerned to
support our assertion that an aggravated shortage economy had
arisen in the DRV by at least the end of the First Five Year
Plan, if not earlier.

Statistical analysis of the DRV economy presents a number
of problems, and this severely limits the reliability of such
investigation. These difficulties are partly to do with the
absence of important information (e.g. accurate free market
price data) but also result from the particular view we have
taken of the importance of the behaviour patterns characteristic of aggravated shortage. The combination of pervasive shortages with extensive free-market opportunities affects economic agents in a great many ways, and understanding this is
vitally important to empirical investigation, not least when
most official writing glosses over such issues. But it does
not often show up directly in official statistics. For example, it would be of great interest, but virtually impossible
in practice, to know precisely the utilisation of mobile
resources - ie those that could easily be shifted between the
Socialist and non-Socialist sectors. For instance - how much
grain was being sold onto the free market ? What proportion of
these sales were being diverted from the state distribution
system ? How much time and effort did state industrial employees actually devote to working to produce planned output in
their factories, and how much did they divert to produce goods
for sale 'outside' ?

These institutional parameters are hard to quantify with
aggregate statistics, but nevertheless cannot be ignored because they have important consequences, most importantly upon
resource utilisation and the dynamic efficiency of the economy. We are still very far from being in a position to carry
out a full-scale econometric investigation, and, combined with
reasons of space, the discussion here can therefore only

attempt to illustrate the major changes that took place (1.).
It examines evidence for the creation of fundamental systemic
stresses as the development effort encountered the constraints
discussed in Chapter 1. It then focuses upon the deterioration
in macro-economic balances, for these reveal, not only the
deep-rooted nature of the problems, but also the pervasive
influence of the developmental effort.

The next chapter discusses the development of production
and sectoral structural change. This confirms the new system's
failure to realise the vastly increased potential output
levels and its inability to generate a stable and sustainable
development path based upon domestic sources of accumulation
and independent of imported supplies of current inputs.

3.2 Systemic malfunction and the creation of an aggravated shortage economy.

(We must) struggle to construct the first step of the
material and technical base of socialism, realise in one
step socialist industrialisation, continue to bring the
North of our country rapidly, strongly and firmly to
socialism.

Source: Resolution of the 8th Plenum,   April 1963, quoted
in **VSH** 1975:221.

The First Five Year Plan (1961-65) saw the effective
institutionalisation of the aggravated shortage economy in the
DRV. The problems that this created for the leadership, and
their apparent inability to respond effectively, show up in
those Plena of the Vietnam Workers' Party Central Committee
that reportedly discussed economic problems (2.).

After a short interval of 'reconstruction' the government
inaugurated a Three Year Plan during 1958-60 during which the
basic foundations of Socialist Construction were to be laid
(3.). The 14th Plenum of November 1958 therefore concentrated
upon the programs of Socialist Transformation of agriculture,
artisanal and capitalist industry, and private trade (4.). An
important step in the control of the free market was the
currency reform of February 28 1959 that replaced 1,000 old
dong with 1 new dong. In May 1959 the 16th Plenum discussed
inter alia the reform of state industry (5.). In December of
the same year the State Council passed the DRV's new Constitu-
tion [VSH 1975:180].

By 1960 the way was clear for inauguration of Socialist
Construction and the Third Party Congress met in September,
declaring that the 'Primary duty of the entire transitional
period in the North is socialist industrialisation of
which the key is the development of heavy industry' [EPU
1975:28]. The Congress sought to avoid the disintegrating
tensions created by the development program by asserting the

need to 'unite central and regional industry', and also to 'unite agriculture closely with industry'. These slogans sought to hide growing economic dislocations under the spurious unifying force of administrative controls.

Thus by the end of 1960 and the completion of the collectivisation of the Red River Delta the basic framework of the Democratic Republic - its three key property-forms - was in place. Rapid rates of investment and non-agricultural employment growth continued. In January of 1961 the 3rd Plenum had to stress the legal and obligatory nature of the Plan as rising tensions started to erode central control; the Plenum also discussed the role of Party economic leadership in grassroots production units [EPU 1975:74]. The 5th Plenum of July 1961 examined the role of the Party in agricultural cooperatives and issues relating to agricultural development [VSH 1975:203]. In the summer of 1962 the Central Committee Plena were greatly concerned with the gathering problems in the international arena [Smith 1985:40 et seq]. But the June 7th Plenum stressed the need for balance in the relation between heavy and light industry and in so doing revealed the deep-rooted problems that were rising to the surface. The Plenum had also to acclaim the need for rapid automation and the general line - 'Develop strongly central industry whilst simultaneously stimulating a strong development of regional industry' - confirms the continuing conservative position (6.). The Plenum essentially did little more than 'concretise' the decisions of the IIrd Congress [EPU 1975:28].

During the important 8th Plenum of April 1963 the Party leadership confronted the gathering difficulties in industry without being able to accept their full implications (7.). The Plenum discussed the Five Year Plan, but reaffirmed the commitment to neo-Stalinist principles with the assertion that 'if you want to mechanise then you must have a machine-making industrial capability, with electricity, iron and steel' [EPU 1975:30]. As an indication of this, priority was given to the following sectors: mechanical engineering, mines, electricity, chemicals and metallurgy [id.:163] (8.).

In these closing years of the First Five Year Plan there are clear signs of the growing inability to finance from domestic sources the current inputs needed for implementation of the development plan. This resulted in disruptions in distribution and forced the 10th Plenum of December 1964 to concentrate upon trade, commodity circulation and prices (see below). By this time, however, the systemic difficulties were well established.

Inelastic supplies of consumer goods and rising free market prices meant that by the end of the Five Year Plan period state employees had seen their real wages fall by over 25% [Tables:132, 136] (9.). Over the next five years such families therefore responded by increasing their 'outside' incomes by nearly 15% annually [Table:133]. This suggests that state employees proportionately reduced their expenditure upon state rations during the worst of the war years. Note the rising proportion of non-state (i.e. free market) expenditure on food over the same period [Table:134]. But whilst the predominantly urban state employees had therefore to supplement their official incomes by taking extra jobs that enabled them to capture high free market incomes, many peasants benefited from their ability to sell private plot output on the free market. This does not show up in the official data, most likely because such trends were frowned upon [Table:137]. But in both state industry and collective agriculture material incentives had already moved strongly against the Socialist sectors by the end of the Five Year Plan.

The main cause of these difficulties was, as we have argued, the state's inability to acquire from the domestic economy those complementary inputs required by the development effort. Demand for such goods derived from two main areas: the expansion of the fixed capital stock in industry and the changing pattern of employment.

3.3 The weight of the development programme

Aggregate data shows that accumulation rose from the already high level of 23.5% of total national income in 1960 to 25.1% in 1965 [Table:22] (10.). Although the great mass of this was, literally, overseas aid, the level of accumulation still appears strikingly high when put beside the estimated 5% surplus above mass consumption that existed in the colonial economy. Realised outlays on 'basic construction' during the five years of the Plan totalled 3.9 bn. dong, with industry taking by far the largest share [Table:56]. The combined gross output of agriculture and industry at constant 1970 prices in 1965 was 5.5 bn. dong , and by 1965 industry was receiving 37.9% of total outlays [Tables:43, 59 and 71]. These figures are, however, somewhat meaningless in isolation from underlying economic conditions, particularly the DRV economy's capacity to absorb the new investment.

By 1965 the programme of investment goods imports meant that the DRV had in place a relatively well-equipped modern industrial sector, centred upon the key 200 modern enterprises managed by the central Ministries [Table:35]. Taken together with the far more numerous locally managed state enterprises, state industrial employment totalled around 220,000 [Table:37]. In 1965 gross state industrial output totalled 1.7 bn. dong at 1970 prices. Examination of Table 46 shows the great diversification that had taken place within this sector. The area now produced machine-tools, electrical motors, pumps, threshers, bicycles, insecticides, bicycle spares, batteries, light-bulbs, thermoses and many other items. By 1965 the DRV was even producing over 100,000 tonnes of cast iron annually.

This industrial growth might conventionally be taken to

indicate the success of the development effort [EPU 1975:33-
35], but this would be misleading. Whilst the basic industrial
capacity was certainly there, many simple complementary inputs
were still imported. A particularly clear example is textiles,
where imported cotton was still required to run the mills
(11.). Since imports were usually insufficient, few state
enterprises worked anywhere near their installed capacity
levels.

Employment generation in the state sector outside industry
placed a considerable load upon both the economy and the
state's ability to meet the corresponding demand for consumption goods. Chapter 4 considers this further. By 1965
there were just over 970,000 state employees [Table:13], and
their numbers had effectively doubled during the Five Year
Plan - total population in 1965 was 18.6 m. [Table:8]. The
increase alone pushed up the demand for marketed (milled) rice
by 0.3 m. tonnnes based upon a crude calculation that uses a
dependency rate of 2.5 and an annual (paddy) rice requirement
of 250 kg. In 1965 the state managed to obtain 1.1 m. tonnes
of staples in paddy equivalent terms from domestic sources, a
rise of 0.3 m. tonnes from 1960 [Table:93]. Between 1960, when
the harvest was rather bad, and 1965, when it was rather good,
paddy output rose 0.37 m. tonnes (around 1.4% annually 1960-
65) [Table:81]. But since over the same period the rural
population was rising at 2.2% annually [Table:8], this
suggests a steady erosion of the intensive subsistence margin
in the Red River Delta. Staples output was growing too slowly.

This piecemeal data serves to illustrate the relative
weight of the DRV development program. Under North Vietnamese
conditions, it is clear that the development programme was far
too ambitious. Any simple international comparison of the
investment rate is extremely misleading. Data describing realised investment in installed capacity means almost nothing in
isolation from the economic conditions that determine how it
is used.

3.4 Institutional evidence for the aggravated shortage economy: the 10th Plenum - 'prices and markets'

It should not be forgotten that during the First Five Year
Plan the North Vietnamese leadership had increasingly to devote their time to the struggle to re-unify the country that
was becoming more and more intense as the Saigon regime came
under greater pressure and the possibility of direct US intervention rose. In the final year of the Five Year Plan (1965)
substantial US bombing forced a partial evacuation of the
major cities and a dispersal of some industrial capacity. It
is therefore extremely important to establish the existence of
the aggravated shortage economy before the end of the Five
Year Plan.

In December 1963 the important 9th Plenum heralded a

commitment to further intensification of the armed struggle in the South [Smith 1985:220 et seq.]. From now on the war rapidly came to dominate domestic affairs in the DRV. The 10th Plenum held in December 1964 [VSH 1975:244] is consequently of great importance, for it revealed the way in which the spontaneous behaviour of the DRV economy had prevented implementation of Party policy.

The covert debate associated with the 10th Plenum is therefore of great interest. It points both to variation in the leadership's responses to the situation and the limits of that variation. The authors of four revealing books still remain at the time of writing (1986) senior members of the Party and state apparatus: Pham Hung (Minister of the Interior), Doan Trong Truyen (General Secretary of the Council of Ministers), To Duy (Chairman of the State Price Commission) and Nguyen Thanh Binh (Secretary to the Party Central Committee) (12.). It is likely, though, that the 10th Plenum cannot be isolated from the on-going conflicts associated with the Sino-Soviet split, and its anti-revisionist position accompanied what was later identified as a slight shift in policy, away from heavy industrialisation [EPU 1975:31 and 176-7] (13.).

Although they are couched in the somewhat impenetrable Marxist-Leninist framework adopted by the participants, the debates reveal rather clearly the institutionalised behaviour patterns of an aggravated shortage economy. They are consequently somewhat more revealing than such textbooks as Nguyen Viet Chau (1963). Thus:

> In reality, a number of state enterprises in both production and distribution have recently shown negative practices: running after material advantage (loi nhuan), careless work, inadequate attention to merchandise quality, running after goods that pay high cash profits (lai), only worrying about implementing the output value plan and not bothering about the commodity plan and output quality, creating a situation where a good is simultaneously short (thieu) and abundant (thua).

Source: Doan Trong Truyen 1965:69.

Clearly, state enterprises were seeking to respond to the material incentives facing them by mixing 'sub-optimisation' strategies aimed at the state planning system (e.g. ignoring output quality since the state guaranteed output disposal) with the diversion of resources into activities resulting in sales that generated cash incomes. This coexistence of orthodox problems familar from the neo-Stalinist planning model with market-oriented (and therefore illegal) activities within the Socialist sectors is the essence of the aggravated shortage economy.

Doan Trong Truyen took a distinctive and in North Vietnamese terms somewhat liberal approach, stressing the positive
role of the free market as a supplement to the collective
economy and the organised market [op.cit.:71]. This accompanied an emphasis, in a long and often rather obscure discussion, upon the role of the Law of Value. He tended to
assert, in keeping with this, the relative autonomy of free
market forces. The way to resolve this issue, in a planned
economy, was for planners to act in accordance with the rules
governing the operation of the free market, rather than simply
attempting to control it through the use of administrative
measures. Thus:

...during the (First Five Year) Plan the Law of Value still
had an objective basis for its existence, and the potential
for exercising a negative influence. This...varied in
strength according to the effectiveness of state management
and the activities of the state economic sectors. The
situation that developed from the middle of 1960 where
there was an excessive and unhealthy expansion of the
unorganised market and unstable free market prices of
staples and foodstuffs shows this...

Source: Doan Trong Truyen 1965:74.

Doan Trong Truyen is very concerned to show that the
existence of markets and exchange is unavoidable, so the key
problem is how to utilise them most effectively and at least
cost [id.:86 et seq.]. This in the end argues against the
simple hostility towards the free market felt both by conservative neo-Stalinists and many lower-level cadres who had seen
their real incomes squeezed by free-market inflation and state
resources diverted to more directly profitable ends. It cannot, however, advance much further without questioning the
entire DRV system. Thus the author naturally endorses the
orthodox line that in the initial stage of the period of
transition to socialism development must start with heavy
industry.
Discussing the state of the Northern economy at the end of
the Five Year Plan, he pointed to many difficulties, which he
rather euphemistically described as external contradictions:

At the present there appear to be many contradictions. For
instance, the state lacks industrial goods to sell in the
countryside so as to buy agricultural produce, whilst
peasants have little agricultural produce to sell to the
state; they buy more from the state than they sell to it.
At the same time, peasants have inadequate income to buy
new means of production...whilst some, with much money to

spare, demand consumer goods.

Source: Doan Trong Truyen 1965:88.

He asserts that, confronted with the proper incentives, North
Vietnamese agriculture was capable of realising an existing
potential for higher productivity and mobilised surpluses
[id.:85]. Carried to its logical conclusion, his argument is,
therefore, a long way away from the orthodox neo-Stalinist
position asserting the determining role of increased fixed
capital. Working through such a line of thought would have
entailed a close re-examination of the incentive structure
within agriculture and the role of collective institutions.
For whatever and as yet unknown reasons, this does not seem to
have happened (14.).

    Indications of the aggravated shortage economy in Pham
Hung (1965) are also relatively clear, although the policy
stress is rather different and the attitude to the free market
much more antipathetic. He accepts that given the simultaneous
requirements of accumulation and consumption, difficulties in
circulation must reflect any inadequacies in output growth
[Pham Hung 1965:12]. This had happened in the DRV, and the
pressure from the free market was therefore understandable. He
confirms the existence of extensive activity on rural markets
and the urban free market towards the end of the Five Year
Plan [id.:30]. In addition:

    At present, for many reasons, some commodities, even those
    coming from the state sector, can be diverted onto the free
    market (15.).

Source: Pham Hung 1965:29.

    Like many others, Pham Hung contrasted the non-market
nature of relations within the state sector with the unorganised and unplanned character of rural markets [id.:29 and
30]. This dichotomous view, related ideologically to class
struggle and the need to 'ceaselessly develop socialist trade
and shift petty-traders to production' [id.:31], de-emphasised
the potentially positive role of prices in informing producers
of the social costs and values of their activities. Since 'in
the process of socialist construction there is a long-term
tension between production and demand that we are unable to
resolve quickly' [id.:33], it followed that goods distribution
had to be in accordance with directly planned supply, and not
necessarily dependent upon either the value ('cost') of the
good or the income of the consumer [ibid.]. This inherently
confused position is expressed most clearly in the notion that
distribution should simultaneously reflect Leninist principles
of remuneration for work actually done and guarantee basic
needs [id.:35]. Thus he could advocate a political compromise
within which:

> We will not cut consumption so we can accumulate, and we
> will not permit the level of production to limit con-
> sumption excessively.
>
> Source: Pham Hung 1965:35.

This approach encouraged perceptions of economic management wherein a certain organic unity should arise in the
state's allocation of scarce products to those deemed to be in
need [id.:42]. Spontaneous extra-plan activities by grass-
roots units contradicted this philosophy:

> The situation where each producer and trading unit cal-
> culates profits and losses in a partial manner when selling
> goods to other units not only does not increase state
> accumulation, it also leads to passivity in the national
> economy.
>
> Source: Pham Hung 1965:41.

But is was to such 'partial' calculations by state enterprises as they dealt directly with each other that the North
Vietnamese economy owed much of its recovery after the Chinese
and Western aid cuts of the late 1970s (16.). And at the time
they tended to raise output above what it would otherwise have
been by increasing the overall efficiency of the economy. But
such behaviour interfered with the methods of directly administered resource allocation required by the neo-Stalinist
model. It also appeared adversely to affect the material
interests of state employees:

> In the past we have allowed prices to rise, (which has) cut
> real incomes and affected badly workers' well-being (suc
> khoe) - this is a major shortcoming.
>
> Source: Pham Hung 1965:68.

Whilst agricultural incomes had tended to rise, except in
areas where there had been harvest failures, state employees
had suffered from rising prices [id.:70].
Nguyen Thanh Binh (1964) took an even more uncompromising
stand, asserting that:

> During the period of transition to socialism, in North
> Vietnam as in many other fraternal socialist countries, it
> is impossible to avoid imbalances between a continually
> growing social demand for consumption goods and a rate of
> increase in output that, although higher, is still in-
> adequate compared with demand.
>
> Source: Nguyen Thanh Binh 1964:9.

These imbalances were manifest on the market, and he

asserted that without what he described as a 'relative' balance it would be impossible to avoid market and financial
instability (i.e. inflation). He took an extremely 'hard'
line, advocating cuts in domestic consumption in order to
raise exports [op.cit.:13], and sharply critical of 'excessive' peasant staples consumption (17.). He was pessimistic
about the chances of raising output, and therefore advocated
the use of administrative means to secure a proper distribution of resources.

These three authors illustrate the way in which policy-
makers were thinking as they confronted the effects of the
development program and the day-to-day operation of neo-Stalinist institutions. Whilst there was some open awareness that
the models themselves were a drag upon output, abandoning them
seems to have been out of the question. In the meantime, their
maintenance appeared to require the continued use of administrative measures to control the free market. Thus the systemic confrontation between the Socialist and 'outside' sectors
of the economy had become an accepted part of the DRV political economy. Market controls and inflation were to be used
to maintain the overgrown Socialist sector's economic position. But, by reinforcing micro inefficiencies and the overall
macro tensions inherent in an aggravated shortage economy,
this merely perpetuated those sectors' relative isolation from
the rest of the domestic economy.

To Duy (1969), writing some years later after the massive
aid program of the post 1965 period had helped prop up state
employee real incomes, clearly holds to this ideological position. He also reveals much historical detail of the distributional system as it had evolved during the Five Year Plan . He
attributed many of the difficulties in managing state distribution to agricultural cooperatives to a decision taken in
1962 to centralise control in the Ministry of Agriculture that
involved taking responsibility from the internal trade companies [To Duy 1969:22-4]. Despite problems with this system
the trading branch was given 'insufficient funds' to offset
the Ministry's lack of supplies and increase state procurement
from agriculture. Presumably this reflected a desire to restrain the growth of the fiscal deficit. The 10th Plenum had
provided the basis for decisions taken in 1967 which attempted
to maintain central control via the Ministry of Agriculture
[id.:24]. This tends to confirm the Plenum's essential conser-
vatism.

In industry, ideological acceptance of the need for coexistence between the Socialist and 'outside' economies continued; indeed, development of petty and local industry was
attributed to the 7th Plenum. Industrial cooperatives had
certain de facto freedoms to dispose freely of output:

(With regard to) cooperatives producing miscellaneous
(linh tinh) goods, state trade and purchase and sale co-

operatives only sign contracts to purchase a part (of output); after the cooperative has fulfilled this contract it has the right to organise disposal (tieu thu) of output by itself so long as it respects state policy, market management regulations and (pays) taxes.

Source: To Duy 1969:54.

This shows how DRV policy sought to maintain the hierarchy of priorities discussed above. State Enterprises retained their ascendancy.

Within an aggravated shortage economy, where fixed capital does not usually constrain output, supplies of current - 'complementary' - inputs are the key input determining levels of production. So long as the basic neo-Stalinist structure remains in place, practical day-to-day operation of the system has in the end to accept this fact. The ideological position observed in the works discussed above in effect reveals the integration of this systemic competition for current inputs into Vietnamese Marxism-Leninism, albeit veiled by the language used. But to someone concerned with these problems on a practical basis, such as To Duy, the basic issue was quite clear:

Guaranteeing materials supply is the factor that determines output.

Source: To Duy 1969:44.

3.5 The state's fiscal deficit - the immediate origins of monetary inflation.

Such statements as the above are not rare. They are strong evidence for the existence of an aggravated shortage economy in the DRV. Other pointers come from the aggregate data on macro-imbalances: the evolution of the fiscal and foreign deficits.

In analysing the financial evolution of the DRV economy it is extremely important to distinguish between different types of monetary transactions. Most important of all is the need to differentiate between the internal 'passive-money' trans-actions of the state system and the 'active-money' dealings that used real cash (18.). In the state's published accounts the two are not usually clearly differentiated, and it is not simple to calculate the cash deficit, which is the main source of liquid funds in the hands of the general public and avai-lable for the finance of marketed non-plan activities. Rough calculations [Fforde 1982:372-6] have suggested that the accu-mulated cash deficit was substantial; Spoor (1985) does not clearly separate out 'active' from 'passive' money, but notes that 'money in circulation grew faster than the growth of the

65

volume of commodities' [op.cit.:134] during the period of the late 1950s and early 1960s. Over the period 1958-62 the volume of money in circulation rose rapidly, laying the foundations for the growth of 'outside' production and other manifestations of aggravated shortage.

The DRV state was, in fact, confronted with a chronically weak tax base and relied heavily upon its trade monopoly and state industry:

> In recent years, the state has taken about 30-32% of national income into its budget as a central source of cash (**von tien te**), and put about 50% of this towards accumulation...About 80-85% of this income comes from the state economy....Most of the income from the state economy rests upon pure income derived from goods produced in light and heavy industry, part similarly derived from agriculture and other economic branches. Some appears directly as enterprise income, some appears as the trading branch sells consumer goods and agricultural products.

> Source: Doan Trong Truyen 1965:238, 238-9.

The two main sources of pressure to expand cash outlays were the procurement of agricultural products and the rapidly expanding cost of wages in the state sector. Table 27 shows how these two categories made up nearly 70% of cash outlays in 1960.

The extremely poor results of the procurement programme during 1959-60 showed how vulnerable the budget was to the need to expand payments to the peasantry. The state's rice purchases were indeed intended to be 'the main source of the peasantry's cash incomes' [Nguyen Viet Chau 1963:281]. During this period, when most of the Northern delta peasantry was joining cooperatives, the volume of rice supplied to the state fell sharply - by just over 8% - whilst the value of agricultural goods purchased by the state rose just over 11%, thus implying a price rise of over 20% [id.:295-296 and 298]. The same source also suggests that the state was increasing its average procurement prices by around 20% annually over the period 1956-61. It was not obtaining comparable increases in grain supplies (rice procurement reached 0.67 m. tonnes in 1958, rose to 0.85 m. tonnes in 1959 but then fell to 0.78 and 0.80 in the two following years [ibid.]). Even these sharp price increases did not keep pace with inflation on the free market [Spoor 1985:42]. Thus from the very beginning of the development program the state was pushing large volumes of cash into the hands of the rural population (19.).

The other main source of cash outflows was the rapidly expanding bill for state employees' wages [Table:27]. Table 13 shows how the total number of 'workers and functionaries' ('**cong nhan vien chuc**'- i.e. state employees) - nearly doubled

between 1960 and 1965; between then and 1975 it rose by nearly
80%. Since wages made up over 30% of all state cash outlays
this again suggests rapid growth.

In judging the state's overall impact on the money-commo-
dity balance in the DRV economy the analysis should also take
into account cash inflows from the sale of commodities either
procured or received as aid [Table:26]. Outline figures com-
puted in Fforde (1982) suggested that the net cash deficit was
around 0.3 bn. dong in 1960, that it recovered to show a
surplus in 1965, but was again showing a deficit of 0.7 bn.
dong by 1975 [op.cit.:44]. The annual cash deficits of the
early 1960s and the mid 1970s were equivalent on a national
per capita basis to just under one month's wages for an un-
skilled state worker [ibid.]. One prerequisite for the expression through the free market of the inappropriateness of
the development program was therefore present - extensive cash
holdings by the population. This resulted from a basic imbalance in one major macro-economic indicator - the state's
fiscal (cash) position.

3.6 The trade deficit and the shift to import dependency for current consumption

The second major indication of the systemic difficulties
facing the Communist leadership's economic plans was the need
for increasing imports of consumption goods and other current
inputs. Whilst it is hard to refute suggestions that the
shifts in the pattern of imports were partly related to issues
relating to the Sino-Soviet dispute (20.), it is more important to confirm the way in which the North Vietnamese economy
came to rely more and more heavily upon imports of current
inputs, especially of food. Table 3.1 shows how the proportion
of consumer goods by value in the official trade data rose
sharply towards the end of the First Five Year Plan.

Of greater importance than developments during the First
Five Year Plan, however, was the shift apparent over the
period from the early 1960s to the mid 1970s. Note that the
official data in Tables 112 and 113 does not permit an
examination of trends during the First Five Year Plan. A
simple measure of the relative importance of imports in an
economy would be the ratio of the value of imports to a
measure of total economic activity. In the North Vietnamese
context such an indicator is made somewhat unreliable by the
lack of a proper measure of aggregate economic activity and by
the use of accounting prices that almost always differ from
those either on the free market or in some sense close to
social values. The following calculation helps to put things
into some sort of perspective.

Probably the best indicator of aggregate economic activity
is the official measure 'National Income' ('Thu nhap quoc
dan'), index numbers for which are in Tables 19, 21 and 22.

Spoor [op.cit.:178] quotes another source that gives a 1959 total of 3.33 bn. dong, but without confirming that the data is in current prices. An estimate for the value of National Income in 1960 may be made by assuming the same percentage growth as for the sum of the gross output values of industry and agriculture and applying it to the figure above [id.:52,

Table 3.1: Share of consumption goods
in total imports

Year	%
1960	12.6
1961	10.9
1962	10.3
1963	16.8
1964	15.3

Source: Le Vinh 1965:12.

Note: The reader should not be unduly concerned by the disagreement between this data and that in Table 113, which is well within the scope of normal variation in official data drawn from different sources. Table 113 does, however, confirm that the proportion continued to rise, so that by the mid 1970s over 30% of imports were means of consumption.

104). This gives a rough estimate for National Income in 1960 of 3.31 bn. dong. Thus at the eve of the First Five Year Plan imports were around 11% of National Income (imports data from Table 113). By the end of the period National Income had risen by just over 88% [Table:19] and imports (21.) by 282% [Table:113], suggesting that imports then amounted to just over 23% of National Income. On a similar basis the reported trade deficit rose from just over 4% of National Income to just over 15% (Export data from Table 112). Whilst the trend to increasing import dependency is unmistakeable, the precise numbers involved serve only to indicate orders of magnitude.

An even clearer indication of the shift to dependency upon imports for current requirements can be seen in the rising levels of food aid. Here the absence of reliable Chinese data muddies the position considerably, but there are two simple ways of approaching the problem: Soviet trade data itself, and the reported difference between the volume of staples procured by the state and the volume of staples distributed by it. Official Soviet trade data in Table 3.2 reveals a sharp rise in food aid.

This suggests that the region had become dependent upon staples imports at a level of around at least 0.35 m. tonnes annually by the mid 1970s. This compares with the recorded deficit on domestic staples transactions by the state and state-controlled trading system of 0.33 m. tonnes per annum

Table 3.2: Soviet food exports to the DRV (Thousand tonnes)

Year	Wheat	Wheat Flour
1958	NIL	NIL
1959	NIL	NIL
1960	NIL	NIL
1961	1.7	20.1
1962	0.8	9.0
1963	0.2	2.7
1964	0.1	1.5
1965	0.1	1.5
1966	0.9	10.7
1967	3.5	39.1
1968	20.2	241.7
1969	18.7	225.0
1970	34.7	426.1
1971	25.0	301.3
1972	NIL	1.3
1973	20.5	251.3
1974	42.4	523.8
1975	16.3	201.1

Source: Foreign Trade Statistical Yearbooks of the Soviet Union.

[Tables:93 and 108]. These estimates ignore the strong possibility of additional supplies from other areas. When these are taken into account the overall shift in the food balance can be assessed to have been from an approximate self-sufficiency in the early 1960s to a situation where perhaps 10-15% of supplies were imported in the mid 1970s [Fforde 1982:49]. Such calculations are highly unreliable but serve to confirm the underlying trend.

The official data on the deficits of the state and state-controlled trading branch shows also the degree to which the productive capacity of the economy did not satisfy domestic demand in the mid 1970s (compare Tables 100 and 108). This is particularly revealing for such important consumer goods as cloth, laundry soap, bicycles and sugar, where sales and other deliveries to the state and state-controlled trading sectors came to be far lower than retail sales by those organs, primarily as a result of aid-financed imports (see Table 3.3).

3.7 Comparison of the DRV economy before and after the years of US bombing

Developments after the Five Year Plan

The worst period of US bombing lasted for the three years from 1965 and ended in 1968 when the Tet offensive in South

Vietnam and growing US popular opposition to the war prevented
President Johnson from standing for a second term and induced
an 'unconditional halt' to the bombing [Litthauer and Uphoff
1972:81]. During this period aid from the Socialist bloc -

Table 3.3: Crude balances in domestic trade of the state tra-
            ding network for some commodities

	1960	1965	1974	1975
State deficit (receipts less retail sales) in:				
Cloth (m. meters)	15.9	-11.4	-55.2	-43.4
Laundry soap (thou. tonnes)	3.5	0.7	-7.3	-8.9
Bicycles (thou. machines)	-45.6	-74.0	-59.0	-31.5
Sugar (thou. tonnes)	10.0	-2.7	-33.6	-30.9

Source: Tables:100 and 108.

mainly the Soviet Union and China - rose extremely rapidly,
pushing aggregate incomes up well above pre-1965 levels (22.).
Despite this, however, there appears to have been some sort of
food crisis in the late 1960s that prompted massive Soviet
food aid and the shift to food imports dependency that continued up until the reunification of the country in 1975.
Bombing in 1971-72 accompanied the push by the Republican
Administration in the US for the Paris Agreements, so by
January 1973 the region entered a further short period of
peace that ended with the fall of the South in 1975.

    Against this background the key comparison is that between
the early 1960s and the period 1973-75. The previous sections
have presented some evidence to support arguments for the
establishment of an institutionalised aggravated shortage
economy in the DRV by the end of the Five Year Plan. Given
this, a clear picture of the state of the DRV economy in
1973-75 is of special importance to assessing the economic
consequences of re-unification in 1975-76.

    This picture is developed in later chapters. Here it is
sufficient to stress again the macro-imbalances outlined
above. In the three years before 1975-76 the DRV state was
running a substantial cash deficit and importing large volumes
of current inputs. This had permitted a substantial growth in
state industrial output and employment which the next chapter
discusses.

3.8 Conclusions

    Reliable assessment of the macro-balances of the North
Vietnamese economy is extremely difficult. But the evidence
presented above on the whole supports the argument that the

Outcomes

area had developed an institutionalised aggravated shortage economy well before the end of the First Five Year Plan in 1965. By 1975, the DRV had experienced a marked deterioration in both the domestic and foreign balances since the Liberation of Hanoi in 1954. The state's fiscal deficits had created a large volume of cash in the hands of the general public and supported the growth of buoyant effective demand for non-plan activities. Party ideology had accepted this.

By the mid 1970s free market rice prices had risen to levels approaching 10 times those offered by the state to cooperatives - Table 111 admits to price rises on the 'unorganised market' of nearly 100% between 1965 and 1974-75. Growing pressure on domestic resources and rising levels of economic activity resulted in a deterioration in the foreign balance. Note, though, that this occurred during a period when the total output of industry nearly doubled: average gross industrial output in 1973-75 was 98% up on the 1960-65 average [Table:30], having risen over 60% between 1972 and 1975 [ibid.]. Rising import dependency was not primarily the result of the substitution of imports for war-hit domestic output, but arose inevitably as an integral part of a dynamic pattern of structural change in the domestic economy. The effects of heavy US bombing during 1965-68 were certainly important, but state output and employment continued to rise sharply over the decade 1965-75 as a whole, placing an increasing weight upon complementary inputs and consumer goods suppliers. Under the circumstances, rising aid imports, by increasing modern state industry's relative isolation from the rest of the domestic economy, led to both an augmentation and masking of the economic pressures already apparent during the First Five Year Plan.

A very basic conclusion can be drawn from this: at the end of the day, fundamental constraints existed, and they severely limited economic development. Under North Vietnamese conditions, the operation of these fundamental constraints led to a generalised tendency for increasingly intense and systemic competition for the acquisition and use of resources in the economy; the authorities were able to survive this by virtue of their ability to acquire large additional resources from abroad. This meant that the identification of the economic structures of the Socialist Revolution with the hyper-nationalism of the war effort ('Nationalism and Socialism are One') could continue. Aid imports therefore served a deeply political purpose.

to p. 97

Footnotes

1. We therefore see ourselves as being in the preliminary stage of the 'Research Program', attempting to build up the institutional familiarity from which to generate systematic and quantifiably testable hypotheses [Portes 1984:3-4]. See

also Le Chau (1966), Leon Lavallee (1971), Spoor (1985) and Vickerman (1984).

2. Plena are numbered sequentially between Party Congresses, which occured in 1951 (the IInd), 1960 (the IIIrd) and 1976 (the IVth). The present authors do not wish to deny the suggestion that these 'economic' Plena, occurring as they did at a time of gathering international tensions resulting from the Sino-Soviet split and the increasingly violent war in the South, must often have been influenced by such factors. Conversely, however, economic issues had their own importance and this should also be taken into account.

3. For a discussion of conditions in the North during the 1950s see T.Shabad (1958).

4. Doan Trong Truyen (1965) p.121. Details of the Plenum Resolution can also be found in TWD (1980) pp.5-14. For details of the Socialist Transformation of capitalist trade see Van Tap (1960).

5. Nguyen Tran Trong 1980:24 confirms that the Plenum 'stressed that industry remained the ultimate priority'. The 15th Plenum of January 1959 had meanwhile heralded the return to armed struggle in South Vietnam [Smith 1983:165/6].

6. The 7th Plenum resolution ('On the task and direction of development of industry') can be found in TWD (1980) pp.97-139. Note that the June date [VSH 1975:162] may be incorrect. According to Smith (1985) pp.45 & 384 the Plenum was in April. The partial stress on local industry did not address fundamental problems.

7. The worked cited as EPU (1975) mentions the 8th Plenum rather frequently (e.g. on pp.31, 181, 191 (note the comments upon the need to prepare for automation (!)), 236 and 308). See also Doan Hai et al (1979) p.25.

8. The Plenum also stressed the need for economic accounting in enterprises [EPU 1975:309]. Excerpts from the Resolution 'On the First Five Year Plan (1961-65)' can be found in TWD (1980) pp.140-56.

9. See Honey (1964) for interesting anecdotal data on prices and wages in the early 1960s. At this stage free market rice prices were already around three times those charged to urban consumers by the state (1.5 dong/kg. compared with 0.4 dong/kg.), compared with wages of between 20 and 60 dong a month.

10. See Prybyla (1966); Spoor (1985) pp.167 et seq. Contemporary authors tend to disagree about the precise level of investment planned for the First Year Plan. According to EFU (1962) expected aid during the Plan was 1.31 m. roubles, covering 108 major projects [op.cit.:158/9]. See also Lavallee (1971) p.58, Le Chau (1966) p.328. The source composition of aid also varied as the DRV manoeuvred between the Soviet Union and China during the Sino-Soviet 'split'. See also Joint Economic Committee (1973) p.776 and (1979) vol.2 p.569.

11. Table 138 shows the relative importance of clothing in

state employee outlays. Tonkin cotton had once been famous for its quality [Gourou 1936:463]. Note the evidence of Table 93 on agricultural goods supplied to the state distribution system, from which cotton is lacking, implying that, as during the French period, all cotton supplies were imported.

12.   When they wrote these books they occupied the following positions: Pham Hung - Politburo Member; Doan Trong Truyen and To Duy - Deputy Directors of the Finance and Trade Department of the Central Committee; Nguyen Thanh Binh - Minister of Domestic Trade.

13.   See also Le Duan (1962) on the value of backward techniques.

14.   The work also discusses a number of other interesting areas, such as the history of the internal trade network [id.:120 et seq.], the effects of the different pricing systems in the liberated and non-liberated areas after 1954-55 [id.:188] and the adverse effects upon exports of the overvalued exchange rate and consequent excessively high domestic price level [id.:195].

15.   In the original - 'can be 'winnowed out' ('lot ra') into the hands of speculators and hoarders'. See also id. p.30 on the growing extent of free market activity, partly as a result of earlier slackness in market management.

16.   One of the authors plans to discuss this in a forthcoming study of Vietnamese Industrial Organisation.

17.   E.g. on pp.15-16 - '...staples consumption has been very wasteful; in many places peasants have consumed staples at leisure (thoai mai) as they wished; people have used paddy anyhow, feeding livestock, to make noodles and cakes, for distillation etc...consumption of goods such as cloth, sugar, milk, flour, tea etc has also been very wasteful...the administrative system is too bulky. This pushes up consumption..'.

18.   This distinction is absolutely fundamental to any understanding of the inter-related exchange mechanisms that accompany aggravated shortage, for 'passive' money, although used for transactions within the state system, cannot be used for purchases on the free market. See Wiles (1977) ch.12, also Podolski (1973) for useful institutional detail.

19.   See Fall (1963) pp.163-4 for interesting anecdotal information on procurement difficulties in 1960-61. Honey (1961) presents a fascinating glimpse of free market developments in Hanoi during 1960 after the poor Xth month harvest. He quotes 'Diplomatic reports' that peasants had started to bring in food during March as prices rose; once they saw that the police were not going to stop such behaviour, there was a sharp rise in traffic. According to the official journal Thoi Moi for 27 August 1962 - 'In 1960 the turnover of these free markets was 12 m. dong. It has risen to 105 m. dong in less than two years. Like a magnet, the free markets (of Hanoi) have attracted as many as 6,000 people who have given up their

old professions for trade' (quoted in Honey (1963) p.6).

20. These issues, and especially any possible relationship between Khrushchevian economic policy and the evolution of DRV policy, are not dealt with here. See, however, Smith (1983) and (1985).

21. The discussion here is somewhat simplified: a full analysis of the overall effects of such imports would have to include the impact of the additional output, as well as other factors. An important caveat surrounds the precise nature of this data. Table 19 gives no firm indication as to whether the data is in current or constant price terms. It seems most likely that they are in constant prices. On the other hand the imports data is most likely in current prices, so that any inflation in the accounting prices used would tend to lead to an over-estimate of the degree to which import dependency was rising.

22. The Systems Analysis Study (quoted in the Pentagon Papers (1967) pp.225-7) maintained that annual economic aid had risen from around $95 m. during the Five Year Plan to $340 m. This, it was thought, more than offset the production losses due to the bombing of an estimated $100 m. annually during 1965-67. For details of the US bombing see Littauer and Uphoff (1972), especially pp.39 et seq. For some details of the yearly plans of the second half of the 1960s and the early 1970s see Lavallee (1971) pp.87 et seq.

Chapter Four

POPULATION GROWTH AND STRUCTURAL CHANGE

4.1 Introduction

This chapter examines the overall pattern of economic change in North Vietnam during 1960-75 and focuses upon movements in the macro-aggregates. It takes the basic conclusions of Chapter 3 as given, and therefore assumes that the DRV economy was characterised by aggravated shortage from at least the early 1960s. The first section discusses population growth and participation rates in relation to variations in sectoral employment. Subsequent sections then examine productivity changes and the sources of growth, both extensive and intensive.

4.2 Population

The recorded population of North Vietnam continued to rise at a rapid rate during the period. Both income security and the general level of social stability were enhanced by a number of factors, such as the end of the war against the French and, in rural areas, by the far more accomodating attitude of the new government to the wider social welfare functions of local corporate institutions. Socialist cooperatives supported this, and the new cooperatives' Statutes clearly stated their extensive role in the provision of social services and income support [Fforde 1984:331]. Families could now take greater risks in expanding their size, at the same time as the generally higher income levels encouraged and facilitated rearing more children. It is likely that a postwar baby boom also pushed up fertility. Population growth averaged 3.0% annually over the period 1960-65, slowing slightly to 2.8% over the next decade as people were killed, either by US bombing or fighting in the South. By 1975 the region's population had risen by just over 52% from 16.1 m. to 24.5 m., an absolute rise of 8.45 m. [Table:8]. These growth rates most probably represented an acceleration from pre-war levels (1.). The data also shows a slow but important degree of urbani-

sation (2.). The rural population, although rising in absolute
terms by some 7.2 m. over the period 1960-75, fell only marginally in relative terms by some 2% to 89.2% of the total
population. North Vietnam therefore remained a predominantly
rural country [Table:8].

Whilst population growth was slowing, the proportion of
the population defined for statistical purposes as being of
working age (16-60 for women, 16-65 for men) declined quite
sharply during the First Five Year Plan, from 46.6% to 44.4%.
There was then no appreciable change between 1965 and 1975
[Table:10]. Despite this, however, the available labour supply
grew rapidly over the period. In rural areas the officially-
defined labour force rose by 1.8% annually during 1960-65, but
3.1% annually during 1965-75 [ibid.]. Over the same periods
the urban labour supply measured on the same basis rose at
annual rates of 3.1% and 4.4%. These trends exacerbated the
authorities' inability to provide economically attractive
opportunities for mobilisation of economic resources into
priority areas by creating a buoyant supply of people seeking
work 'outside' the Socialist sectors. 3.45 m. people came of
working age between 1960 and 1975; of these, 0.74 m. were in
the urban areas.

4.3 Changes in sectoral employment

The official data on employment shows without doubt that a
substantial proportion of this rising labour supply was not
employed either in the Socialist or even the regulated (and
therefore recorded) sectors of the economy. Total industrial
employment in the state and collective sectors rose by 6.9%
annually during 1960-65 and 3.5% during 1965-75 (absolute
gains of 0.17 m and 0.25 m. respectively [Table:37]. Non-in-
dustrial state employment (of 'workers and officials' (3.))
rose far more substantially, by 14.7% annually 1960-65 and
6.6% annually 1965-75 (absolute rises of 0.35 m. and 0.64 m.
respectively [Table:12]. Non-agricultural employment therefore
grew fast enough to generate sharply rising demand for food,
but was inadequate to absorb the increased labour supply (4.).

Recorded agricultural employment stagnated throughout the
period. During the First Five Year Plan the collective sector
(the agricultural producer cooperatives) absorbed some 0.32 m.
people, with numbers in the individual sector falling by
0.24 m. [Table:72] (5.). State farms took on a net additional
0.06 m., so that total agricultural employment rose an average
1.2% annually, or 0.33 m. During the next decade, however, the
collective sector was no longer able to compensate even for
those small numbers still moving out of the individual sector,
and despite some further growth in the (still almost negligible) state farms sector, total agricultural employment
actually declined by 0.14 m. during the period 1965-75 [id.].
Thus over the period as a whole total employment rose an

average 0.2% annually, an absolute gain of only 0.19 m. Within agriculture the producer cooperatives retained their dominant position in the official employment data, reportedly employing around 90% of the agricultural labour-force throughout the period. The crucial question arises, however, as to what proportion - if any - of their working time was actually spent working for cooperatives rather than on their own account (see below, Chapter 6).

Table 4.1: Absorption of the rising labour force, 1960-75

Million	1960-65	1965-75	1960-75
1. Increase in population of working age	0.77	2.68	3.45
2. Increase in identified employment:			
State and Collective Industry	0.17	0.25	0.42
Non-industrial state employment	0.35	0.64	0.99
Total agriculture	0.33	-0.14	0.19
(of which collective)	0.32	0.09	0.41
Petty trade, services and industry (excluding the collective sector)	-0.11	0.06	-0.05
Collective industry	NIL	0.16	0.16
Total Increase in identified employment	0.74	0.97	1.71
Residual	0.03	1.71	1.74
Army (regular forces)	n/a	0.25	n/a

Sources: Pike 1986:190; Tables 10, 12, 37, 68, 72 and 97.

Note: According to Pike (1986) p.80, the regular force strength rose only 0.18 m. from 1955 to 1965.

The remaining official categories of employment are petty-trade and services, petty industrial production and the full-time armed forces. Table 97 gives data for the first, and shows a small decline over the period. Note that this table refers only to those either 'registered' or 'participating in some collective form', and therefore excludes un-registered free-market and other activities. Indeed, Table 37 shows that those recorded as active in the regulated 'individual' industrial sector - the official petty-producers - were very small in number, and furthermore shed 0.03 m. during 1960-65 only to re-employ 0.01 m. during the period 1965-75. This is almost certainly an under-estimate, but note the rapid (19% annually) growth between 1968 and the first year of peace - 1973. Data on the regular army is not officially available for the DRV, for obvious reasons. US estimates suggest an approximate figure of 0.4 m. in 1965 rising to 0.65 m. in 1975 [Pike 1986:190]. In any case, troops stationed in base areas far from the front were often active participants in the civilian economy.

The above data implies that only around one half of the rising labour force was absorbed into some form of officially recognised employment over the period 1965-75 (see Table 4.1). The remainder was available for 'outside' work.

4.4 Changes in labour productivity

Aggregate data on sectoral output in the DRV follows Soviet methodology and measures gross production rather than net (i.e. 'value added' [Chen 1966]). When rising imports support industrial activity this raises major problems of interpretation and analysis. In addition, there is no way of obtaining official measures of aggregate income flows to assess the relative importance of planned and non-planned activities. At the same time analysis of the 'sources of growth' is inhibited by the lack of any real measure of factor returns. Thus a proper comparison of the comparative economic efficiencies of state, collective and petty production is almost impossible - the aggregate data is simply absent. What follows, therefore, is an attempt to indicate possible trends, and, perhaps more importantly, to demonstrate what the data does not show.

A major additional difficulty with the assessment of changes in labour productivity comes from the need to assess the implications for the First Five Year Plan of the fact that its closing year - 1965 - saw major disruptions as US bombing began. In that year, however, gross agricultural ouput (henceforth GAO) rose 3.3% [Table:73] and gross industrial output (henceforth GIO) rose 9.2% [Table:30]. The latter was not an abrupt deceleration from the previous year, whilst the former compares well with the 1960-64 average of 4.3%. This suggests that 1965 can be included in the period 1960-65 for the purposes of comparison with 1973-75 without excessive loss of accuracy.

Industry

During the First Five Year Plan GIO averaged an annual rate of growth of 13.6%. As Spoor (1985) and Vickerman (1985) point out, however, this was rather unstable, with a peak of 25.3% in 1962 and a trough of 8.4% in 1963 [Table:30]. During 1973-75 GIO growth was even faster, averaging 17.7%, whilst over the intervening period of intermittent bombing GIO fell sharply to a trough around 10% below the 1965 peak in 1968, but then recovered to a new peak around some 20% above it in 1971, before falling again during the 1972 bombings. This meant, however, that GIO grew on average by 5.9% annually during the 1965-75 decade. The war did <u>not</u> halt economic growth. It is therefore not entirely inappropriate to consider the pattern of economic development during the years 1965-73 as an integral part of the whole period.

Industrial gross labour productivity growth averaged 8.3% during the First Five Year Plan compared with 11.7% during 1972-75. Over the period as a whole, however, productivity growth averaged only 4.3%, which may be proximately explained by the way in which industrial employment continued to rise during 1965-72 (by 2.5% annually) whilst GIO on average stagnated, growing by 1.2% annually [<u>Tables</u> 30 and 37]. This suggests that there was considerable under-utilised wartime investment, since official employment generation in a neo-Stalinist system results primarily from the additional vacancies that accompany the expansion of industrial capacity. This conclusion is supported by the way in which the value of fixed capital in industry (6.) reportedly rose 16.6% annually during the First Five Year Plan, and by 9.0% during the war years (1965-72), whilst during the period 1972-75 it only rose 4.2% annually [<u>id.</u>]. This suggests that the 1972-75 aid programme concentrated upon current inputs rather than further additions to the capital stock. The additional capital stock both created demands for current (non-labour) inputs that could not be met by domestic suppliers in the domestic economy and provided one basis for the rapid output growth of 1972-75.

For the period as a whole labour productivity growth in the entire industrial sector averaged 4.3%. Coupled with employment growth of 3.9% annually, this entailed a rapid annual average increase in GIO of 8.4%.

Agriculture

Table 72 gives data on the development of GAO (7.). This shows an average annual rate of growth of 4.1% during the First Five Year Plan, falling to 0.8% through the war years (1965-72) and then stagnating during 1972-75 at 0.4%. Throughout the period agricultural output growth also became increasingly unstable, falling by 2.2% in 1963 and by 5.0% and 4.9% in 1973 and 1975 respectively. Whilst gauging the underlying trend through 1973-75 is particularly difficult, the average level of output in those three years was, at 3.06 bn. dong, some 16% above the average during the First Five Year Plan. This compares with a total population some 40% higher [<u>Table</u>:8]. Since the reported agricultural labour force grew by only 1.2% during the First Five Year Plan [<u>Table</u>:73] labour productivity saw an average rise of 2.9% annually. During the war years the number of workers in agriculture fell by an average 1.6% annually, but this was made up of a total decline of nearly 1 m. between 1965 and 1970 followed by a rise of 0.36 m. thereafter. During 1965-72 gross output per worker rose by 2.5% annually whilst through 1973-75 it fell by 2.5% annually.

Table 4.2: Comparisons of sectoral gross labour productivity growth

Sector	1960-65	1965-72	1972-75	1960-75
Agriculture	2.9	2.5	-2.5	1.6
Industry	8.3	-1.3	11.7	4.3
Total	5.9	2.1	5.0	4.0

Sources: Tables 30, 37, 45, 72 and 73.

This overall pattern reveals deep economic problems, above all the imbalance in the overall development pattern between the drive to increase industrial output and the necessary accompaniment of 'balanced' economic growth: rising domestic supplies of means of consumption. Since the economy was already out of balance by 1965 the rapid industrial productivity growth during 1972-75 appears, in hindsight, a grave error.

4.5 Sectoral output and the 'sources of growth'

The inevitable question that arises from the above is how the DRV was able to generate gross industrial output growth despite stagnation in the agricultural sector. Food remained by far the most important part of consumption expenditure for state employees and food purchases were around 70% or more of total outlays for such families throughout the period [Table:134].

In order to appreciate how this was done it is necessary to look, despite the difficulties involved, at the sources of growth in the macro-economy. Here the distinction must be made between the 'extensive' and 'intensive' growth patterns that characterised different sectors at different times. Broadly speaking it is sufficient to distinguish between them in the following way:

'Extensive' growth is characterised by the more effective use of economic resources by shifting them from sectors where their marginal contribution to output is low to sectors where it is high. A ready example is the steady transfer of rural labour into urban industry seen in Eastern Europe throughout the earlier part of the postwar period.

'Intensive' growth, on the other hand, must rely upon the more intensive use of economic resources basically fixed sectorally, typically by the use of increased levels of produced inputs and improvements in technology and management (8.).

Viewed from this perspective, what is most striking about the pattern of growth of both industry and agriculture in the DRV is the relatively small contribution of extensive growth and the correspondingly greater significance of higher levels of produced inputs in both sectors during circumstances where, if capital availability had been constraining output, almost all growth should, on a conventional analysis, have been extensive.

Aggregate labour productivity rose from 588 (1970) dong in 1960 to 1,081 (1970) dong in 1975 (9.). A simple measure of the extensive growth component derives from consideration of the effects of the higher level of industrial employment in isolation from rising labour productivity in that sector. Had labour productivity not been rising at all in industry, the increased employment would have been expected to produce only 2.21 bn. (1970) dong in 1975, rather than the actual output of 4.17 bn. (1970) dong. This suggests that only around 40% of the gain in labour productivity may be attributed arithmetically to pure extensive growth (10.). Instead, higher capital inputs in industry push up labour productivity and lead to higher output through more intensive growth.

Rising per capita output in agriculture reflected not inconsiderable increases in non-labour inputs which helped compensate for a declining reported sown acreage. Tables 74 and 75 show, for instance, an average annual increase in state investments in agriculture of nearly 10% over the period, coupled with substantial hydrological installations 'in use' by 1975; Table 76 reveals the degree to which the agricultural machine stock had been built up by the late 1970s. These issues are discussed further below, but whilst it is hard to balance such evidence against the considerable damage done to the rural infrastructure by US bombing, it is evidently true that there were, in some areas, major improvements in the capital available to agricultural workers during the period 1960-75.

Overall, these perhaps striking results are quite comprehensible if the basic constraints facing the area are recalled. High population density and a low level of mobilisable agricultural surplus meant that the macro-economy was subject to considerable tensions as the increasing demands for current inputs to the growing urban-industrial sector could not be met from domestic sources of supply. As mentioned above, the two main consequences of this were an increased dependency upon imports of goods for current use and consumption and the creation of inflationary pressures. It was therefore natural that a shift to an intensive growth pattern should occur, where the modern industrial sector, unable to obtain additional current inputs, tended to substitute for them either increased imports or more capital-intensive production. Thus it became further isolated from the rest of the domestic economy, in contrast to the largely unrecorded petty industrial producers who (as discussed in Chapter 5 below) became adept at absorbing labour unemployed or underemployed in the Socialist sectors by using extremely low capital:output ratio technologies. This analysis also reveals the inherent difficulties involved in the use of gross output data, for it is probable that imports rose so fast at times that net industrial output growth was in fact negative, despite rapid growth in gross output.

Footnotes

1. See ch.1 footnote 7.

2. No clear definition of 'urban' is given in the official Statistical Dictionary [Statistical Office 1977].

3. Throughout the text the Vietnamese term 'cong nhan vien chuc' is translated as state employment, although a literal translation would be 'workers and functionaries/officials'.

4. Note that the overall increase in total state and collective industrial employment was far greater than the growth in the reported urban labour supply. The precise reasons for this are unknown.

5. Tran Dang Van (1964) reported sharp increases in the numbers of non-agricultural rural workers and the problems they were causing to the quality of labour supplied to the socialist sectors.

6. The Footnote to Table 30 implies that the fixed capital data is at current prices; that to Table 17, which presumably gives fixed capital net of capital in non-material production in industry, suggests that the basis for the calculation of the measures is installation costs. Inflation in industrial capital goods prices over the period was not great: agricultural means of production prices rose on average only just over 1% annually during 1964-75 [Table:109].

7. The footnote to Table 73 states that output 'only includes the value of material output of the peasantry'; note, though, that whilst this series shows an average annual increase of 1.9% for the GAO of Agriculture and Forestry combined, the implied growth of the contribution of Agriculture and Forestry to 'Total Social Product' [Tables:19 and 20] is 4.6% annually over the same period. Note also that 'Total Social Product' grew by 5.8% annually over the period 1960-75, whilst the total of GAO and GIO rose by 2.9% annually. [Tables:43 and 73]. It is possible that the 'Total Social Product' data is in current prices, but the wide gap is otherwise unexplained.

8. The problem of the transition from 'extensive' to 'intensive' growth is commonplace in contemporary discussions of the growth problems faced by the developed centrally-planned economies of Eastern Europe and, of course, the Soviet Union. The basic cause of this is said to be the way in which most 'surplus' labour in agriculture has been moved into industry, leading to severe difficulties in raising aggregate labour productivity through crude inter-sectoral transfers of labour.

9. This rather approximate calculation is based upon a simple aggregation of GAO and GIO data from Tables 30, 43 (to obtain the data for 1960 and 1972 - as used in Table 4.2 above) and 73, coupled with employment data from Tables 37 and 72. GAO, as elsewhere, is derived from the column in Table 73 headed 'Agriculture' and therefore excludes non-agricultural output by the peasantry as well as forestry output.

10. The simple calculation is as follows and based upon the same data as footnote 9. Per capita industrial gross output in 1960 was 2,435 (1970) dong. If the 1975 industrial labour force had worked at that same level of productivity GIO would have been only 2.21 bn. (1970) dong instead of 4.16 bn. (1970) dong. It follows that average total labour productivity would then have been only 786 (1970) dong, rather than the recorded level of 1,081 (1970) dong.

Chapter Five

INDUSTRY

5.1 Introduction

The pattern of industrial development in the DRV was
determined both by the general issues surrounding micro and
macro policy and by circumstances peculiar to the sector.
Amongst specific examples of the latter were: first, the
survival from the dynastic and colonial periods of a great
variety of petty-production techniques; second, the early
establishment of state enterprises dependent upon administrative methods for their resource supplies; third, the existence
of a number of central organs who had competing interests in
the control and utilisation of 'their' industrial capacity.

The traditional artisanal sector managed to survive relatively intact during the colonial period. Although most of its
workers were collectivised in the late 1950s, this created the
potential for rapid and extensive growth in small-scale production as the balance of incentives moved in its favour. This
facilitated the processes already described in previous
chapters: a dynamic interaction between the various sectors of
the DRV economy that resulted, inter alia, in institutional
adaptation in accordance with local interests.

Such problems in policy implementation at the micro level
then reinforced the effects of resource misallocation at the
macro level. Of direct relevance to industry was the excessive
investment in the production of means of production (Group A),
and, within that sector, the excessive stress upon production
of 'means of production to produce means of production'. By
depressing real wages growth and shifting the balance of
incentives against effective participation in the Socialist
sector this reinforced the more fundamental constraint of a
low supply elasticity of agricultural surplus. This then gave
added impetus to the creation of aggravated shortage. Producers dependent upon the state for inputs found themselves
confronted with severe constraints upon current input availability. Chapter 3 showed how foreign aid imports perpetuated
the underlying problems by easing this constraint and further

84

isolating state industry from the rest of the domestic economy. These long-term trends clearly reflected deep systemic tensions within the DRV economy. At certain times, however, and for different reasons, certain of the constraints were relaxed. Thus during the late 1950s and very early 1960s it appears that the beginnings of the implementation of the Stalinist growth strategy had not yet really encountered binding constraints: free market grain prices were at times below those offered by the state (indeed some food exports were recorded); post-independence 'reconstruction' had not yet created the large employment increases that placed such stress upon the state's ability to supply consumption goods; the early stages of agricultural collectivisation had not yet depressed output below potential. Again, in the late 1960s the massive wartime aid program, coupled with the inevitable reduction in accumulation pressure as US bombing destroyed modern industrial capacity, helped reduce the tensions in the system. After the Paris Agreement of 1973 and consequent aid cutbacks difficulties mounted rapidly, fuelled by the effects of wartime inflationary finance.

5.2 Artisanal and modern industry before 1954-55

Artisanal Industry

French studies point to the existence of a substantial rural artisanat during the 1930s [Gourou 1936:448-539] that operated along traditional lines. This was made up of a great variety of small-scale producers, both craftsmen and ordinary peasants working in slack seasons. Here a division of labour amongst specialising communes was well established for certain products. The artisanat's survival was helped by the lack of French interest in the development of a mass market for consumption goods amongst the rural population [Fforde 1983:47-9]. Families that concentrated primarily upon farming were often extensively involved in artisanal production.

The most significant area where modern producers had supplanted traditional suppliers was in cotton thread, much of which was supplied to petty-weavers from the Nam Dinh mill that used imported cotton (1.). Cotton goods and silk were the two sectors in most notable decline. Gourou estimated that 200,000 out of an estimated total Red River Delta population of 6.5 m. were involved more-or-less full time in rural petty industry. Of these over one-third worked in specialised villages [id.:527]. Gourou thought that artisanal work tended to be concentrated in areas with the poorest land, but found the pattern of activity very hard to explain. He noted that it tended towards regional concentration, especially in Ha Dong province (now part of Ha Son Binh). Areas of activity included: textiles, based largely upon imported cotton but also using the high quality Tonkin cotton (around 55,000 workers); silk, where workers had high status; food preparation (around 55,000 workers); illegal alcohol distillation had gone underground after the French shut down production in those villages that previously specialised in it; basketware was an area of great importance at the margin of profitable specialisation by farming families; wood-working, with over 30,000 labourers many of whom were itinerant; paper work, of great importance in religious ritual, was found in only three communes; because of the very limited use of metal there were around 7,500 metal workers who largely worked on scrap; potters were, like paper workers, very concentrated in certain specialised villages - much of the Red River's supplies were imported from Thanh Hoa province.

The survival and development of artisanal production during the colonial period is very interesting. In employment terms it was considerably more important to the colonial economy than modern industry. The most important implications for the post-war economy were as follows:

First, that these petty-producers, based primarily upon methods of production requiring low levels of fixed capital and aimed above all at the production and reproduction needs of the peasants themselves, possessed a ready potential for rapid extensive growth should suitable conditions arise.

Second, the varied organisational forms that had evolved over the centuries (for example - part-time work, individual or family-based specialisation, village specialisation and, in the case of Nam Dinh textiles, integration into a production sequence part of which was carried out using large-scale modern technology) showed a process of adaptation that had resulted in institutions appropriate to the technology and resources available. This suggested that further adaptation would likely result in the future, if possible and advantageous.

Modern Industry - the colonial and Vietminh legacies

In North Vietnam the development of large-scale industry and modern technology was extremely limited. French colonial investment had sought only to exploit opportunities in world markets and in the supply of goods to high income sectors. This, it can be argued, was in keeping with the particular requirements of the metropolitan economy at the time [Fforde 1983:47-9].

During the Vietminh war the nationalists started up a number of production facilities, primarily in areas aimed at serving the war effort, but also directed at civilian consumption - especially in bureaucratic means of production such as paper (2.). When the Vietminh troops abandoned the urban areas in 1946 they took some industrial capacity with them, such as the Truong-thi railway engine plant and the Dap-cau paper factory. But the peasantry became far more dependent upon artisanal production as the war interrupted trade and the French attempted to isolate the nationalist areas. Vietminh industry grew up in an attempt to compensate for this, but stressed large-scale - i.e. non-artisanal - industry (3.). But a realistic view of the development potential of rural industry stemmed from recognition of the artisanat's low capital needs and effective methods of labour utilisation [id.:13].

Army installations required substantial material inputs from the mines as well as larger-scale plants with higher capital-output ratios. Recent writings have suggested that perhaps 50% of the rifles used at Dien Bien Phu were manufactured in Vietminh military factories [Nguyen Anh Bac 1985:2].

Not unexpectedly, debate about the correct degree of centralisation arose early. Some people reportedly argued for excessively large units; counter arguments, according to Pham Dinh Tan (1962), were that smaller and dispersed units would be better able both to utilise capital and to dispose of output. Such a policy would also help to integrate production into the local economy, thus encouraging regional self-sufficiency and mitigating the effects of the French military blockade. The decentralisers apparently won the day, and excessive centralisation was condemned in October 1947 by an Order from the Party Centre [Pham Dinh Tan 1962:16-17]. From 1947 a major expansion occurred and by 1949-50, when their numbers peaked, there were reportedly around 40 so-called 'national factories' in the Northern liberated areas who were primarily producing for civilian needs [id.:19]. These covered: - the extractive sector: primarily the mines; three metal-manufacturing plants, of which the Tran Hung Dao factory in Tuyen Quang was the most important; four textile mills; a couple of pottery kilns; fourteen paper plants; two soap plants; a match factory; two tobacco factories; and three plants producing tea, leather and wood.

Recognition of the DRV by China and the Soviet Union on January 18 and 30 1950 respectively led to profound changes in industrial organisation. Economic and financial work became far more disciplined and ordered [id.:22] and a number of the most inefficient units were closed. The 1st Plenum after the January-February 1950 Congress stressed the need for more effective economic management, emphasising: fiscal retrenchment by raising taxes, cutting staff and introducing financial accounting; the introduction of an effective banking and credit system; and the organisation of state trade, price management and economic warfare.

After 1950-51 almost no new national factories were established. This was partly facilitated by rising imports across

the Chinese border, but also reflected the poor economic
results experienced by many factories. The arrival of foreign
experts and pressure for effective use of available resources
placed greater emphasis upon controlling costs and managing
revenue sources [id.:23-24]. At the same time there were two
contradictory movements in the pattern of control. Before
1950-51 central organs had managed production units in a
rather chaotic manner that partly reflected their own particular economic needs. For instance, the Trade Unions managed
the Lam Son coal mine, the Financial Department of the Party
Central Committee managed the Ngoi Lua and Hoan Tien paper
factories and the Revolutionary Administrative Committee of
Quang Binh managed the Quang Xuan textile plant. This partly
reflected the scattering of resources and demand throughout
the Vietminh movement. After 1950-51 all production units that
were neither shut nor turned into collectives were turned over
to the Ministry of Industry and Trade [id.:27]. In practice,
however, management was still not centralised, and units were
responsible to the relevant Regional Industry-Trade Office
(Khu Cong Thuong) (4.). Regional autonomy was reinforced by
the inability of any central organisation to ensure reliable
supplies of means of production and consumption to production
units, which remained largely dependent upon local sources.

The legal framework covering the Socialist (state) enterprises reportedly dates from a Provisional Governmental Decree
of October 1952 (No. 214/TTG) which established the 'state
economy' ('Doanh nghiep quoc gia'). This was soon followed by
a second Decree (No. 215/TTG of November 1952) setting up
management organs in the factories - the Enterprise Management
Committees (Uy ban quan ly xi nghiep) - to supplant the previously 'advisory' Enterprise Committees (Uy ban Xi nghiep)
set up by Order 118/SL of October 1949 [EPU 1975:17].

The above picture does not really reflect the operation of
a centralised 'alternative state', for most activities resulted from purely local needs. The area where the Vietminh
did, however, establish some sort of integrated and sizeable
economic activity was in the production of military materiel.
Unlike civilian producers, such units did not have to worry
about either output disposal or profitability. As the highest
priority area their position was secure. The larger units had
labour forces of over 1,000, whilst the smaller ones employing
100-300 workers were supplemented by a number of repair shops
employing 10-50 [Pham Dinh Tan 1962:31]. This compares with
levels of employment in the larger civilian factories of 100-
300 workers [id.:42].

Conclusions

By 1954 the Vietminh/DRV administration possessed elements
of the basic framework for the creation of state enterprises
after the Soviet model. This framework reflected certain basic

requirements, especially those of key elements within the Vietminh, above all the Army. Important changes had taken place in industrial organisation, such as it was, when the arrival of Chinese Communist forces on the Northern border and recognition by the rest of the Communist bloc set conditions to the pattern of economic assistance. Although the level of modern industrial development remained extremely weak, the extensive artisanat retained considerable vitality.

5.3 Creation of the mature system and its operation: 1955-75

By 1975 the industrial management system had not changed significantly since the late 1950s (5.) Its basic principles of operation were quite conventional, and focused upon operating the rather large modern state factories whose fixed capital had been supplied by fraternal Socialist countries. Official texts usually differentiate between industry, in the strict sense - cong nghiep - by which was meant large modern plant operated under the state enterprise property form, and by contrast small and artisanal industry - tieu, thu cong nghiep - which was operated under the collective or individual property form. Thus such important textbooks as the 'Textbook on Industrial Economics' of the Economics and Planning University [EPU 1975] almost completely ignore non-state industry.

This and other works describe the formal operation of the system of management of state enterprises and provide illuminating insight into both the thinking behind it and the problems encountered in practice. The basic thrust was the desire to establish state industry's leading role in the national economy, above all by increasing its stock of fixed capital [EPU 1975:47-56]. In practice, however, the high levels of spare capacity utilisation meant that effective utilisation of resources mobilised into state industry was of major concern. Thus ways had to be found of increasing the contribution to output of fixed and circulating capital, as well as labour and other current inputs. In addition, the basic micro target remained in practice quantitative output maximisation (6.). The poor economic results of state enterprises [Nguyen Nien 1973:46] reflected the problems that typically arise from this system of economic control [Nove 1977:ch.4; Conyngham 1982; Kornai 1980].

Enterprise maximands: indicators and targets

Statements about the precise planning targets used in the DRV cannot be understood without some reference to the hierarchical administrative relations that existed between enterprises and superior levels (7.). The key management cadres in enterprises were viewed as the 'property' of the Ministry that acted as the enterprise's 'Head' - the 'Bo chu quan' (lit. - the 'Head Management Ministry'), and their careers were largely dependent upon its evaluation of their behaviour. Such Ministries were similar in their formal position to the Province, if the enterprise was locally managed. At the same time, such Ministries were differentiated from the so-called 'functional' organs such as the State Planning Commission and the 'branch-managing' Ministries both of which tended to compete with the 'Head' Ministries for influence and control. Over time the balance of power appears to have shifted against the latter (8.), who up until 1960 had managed all the materials used by them [EPU 1975:206 et seq.]. Thus, for instance, plant belonging to such Ministries as those of Transport, Culture and Health tended to be taken over by branch Ministries.

These complex links, within which precise spheres of responsibility were not capable of clear definition, accompanied a similar lack of clarity in the stipulation of the targets at which the enterprise should aim. In neither of the two textbooks 'Textbook on industrial economics' [EPU 1975] and 'Planning the National Economy' [EFU 1962] is there a clear statement of this. The most basic indicator, however, was output quantity, initially established at the macro level through consideration of the resources available, and then passed down to the enterprises [EFU 1962:146]. By the early 1970s some development of the formal system had taken place, and the more closely managed units then paid some attention to three legal indicators (chi tieu phap lenh). These were : 1. the realised value of merchandise output (gia tri san luong hang hoa thuc hien); 2. the principal products made, measured in volume terms (san pham chu yeu tinh bang hien vat); and 3. the total value of the wage fund (tong quy tien luong) [Nguyen Nien 1973:50]. But there is little evidence that this system was in effective operation. It is reasonably safe to assume that Ministries sought to make enterprises produce to a simple quantity target those 'principal products' (9.) that the state had decided were only to be distributed by its distribution and supply organs.

Industrial management remained heavily constrained by the limits placed upon the acquisition and disposal of economic resources. The real underlying aims of the people who worked in state enterprises generally led them to avoid instructions from higher levels that sought to make them do things that were not in their immediate interests. Here the way in which higher levels supplied resources to them were of great importance.

The acquisition of capital and state investment policy

The stress paid by received neo-Stalinist theory upon the key role of fixed capital meant that it received considerable attention. State investment policy at the macro level, with some variation over time, greatly favoured industry over other

sectors of the economy, and, within industry, those branches
that produced means of production (the so-called Group A
sectors (10.). Investment cutbacks towards the end of the
First Five Year Plan were at the expense of the means of
consumption branches - the so-called Group B (11.).

In a low-income developing economy a theoretical bias in
favour of large and modern plant naturally resulted in a
somewhat ambiguous attitude towards the choice of techniques.
Whilst 'better' technology was seen as increasing the capital-
intensity of production - thus pushing up labour productivity
- it was also seen as expensive, since it increased inputs of
capital [EPU 1975:129-30]. There was no simple answer to such
questions: the basic assumption tended to be that economies of
scale were large, which ignored the strong likelihood that
some of the very smallest production units - especially those
in the collective and individual sectors - were capable of
producing at apparently far lower capital:output ratios than
their larger competitors. Major reasons for this, of course,
were their far better utilisation of labour and other current
inputs which resulted from different incentive structures. An
illuminating discussion of the advantages of size in the
'Textbook of Industrial Economics' entirely ignores such
issues [EPU 1975:261-6]. Such myopia is, unfortunately, quite
consistent with the modernising idealism of the neo-Stalinist
model.

From the point of view of the individual enterprise, a
major difficulty lay in establishing effective control over
the use of assets once they had been installed. By the early
1970s the system was under attack from some quarters on the
grounds that 'superior organs interfered directly and deeply
in enterprise economic activities' [Nguyen Nien 1974:7]. This
meant that 'Head' Ministries could effectively prevent assets
from being transfered through the state system to areas where
they might be put to better use (average levels of capacity
utilisation were said to be 40-50% [id.:11]). A key reason for
this was that enterprise rights over fixed assets had not been
fixed with any clarity, so that the 'Head' Ministry could in
principle do what it liked [ibid.]. One frequent result was
that the enterprise simply gave up, and its people did nothing
for much of the time. Alternatively, the enterprise could use
its assets to produce something quite different and thus move
outside the sphere of responsibility of the 'Head' Ministry -
for instance by inventing some sideline product - or simply
break the law by, for example, using circulating capital to
make things that could be sold or swopped [id.:12]. A revealing example of the lack of an effective system for controlling fixed assets was the absence of regular stock-taking
[id.:13] (12.).

The overall pattern of events appears in hindsight to have
been fundamentally chaotic and certainly not 'planned'. State
enterprises were set up and equipped with aid-financed equip-

ment and then expected to operate in an increasingly tense economic environment where domestic supplies of various current inputs through the state distribution system were becoming more and more unreliable. If such supplies could be imported, then some of the installed capacity could be utilised, but typically much of it could not be. 'Output maximisation' was therefore deeply conditional on supply availability. Since this was unreliable, state enterprise activity often depended upon the extent to which local substitutes could be found in order to give the existing work-force something to do. In an aggravated shortage economy this often involved the creation of illegal 'circuits' ('vong') relying upon free-market transactions. Such behaviour was limited by the extent to which such activities were politically tolerated. Acceptance of it, however, could be secured through appropriate use of the resulting output (especially if it consisted of consumption goods). Deals done with agricultural cooperatives could see food swopped for scarce industrial goods. With the possibility of such behaviour always present, it is no wonder that there was no clear legal definition of enterprise rights with regard to 'their' fixed assets.

Acquisition and use of current inputs

The neo-Stalinist model bases itself upon a reasonably effective control of the distribution of current inputs to production. For the DRV's economic planners, proper resource allocation depended in theory upon the use of technical-economic norms giving the simple arithmetic ratios between planned output levels and the corresponding input requirements of the production unit. Thus planners should have been able to construct aggregate material balances between the supply and use of each major category of resource, permitting them to plan directly the production and distribution of resources needed to meet the given aggregate output targets. Pressure both for less inefficient (i.e. more intensive) resource use and for additional resource mobilisation was to come from the setting of progressive (tien tien) norms, which required extra effort at the micro level if plan targets were to be attained. This was a vital source of increased labour productivity and better resource use within the system. In practice, the low levels of capacity utilisation and generalised inputs shortage meant that this mechanism could not operate at all effectively.

The proportion of current inputs available to the DRV economy that was actually under the direct and unified control of the state trading and distribution network varied throughout the period (13.). During US bombing and immediately afterwards high levels of aid imports helped prop up the authorities' position against the growing pressure from spreading non-planned activities. There were two major criticisms of the methods used to allocate available supplies. These were, first, that planning was poorly managed, so that supplies were not sent where they were most needed. This reflected particularist pressures from 'Head' Ministries and other organs. Second, the management of the state's system of materials supply was weak - in other words, that materials were both wasted and siphoned-off illegally onto the free market [EPU 1975:205].

The central state system in any case only formally covered a limited number of products. Many other items not produced by the state were in effect managed by the Ministries or provinces 'subject to the operations of the Ministry of Internal Trade in its attempts to control prices and markets'. In the absence of clear guidelines and precise stipulation as to the products covered this led to considerable confusion. Enterprises could - and did - establish direct relations with non-state suppliers or even somewhat autonomous elements within the state distribution system in order to acquire non-listed goods [id.:208]. The way in which the centralising principles of the unified neo-Stalinist model became muddied is brought home by the observation that by the mid 1970s many - if not most - of the State Planning Commission's rights in the allocation of materials had been delegated (uy nhiem) to organs specialised by product type that operated comparatively independently, such as the Petrol Department [id.:211].

Labour

The attitude of labour to work in state enterprises was ambiguous. Whilst a job was keenly sought after because it gave access to goods and services in short supply, such as housing and medical services, the value of monetary wages had by the mid 1970s become so low compared with the prices of non-rationed goods that direct material incentives to work effort were very weak. Real wages of state employees had fallen sharply during the First Five Year Plan and by 1975 were nearly 25% below their 1960 level [Tables:133 and 136].

Labour remuneration theory in the DRV remained traditionally Leninist ('payment acording to work done'), and whilst non-material incentives in the form of patriotic emulation et al were from time to time important (14.), the system of labour management placed great stress on the utilisation of material incentives. The 1963 8th Plenum stressed these issues, possibly in the context of the Sino-Soviet debate, advocating an expansion of piecework and a rationalisation of the grading system [EPU 1975:166]. A Provisional Statute on Worker Protection in December 1965 gave workers - in principle - considerable safeguards against bad labour conditions.

The system of labour remuneration reportedly dates back to the 13th Plenum of late 1957. It sought to meet four basic aims [id.:167-9].

93

First, distribution should be in accordance with the work actually done but also take account of both the basic needs of different types (lop) of workers and the financing of enterprise-based social services.

Second, the wage system had to reflect the country's ability to pay, in the then current conditions.

Third, the average level of wages should allow for a balance between consumption and accumulation.

Finally, wages should be set in the light of particular economic difficulties.

From 1960 to the mid 1970s the system remained largely unchanged [id.:172 et seq.], and was made up in principle of three main elements: a system of technical levels (cap bac ky thuat), a wage-scale (thang luong) and a wage-rate (muc luong) which in combination established the rate of cash remuneration per unit of time. Thus a given worker was placed at a certain technical level depending upon the complexity and importance of his work. Wage scales differed between different groups of industries, and within them the number of levels (bac) also varied. The proportions between the positions on the scales also varied. The state, when it did so, only fixed the monthly wage-rate, whilst daily and hourly rates were set by the Enterprise or the 'Branch' Ministry on the basis of the monthly rate. Enterprises also had freedom to vary piece-work rates subject to the permission of the Ministries [id.:174].

In addition to the grade-wages (tien luong cap bac) of the workforce, the wage-fund of the enterprise had also to finance a number of supplements (phu cap) that had become a major element of costs by the early 1970s. These included subsidies paid to workers with large families, regional subsidies, payment for extra responsibility (such as foreman - to truong) and for overtime. Almost all payments to the workforce were made on a cash basis, and the State Bank should have made a regular monthly inspection [id.:201].

Data on the development of state employee incomes is extremely interesting, and can be taken as a reasonably close proxy for industrial workers' wages. The first point to note is the way in which [Table:133] so-called 'Other income sources' increase rapidly (by an average 14.8% annually) after 1965 after falling over the period 1960-65, so that by 1975 they were nearly 17% of total household incomes. This is probably an underestimate, since much of these earnings were quasi-illegal. Over the same period employees' pay rose only 1.8% p.a. Second, this was accompanied by a sharp fall amidst large fluctuations in the proportion of expenditure met from the state distribution network [Table:135] over the period 1965-75 (note especially the decline during 1965-1968 - from 73.4% to 59.7% - in the share of food expenses met by the state). Real income data is also available from another source and shows that average monthly incomes for state employee families moved as shown in Table 5.1.

Real incomes stagnation between 1965 and 1975 is confirmed by this data. What is clear, however, is that the real value to state employees of their wages declined sharply over the entire 15 year period whilst industrial gross output rose.

Table 5.1. Monthly incomes of state employee families

Year	Average per capita income, dong	Average real per capita income, dong (*)
1960	21.4	20.4
1965	21.7	16.3
1970	23.5	15.6
1975	27.6	16.3

*No base year given.

Source: Dao van Tap (ed.) 1980:65.

This again suggests that the major source of industrial growth in the DRV economy was the high supplies of inputs from overseas that encouraged an intensive pattern of growth.

Grass-roots reality: the Hanoi engineering branch

The day-to-day effects of aggravated shortage upon the economic efficiency of State industry could be illustrated in many ways. Limited space precludes a detailed empirical discussion, but an illustrative example comes from the experiences of the Hanoi engineering branch. These are reasonably well documented [Le Sy Thiep 1967]. This group of largely aid-financed factories was intended to play an important role in the development of regional industry, supplying spares and equipment to local agriculture and food and light industries. They had been on the whole unable to do so, and operated at shockingly low levels of capacity utilisation:

Why is it that the capacity of the branch is still not fully used, whilst the input requirements of other branches are insufficiently met?

Source: Le Sy Thiep 1967:14.

The source gives a number of reasons for this, which are extremely revealing. First, there was no concrete plan that fixed the pattern of investment and material supply for the city's economy. As a result, there was great confusion amongst enterprises as to who, according to the planners, they should have been supplying. As a result, and this had been 'happening for years', they frequently had to set about finding their own customers. With inadeqate supplies of complementary inputs from the state's trading organs, many could only work for six months each year. Some enterprises produced anything they could in order to meet formal plan targets, which then could not be sold. Second, and in much the same vein, their customers did not research their own needs properly, so that the state trading organs were unable to maintain stable distributional relations. With supply and demand thus separated, it is not surprising that the third reason given for the appalling state of affairs was the absence, when output plans were issued to enterprises, of any attempt to make a material balance. The branch therefore 'had no basis for putting out production duties and no basis for organising specialisation amongst enterprises' [op.cit.:15]. This meant that the environment within which enterprises operated led them to extremely inefficient and ineffective internal organisation. Finally, the chronic shortages of inputs forced engineering enterprises either to seek out supplies for themselves, or to give up. Typically, workers turned up for 5.5 to 6 hours daily, and enterprises actually operated for 3 to 4 hours [ibid.].

5.4 The artisanal and collective sectors

The artisanal and collective sectors of industry behaved quite differently from the state enterprises. They did not receive the large levels of imported inputs and supplies derived from administrative procurement that allowed the latter partly to escape the economic implications of the adverse shift in the balance of material incentives. As agents active in areas where resource suppliers had considerable freedom of disposal, the artisanal and collective sectors faced far greater pressure to generate incomes and supplies that fitted in with local interests. Section 5.2 above showed how the extensive and well-developed artisanal sector of the traditional economy had survived during the colonial period. After Land Reform growing agricultural production probably stimulated local production for exchange and by the late 1950s the numbers involved had grown substantially. Estimates for the total on the eve of Socialist Transformation go as high as 0.47 m. [Spoor 1985:229, quoting M.M.Asvenev 1960:72].

The drive to control this sector took three main directions: the registration as 'individual economic units' of those who were allowed to remain outside collectives, collectivisation of any others who were to remain active in the sector, and the re-employment of the remainder by the agricultural cooperatives, state farms and industrial enterprises. In this way the authorities hoped to exercise control. In practice, the great ease of capital transfer within this sector, where capital requirements were never large and where production activities were frequently bound up closely with trade, farming and livestock-rearing, meant that economic activity was hard to control.

By the end of the First Five Year Plan the official data showed that, despite the formal completion of Socialist Transformation, there were still 56,000 registered 'individual' industrial artisans [Table:41], supplemented by over 200,000 specialised workers in a variety of collective forms. The numbers economically active who used these units as a way of avoiding state regulation (by simply registering without submitting to state control) were probably far higher. Whilst the limit on employment was very low, family labour was largely unregulated (15.). In addition, such activities go a long way towards explaining the buoyancy of state employees' 'Other incomes' mentioned above. The discussion in Chapter 4 revealed the large increase in numbers not in identified employment over the period 1960-75, and petty-production, along with petty-trade, must have absorbed much of this. In so doing, of course, it offered those opportunities for gainful economic activity that were lacking in the Socialist sectors and thus helped to attract resources into such 'outside' ('ngoai') activities. The actual size of such activities will never be known precisely, because of their quasi-legal or illegal nature. Their buoyancy and presence are, however, widely marked in the available data. One striking example is the statistics on sales by private restaurants (admittedly not strictly an industrial sector) which, for reasons as yet unknown, show a nearly six-fold growth between 1969 and 1970 [Table:106].

5.5 Conclusions - North Vietnamese industrial development to 1975

By 1975 North Vietnamese industry demonstrated clearly the compounded effects of the attempt at accelerated industrial development in a low-surplus area. Wartime bombing had both masked and intensified these problems by encouraging large supplies of current inputs from other members of the Socialist bloc. These isolated modern state industrial enterprises from their natural sources of supply in the domestic economy whilst facilitating the development of unplanned activities associated with the so-called 'outside economy'. Such activities were based upon petty-production and trade both in industry and agriculture. Growth in the state sector was therefore intensive rather than extensive and gross labour productivity there grew rapidly during the closing years of the period 1965-75.

Over the period as a whole the DRV economy was unable to support either the pattern or the speed of industrial growth. The rigid and foreign institutional forms of the centralised state industrial management system stood in sharp contrast to the complicated interrelationships characteristic of 'outside' activities, where the enormous variety of organisational forms based upon both individual and collective property forms

to p.101

97

reflected their appropriateness to North Vietnamese economic conditions.

Footnotes

1. The French established the large mill at Nam Dinh in order to obtain the market for raw cotton imports that other Western producers had originally identified.

2. One interesting survey of developments in this area [Pham Dinh Tan 1962] also provides an implicit early critique of developments during the First Five Year Plan. Prof Tan stresses that the book is not a detailed history, but seeks to 'draw out the main lessons' [op.cit.:5] . See also Bui Cong Trung ed. (1960).

3. This points very early to the way in which the conventional North Vietnamese interpretation of the word industry corresponded to a conception of industrialisation that stressed large modern plant. In this way an 'essentialist' meaning of socio-economic development is reinforced, naturally de-emphasising a more functional definition, for example in terms of sustainable long-term increases in per capita output and the most appropriate way of obtaining them. See the discussion below on the meaning of industry (cong nghiep) in modern Vietnam.

4. The 'region' - 'Khu' - was an organisational level above the province that also provided the main basis for large-scale military activity.

5. One of the authors discusses the detail and meaning of the attempts to renovate the DRV industrial management system during the early 1970s in a forthcoming study of Vietnamese Industrial Organisation. There were, however, no fundamental changes until the very early 1980s (e.g the important Decree 25-CP of 21st January 1981 'A number of measures and policies aimed at continuing the development of the right to autonomy in production and trade and the right to financial autonomy of state enterprises'. One area that received attention was the creation of enterprise funds. By the mid 1970s certain targetted enterprises possessed three funds into which a certain proportion of their profits were to be paid: a 'welfare' fund, a 'development fund' and an 'incentive' fund. Another area of concern, where again little was actually done, was in the supply of subsidies to loss-making units. By the early 1970s the system in force in practice met most losses in full from the state budget (the 'thu du chi du' system - 'enough income, enough expenses') and enterprises were under very little pressure to keep proper accounts; a stricter system ('gan thu, bu chi' - 'deduct incomes, absorb expenses') that sought to discipline enterprises was being tried in the mid 1970s [EPU 1975:294-5].

6. This resulted in considerable intellectual confusion, since without a net output maximand the economic value of

input substitution cannot be properly assessed. It might usefully be added that without some ordinal measure of the social
value of output it is very difficult to assess the relative
social value of the different input combinations provided by
alternative technologies [Giffen 1981]. See also Ellman (1979)
pp.133-43;

7. The following discussion has greatly benefited from
interviews with Vietnamese economists in Hanoi during 1979 and
1980.

8. By the early 1970s the 'branch-managing' Ministries
were: the Ministry of Machinery and Metallurgy; the Ministry
of Industrial Coal and Electricity; the Ministry of Light
Industry; the Chemical Department; the Ministry of Staples and
Food [EPU 1975:72].

9. For the list of these products as it was in the early
1960s see the Supplementary Table at the beginning of Part II.

10. Spoor (1985) pp.85-101 collects much of the available
evidence. See also Leon Lavallee (1971) pp.35 et seq.

11. The data on realised investment in Table 63 shows how
basic construction in industry rose by 41.8% between 1960 and
1965; for Group A, it rose 64.4%, but for Group B, it fell
27.9%.

12. See Spoor (op.cit.) p.89 on the 'voluminous' levels of
private enterprise stocks revealed by the April 1961 asset
census, which was probably not repeated until the early 1970s.

13. It is noteworthy that, according to US sources, the
DRV never managed to attain a unified system of logistical
supply of imported military materiel [Pike 1986:52-3].

14. E.g. the famous 'moi nguoi lam viec bang hai' ('every-
body does the work of two') movement.

15. The exact limit is, revealingly, hard to establish.
Personal interviews in Hanoi during 1979 put it at '1-2' and
confirmed the importance of family labour in the sector.

Chapter 6

AGRICULTURE AND FORCED DEVELOPMENT: THE PEASANTRY COPES

6.1 Introduction

Looking back over nearly 20 years (it is clear that)...in
many cooperatives...a number of cadres lack the collective
spirit and embezzle and waste (collective property); The
situation of cooperators taking over collective land
without permission is...generalised and has been so for
many years; For a long period (more than 10 years) the
method of management has been to allocate out to the
brigades...(who) have held land, labour and (production)
expenses and have organised production by themselves,
frequently independently of the cooperative's plan; Apart
from a number of cooperatives, almost all produce without
regulations and without work norms; (Cooperative)
managements tend only to plan for the next harvest.

Source: Dinh Thu Cuc 1977:passim.

The cooperative's (My Tho, Binh Luc district, Ha Nam Ninh
province) way of planning and accounting was usually lying
and inadequate; the district never checked the figures
properly...The management did nothing but act as representatives of the brigades in dealing with the state in the
work of buying raw materials, borrowing money...(and)
supervising vaguely the encouragement of brigades to raise
the proportion of new seeds, transplant at the correct
time and so on...The plan was constructed in order to
obtain the approval of superior levels and (to provide a
basis) to ask for supplies of raw materials and loans..
The Party was usually absorbed in replacing the cooperative in organising economic activity. When a job was done
wrong but in accordance with local interests and using a
resolution of the collective, then it was very hard for
the superior level to maintain control.

Source: Dang van Ngu 1974(A):pp.15-16.

> Up until recently many groups of villagers had informed
> the Management Committee (of My Tho)...about frequent
> incidents of embezzlement by cadres, but these were not
> quickly dealt with.
>
> Source: Dang van Ngu 1974(B):p.28.

Agriculture provides the most revealing example of the
institutional adaptation of neo-Stalinist models. Here endogenous response to their fundamental unsuitability took two
main directions. First, a widespread 'nominalisation' of
collective structures sought to strengthen local control over
them and correspondingly weaken the influence of higher levels
in the Party/state hierarchy. Once established, this relative
autonomy then facilitated significant pressure for a return to
more economically viable methods of socio-economic organisation. Under North Vietnamese economic conditions, these
stressed family-based production and mutually advantageous
exchange rather than collective production and administered
distribution and supply. Both these trends shared a tendency
towards wide variation in social organisation which contrasted
with the uniform blanket approach of official policy that
viewed agriculture as more or less homogeneous.

One very important reason for the particular direction
followed in the adaptation of neo-Stalinist models was the
multi-sectoral character of collectivised agriculture's institutional forms, which formally permitted petty-commodity production on the so-called '5% land' - the private plots left
for cooperators to exploit on their own account. Acting in
response to material incentives that increasingly inhibited
voluntary participation in collective production, cooperators
sought, often successfully, an expansion of these plots beyond
their Statutory limits. Such strategies required protection
against interference from higher levels and supervisory
bodies, and the cooperatives themselves frequently played this
role and acted as 'protective intermediaries'; as such, their
real social functions became quite different from those intended by official policy. By permitting a partial return to
more economically beneficial methods of organisation this
provided one of the most important elements of the process of
endogenous response whereby rural institutions began to re-
establish the link between technology and organisation that
the French colonial presence had broken. Experience increasingly showed that, as elsewhere, family-based control of most
elements of the production process coupled with a market-
oriented and therefore voluntary distributional system was
more economically viable than collectivised production and
administrative allocation of resources [Bray 1983; Nolan and
Paine 1986(B)].

A major constraint upon rural development was the authorities' hostility towards accumulation in non-Socialist sectors. This meant that the economically attractive areas of the rural economy - the private plots and the free market - were greatly constrained in their access to modern inputs and financial credit which remained subject to state monopoly control. Since the producer cooperatives were deemed Socialist the authorities saw them, despite their inefficiency and wide unpopularity, as the principal legitimate site of rural accumulation.

By at least the end of the First Five Year Plan it was reasonably clear that collective production units had proven themselves generally inappropriate to North Vietnamese conditions. The economies of scale promised by their exponents were insignificant if not negative in some cases, and their clumsy and over-complicated remuneration systems were incapable of overcoming 'free rider' and other problems so as to secure an effective labour supply and proper use of other current inputs. Their dense management systems created too many jobs for idle cadres, whose incomes were a direct cost to the cooperative, and whose presence obstructed the quite genuine attempts of many other cadres to operate the collectives as efficiently as possible. In practice, however, cooperatives suffered from certain insurmountable difficulties. The use of internal accounting systems that valued resources both rather ineffectively and incorrectly meant that resources actually mobilised into the collective economy were rarely used efficiently. In addition, management cadres confronted continual difficulties in their attempts to enforce the cooperatives' formal property-rights and obtain adequate control over collective economic resources. Although peasants probably valued certain of the cooperative's collective functions, their survival in the main resulted from the political requirements imposed by the Communist leadership. This accompanied the ideological association of cooperatives with the Socialist Revolution and, therefore, with the struggle for National Liberation that propaganda linked more and more closely to the Socialist Revolution. The way in which peasants and cadres actually operated the agricultural producer cooperatives on a day-to-day basis was therefore closely bound up with the shifting balance between the inclinations of the top leadership, as reflected in official policy, and the development of various local strategies designed to cope with an evolving environment of which those policies were an important part.

When peasants confront the wide-ranging transformational intentions of a Communist government both the concept and the practice of endogenous institutional adaptation are closely linked to the wider question of policy implementability. This has major political implications. A key element of North Vietnamese peasant strategies was the attempt, often successful, to maintain control over local affairs by turning

into protective intermediaries those unwanted elements of the
Socialist institutions that the authorities wished to utilise
as a means for controlling the rural political economy. Thus
the real economic functions of cooperatives, in so far as
local interests determined them, included such important tasks
as permitting excess private-plots (the so-called '5%' land)
through inaccurate and deliberately misleading reports to
higher levels. Most peasants probably did not see anything
wrong with the generalised illegal behaviour that resulted.
But state policy was presented as a historically necessary
realisation of the Party Line, which was, furthermore, asserted to be both ethically and scientifically 'correct'. The use
of showpiece models emphasised the intended universal applicability of prescribed cooperative management methods. Official
policy's widespread unimplementability therefore had important
implications for the validity of 'Mac Le-nin'.

The wider perspective suggests an interpretation of these
particular conflicts as an example of peasant resistance to
state power [Fforde forthcoming]. In North Vietnam, this resistance inevitably focused upon the local expression of the
state's social and economic power: the neo-Stalinist models.
Once the rural areas were collectivised these institutional
forms provided the framework for subsequent struggles to control output disposal and access to means of production. A
failure to prevent them from operating according to prescribed
policy meant that peasants lost most control over access to
means of production, over output distribution and the labour
process itself. But a successful resistance effectively
stripped producer cooperatives of much of their influence and,
more importantly, obstructed their capacity for allowing
higher levels to interfere in communal or sub-communal
affairs. Such 'nominalisation' of the Party/state apparatus'
local economic organs required an ability to manipulate administrative structures. Whilst these institutions in principle conferred great social power upon the Party/state
hierarchy, centuries of experience with corporate villages and
the avoidance of unwanted demands enhanced peasants' ability
to resist. One of the important aspects of the historical
inheritance discussed above can be seen in the way in which
the North Vietnamese peasantry's experience with centralised
states acted to constrain extractive economic policies aimed
at the mobilisation of agricultural surplus. Institutional
adaptation and the creation of protective intermediaries in
order to prevent loss of control over the rural economy constituted the way in which this constraint actually operated at
the micro level.

For reasons of space, this chapter examines these
processes in only limited detail. The next section looks at
the basic institutional model - the agricultural producer
cooperative - and considers its appropriateness to the North
Vietnamese context. The following section discusses the tra-

103

jectory of the macro-environment facing cooperatives and their management cadres, linking this to the observable data on cooperative nominalisation and the deep-rooted problems that constituted the Agrarian Question that confronted the authorities in the mid 1970s. A central aspect of this was the day-to-day reality of aggravated shortage in the rural political economy, where adapted collectives and state controlled distribution coexisted with highly attractive possibilities for family-based production and sales on the free market [Challiand 1969:132-6].

Few Western scholars have studied North Vietnamese producer cooperatives. This fact is in itself surprising, given their important wartime functions in troop mobilisation. Early and valuable works such as Tran Nhu Trang (1972), Elliott (1976) and Woodside (1970) do not study the problem from an economic perspective and inevitably ignore the deep-rooted problems resulting from aggravated shortage, but nevertheless provide much interesting detail. Moise (1977 and 1983) and White (1981) deal with the Land Reform period only. More recent work (Vickerman (1985); Fforde (1982); Spoor (1985)) has started to open up the subject, but proper fieldwork is still lacking. Houtart and Lemercier (1984) and Challiand (1969) supply further information, but again do not deal with the key issues of institutional adaptation and entrenched distributional conflicts characteristic of an aggravated shortage economy. And it has to be stressed that many of the present work's conclusions are still rather weak. In the present state of knowledge this is unfortunately inevitable.

6.2 Overview of agricultural development 1960-75

It is important to recall from the outset the basic parameters of agricultural development in the DRV: the relative stagnation of a very poor area long characterised by demographic saturation and accorded low priority by an essentially industry-oriented post-independence development strategy. Previous chapters have stressed the growing isolation of the precociously-developed 'modern' sectors from the rest of the domestic economy. For state industry and the state bureaucracy this meant an increasing dependency upon imported current inputs to maintain minimal activity levels. But for the impoverished delta peasantry the continuing pressure from the state for supply to the resource-starved priority sectors meant that in order to generate the higher retained output levels required by the rising population they had to adopt strategies designed to minimise loss of control over both production and distribution. Agricultural cooperatives were in fact intended as a means for bringing cooperators' economic activities under collective - and therefore, where necessary, state - control. Peasant resistance strategies therefore had to confront this sustained attempt to establish effective structures and avoid loss of control over both production and distribution.

Chapter 3 presented arguments for the growth and continuing existence of an aggravated shortage economy in North Vietnam from at least the early 1960s. One element of this was the relatively slow growth of agricultural consumption goods output compared with the rapidly rising demand from those newly employed in state industry and the bureaucracy. Increasing dependence upon staples imports reflected this fundamental imbalance. Over the period 1960-75 as a whole labour productivity growth in agriculture averaged around 1.5% annually compared with nearly 4.5% in industry [Table 4.2].

On closer examination, there are a number of interesting - if not surprising -aspects of DRV agricultural development. One particularly surprising feature is the rather high levels of state supplies to agriculture (especially during 1965-72), and the relative absence of any corresponding yield gains. This is prima facie evidence for poor utilisation of such resources, and the likelihood is that inadequate supplies of other factors of production were in fact constraining output growth.

Cultivation

In 1974 the rice-growing area of the DRV was about 1.1 m. ha., supplemented by another 0.2 m. ha. that was also used to grow other crops [Table:67]. Direct precipitation remained the major source of water for the fields. Under ordinary circumstances a factor acting to stabilise the cultivated rice area in the face of fluctuations in the pattern of precipitation was the balance between the major 'Xth month' crop and the minor 'Vth month' crop. Put simply, rain that flooded one crop would leave water in low-lying areas for the other, whilst less rain meant that conditions for some main crop rice would improve [Chassigneux 1912]. Farmers gained additional flexibility from their ability to choose seeds with differing growth rates. But the issue of water-control at the local level remained of great importance, and the rising stock of pumps coupled with state infrastructural investment at various levels should have contributed substantially to the gains in rice yields per sown ha. These reportedly rose from an average of 1.82 tonnes/ha. in 1960-65 to 2.23 tonnes/ha. in 1973-75 (+22.5%) [Table:80]. This was offset, however, by the combined effects of a fall in the sown area and a decline in the production of non-rice staples. The former fell from an average of 2.38 m. ha. in 1960-65 to 2.20 m. ha. in 1973-75 [Table:79]. The latter fell from an average of 0.85 m. tonnes of paddy equivalent in 1960-65 to 0.74 m. tonnes in 1973-75 [Table:84]. Total staples output therefore grew only marginally, from an average of 5.19 m. tonnes of paddy equivalent in 1960-65 to 5.65 m. tonnes in 1973-75 (+8.8%),

and far too slowly to keep pace with either the rising
population or the increasing non-agricultural labour force
(1.).

The fall in the sown rice area is conventionally explained
by reference to the destructive effects of US bombing. This is
unlikely to be the sole explanation, however, since there is
considerable evidence to suggest that many cooperatives reported declines in the sown area in order to hide illegal increases in the private-plots at the expense of the collective-
ly farmed area (2.). This suggests that reported national
output was, for this reason alone, likely to have underestimated staples output. Against this, however, has to be put
the likelihood that local interests could seek both to under-
report output so as to reduce procurement pressure, and to
over-report in order to secure plan fulfilment bonuses. The
net outcome of these conflicting pressures is unclear.
Furthermore, it is likely that the combined effect of these
factors varied over time. Here the fall in the output of non-
rice staples is particularly interesting. During 1960-65 this
grew from 0.5 to 1.0 m. tonnes of paddy-equivalent. It then
averaged 1.0 m. tonnes annually during 1966-68, when the
effects of US bombing in the rural areas were at their peak.
But by 1969-72 the average was down to 0.8 m. tonnes, and in
1973-75 a further fall, to 0.7 m. tonnes, had occurred
[Table:84]. This data appears rather inconsistent with the
idea that state procurement was placing increasing pressure
upon cooperator real incomes, and suggests rather that farmers
successfully shifted back to rice, the more readily marketable
crop, after the period of severe bombing in 1966-68, before
procurement pressure was eased by the arrival of large-scale
imports of food intended primarily for the non-agricultural
population. Table 6.1 shows how the reported level of staples
availability from domestic suppliers had fallen to crisis
levels by 1968. It appears likely that this coincided with a
fall in procurement pressure and a recovery of rural real
incomes. Rising imports of food aid masked the underlying
problems with the collectivised system by isolating state
employees from rural producers. Here the subsequent fall in
non-rice staples output is consistent with the idea that
producers will tend to shift away from lower-value and lower-
preference crops as subsistence pressure falls.

Animal husbandry

Livestock were of great importance to the delta peasantry.
Ploughing, harrowing and transport required the use of buffalo, and also, although less frequently, the chill-prone oxen.
Pigs were reared primarily for sale to raise cash, and consumed at important feasts; they were often the major source of
cash income for a peasant family. There was a sharp fall in
the recorded gross output of the livestock element of agri-

culture in 1961, just after collectivisation [Table:72], which
is probably associated with above-average slaughterings during
the collectivisation period itself. At this stage there was
little pressure for the collectivisation of peasants' pigs,
although draught animals were meant to become the property of
cooperatives [Fforde 1984:327]. The DRV buffalo and ox herds
both fell in 1961; the pig herd did not [Table:92]. Most
draught animals came from the uplands, and it is noticeable
that the ox herd never returned to the 1960 level [id.].
Comparing the 1960-65 and 1973-75 averages, the data shows an
18% rise in the buffalo herd, a 17% fall in the ox herd
(implying a rise of 5.9% in the total draught animal stock)
and 49.5% rise in the pig herd [id.]. Prior to 1973 the
collective pig-herd grew faster than that of the family
sector, but subsequently all of the growth took place outside
the cooperatives (3.). This was quite contrary to official
policy at the time, and reflected the growing attraction to

Table   6.1:   Reported   levels   of   staples   (rice   equivalent)
              availability from domestic suppliers

	Population m.	Staples production m. tonnes	Monthly per capita supply (kg.): A. Unmilled	B.Milled
1960	16.10	4.698	24.3	15.8
1961	16.57(*)	5.201	26.2(*)	17.0(*)
1962	17.06(*)	5.173	25.3(*)	16.4(*)
1963	17.57(*)	5.013	23.8(*)	15.5(*)
1964	18.09(*)	5.515	24.4(*)	15.9(*)
1965	18.63	5.562	24.9	16.2
1966	19.20(*)	5.100	22.1(*)	14.4(*)
1967	19.78(*)	5.398	22.7(*)	14.7(*)
1968	20.38(*)	4.629	18.9(*)	12.3(*)
1969	21.00(*)	4.709	18.7(*)	12.1(*)
1970	21.84(*)	5.279	20.3(*)	13.2(*)
1971	22.30	4.921	18.4	12.0
1972	22.66	5.742	21.2	13.8
1973	23.14	5.190	18.7	12.1
1974	23.95	6.277	21.8	14.2
1975	24.55	5.491	18.6	12.1

(*) Estimated by assuming constant rate of population growth
    between years where there is official data.

Source: Tables: 8 and 78. Population between those years given
in Table:8 calculated by assuming constant growth between
years. The ratio used to adjust to a milled rice equivalent
basis is 0.65. This includes an allowance of 5% for seeds etc
on top of the 70% conventionally used (information provided by
Hanoi University, 1979; see also Fforde 1982:378).

peasants of the free market and own-account activities, combined with the authorities' inability to enforce central policy.

Incentives and the conflicting attractions of collective and own-account activity

On balance, it appears most useful to view the period 1960-75 as characterised by a broad secular shift against participation in collective production and the supply of surplus staples to the state, and therefore in favour of freely-marketed output produced on the expanded private-plots. This tends to be confirmed by the data on the state's share of cooperator purchases and sales [Table:139], where the state saw its share of purchases by cooperators fall from a peak of over 50% in 1965 to an average of 44.8% in 1973-75; its share of cooperator sales, on the other hand, also fell from a peak of nearly 39% in 1975 to just over 30% in 1973-75. Thus by 1975 over two-thirds of cooperator sales were to the free market.

This on the whole probably meant that farmer real incomes on average rose over the entire period 1960-75, and furthermore that living conditions in the rural areas remained in many ways better than those in the cities. Neither population group was particularly well off, however, and particular subgroups suffered badly at times. The data on expenditure patterns, which is not, however, likely to be reliable, supports this conclusion, for by 1975 the share of cooperator family expenditure on food was below 60%, compared with over 70% for state employees [Tables:134 and 138].

These trends had obviously important implications for the pattern of incentives facing state employees. But, confronted with major problems in agriculture, it is reasonably clear that the state responded positively by attempting to improve the terms of trade that its trading organs offered to farmers. Thus whilst the general level of controlled retail prices of staples and food rose over 30% during 1964-75, the average prices paid for agricultural means of production rose only 13% [Table:109]. Retail outlets directly controlled by the state actually cut the prices of agricultural means of production by around 7% over the period 1964-75, whilst the general price index hardly shifted [Table:110]. Other statistics confirm this trend, suggesting a rise in state purchasing prices of the order of 50% over the period 1965-75 when state selling prices were broadly unchanging (4.). Recorded data on price movements in the unorganised market shows, however, both how the 'outside' economy was operating at far higher price levels, and also a relative movement in the free market terms of trade against producers, for prices of agricultural means of production rose nearly 188% over the period 1964-75 compared with 85% for staples and food [Table:111]. The record regarding the terms of trade offered by state trading organs is therefore not one of passivity, but of a somewhat impotent attempt to avoid the effects of the macro-economic tensions created by the development programme of the early 1960s. Aggregate information on supply levels is unavailable.

The overall picture of stagnation in the level of surplus products mobilised into the state distribution system is, however, not true either in the particular case of industrial crops or that of 'hard commodities' such as coffee. State farms rather than the cooperatives were responsible for producing much of the latter. The relative value of non-staples food crops received by the state did, however, on the whole tend to decline [Table:99]. Here a direct comparison can be made between reported output levels and the data on state procurement of Table 91. Table 6.2 below shows how the state managed to maintain control over jute, rushes, tobacco, tea and coffee. Sugar procurement fell back sharply as a share of reported output towards the end of the First Five Year Plan but the state had recovered its position by 1974-75. In all these six categories the state directly controlled more than half of domestic production. But for soybeans, peanuts and rice the state's relative position deteriorated. By 1975 the state procured only just over 14% of reported domestic rice production compared with over 20% in 1965. It is worth noting

Table 6.2: State procurement expressed as a percentage of reported output

	1960	1965	1974-75 (avge.)
Staples	18.7	20.2	15.2
Of which Rice	20.0	23.3	17.0
Jute	76.9	83.0	92.2
Rushes	71.9	63.6	84.5
Sugar	69.4	49.3	64.7(*)
Peanuts	37.7	52.4	49.3
Soybeans	33.0	34.1	19.7
Tobacco	57.1	84.6	83.8
Tea	60.5	73.3	57.6
Coffee	82.4	88.0	132.0
Pork (kg. per head)	11.7	12.6	15.2

(*) 1974 only.

Source: Tables 78, 81, 86, 87, 88, 89, 91 92 and 93.

that neither soybeans nor peanuts were on the list of 'planned goods', and therefore were goods where the state's monopsony position was weaker. Aggregate calculation of the state's ability to obtain supplies of meat, above all pork, is difficult. Examination of the simple ratio between the series on meat supplied to the state with that on the DRV pig-herd shows a rise over the period 1960-75 from 11.7 to 16.6 kg. per head. Since around 90% of pigs remained in the private pig-herd this was an area where state procurement organs had to provide incentives that were competitive with the free market. Active cooperative managements often devised alternative strategies, and these are discussed in the next section.

The reasons for stagnation: agriculture after the Paris
                                  Agreements

By the time of the 1973 Paris Agreements North Vietnamese agriculture was in a position to set about re-establishing itself and restoring production lost due to war-damage. But isolating the direct consequences of the war from the adverse effects of the adapted collectivised system is extremely difficult in the absence of a formal model. But it is interesting to note that the average level of real gross agricultural output during 1973-75 was in fact some 15% above that during the First Five Year Plan [Table:72]. Output had surpassed the previous (1965) peak in 1972.

One of the main statistical origins of the stagnation in staples output was the fall in cultivated area. Although there are reasons for attributing part of this to mis-reporting, bombing of the north-central provinces (Nghe An and northern Binh Tri Thien) is known to have had a particularly severe impact upon farmwork. Table 79 suggests that a total loss of 0.1 - 0.2 m. ha. was reported (the fall in the area sown to the main rice crop), largely offset, however, by increased use of the Spring and Cham ('Vth month') sowing. Here a number of pointers suggest the role played by the structural difficulties of the adapted collectivised system in restraining output growth by preventing utilisation of increased inputs, though these questions have really to be answered by micro-level investigation. The main basis for this is the rather surprising increases reported in the availability of various inputs. First, however, there is the slow recovery of the sown rice area in the period after the signing of the Paris Agreements: by 1975 this was still only 92.5% of the previous peak (1964) [Table:79] and had showed only marginal growth from the early 1970s. But this must have been at least partly to do with the difficulties involved in repairing damaged local water-works and other infrastructure. Second, Tables 74 and 75 show a substantial state investment in agriculture, both in water-control and industrial inputs. By 1974 state water-works actively supplying water to agriculture reportedly covered some 37% of the total yearly-cultivated area, equivalent to some 53% of the rice land area [Tables 67 and 75]. These are large numbers, especially compared with the colonial situation. And Table 76 shows a machine stock that is not only rather respectable, but, as other data confirms, represented a substantial increase over the period since the early 1960s (see Table 6.3).

Thus to put against the decline in resource availability represented by the loss in cultivated area attributable to US bombing there is evidence for increased resource availability in addition to the rising labour force already mentioned. There is, furthermore, some evidence for the use of improved rice strains as well as higher supplies of industrial fertilisers and insecticides. By 1975 domestic production of chemical fertilisers was some 3 times the 1965 level at over 0.4 m. tonnes, whilst insecticide output was 27% up on 1965 [Table:46].

The evidence therefore suggests that whilst part of agriculture's apparent stagnation was certainly attributable to the direct effects of US bombing, it was also in part to do with the inability to utilise the increased inputs available, which included labour, machines, water-control, seeds and industrial chemicals. Apart from labour, these inputs were supplied through the state distributional system and placed under the formal control of the producer cooperatives that were intended to play a dominant role in the rural economy. Micro evidence shows that these Socialist institutions undoubtedly created great obstacles to attaining better resource utilisation, and a full explanation of the collectivised

Table 6.3: Machinery and electricity available to agriculture
(excluding state farms)

	1965	1975
A. Machines per 1,000 workers in cooperatives		
Motors	0.5	4.5
Pumps	1	4.5
Standard tractors in use	0.2	2.6
Threshers	-	1.5
Mills	0.5	1.5
B. Electricity supplied per 1,000 workers in cooperatives, m. kW-hr.		
	0.01	0.03

Source: From a table in Fforde 1982:383, based upon data provided by Hanoi University, 1979.

system's poor performance has to take account of this. The terms under which these resources were supplied, and the balance of incentives acting upon cooperators who controlled

important complementary inputs, most especially labour, prevented an effective use of economic resources. Whilst cooperative nominalisation and illegal extensions of own-account
activity to some extent reduced these effects, as did similar
behaviour elsewhere in an aggravated shortage economy, the
overall system still operated well below potential.

The next section examines the micro institutional framework in some detail. This provides a basis for understanding
the various conflicts that took place as local interests
sought to retain control over output and distribution. These
confrontations focused upon the relation between sub-units of
the agricultural producer cooperatives and the cooperative
itself, and the interaction between cooperators' family-based
own-account activities and the collective.

6.3 The basic institutional models: agricultural producer co-operatives and state farms

The basic triad of property-forms associated with orthodox
Communist theory (Chapter 2) was introduced into agriculture
quite rapidly. It took the form of agricultural producer
cooperatives (hop tac xa san xuan nong nghiep), state farms
(nong truong) and a residual private or individual (ca the)
sector. Of these the first was by far the most important, and
by the early days of the First Five Year Plan (1961-65) the
great majority of delta peasants had, with their land, joined
cooperatives [Table:69]. Many of those who remained outside
the collectives were non-ethnic Vietnamese in the upland areas
who used relatively land-extensive 'slash and burn'
techniques. Comparison of the per capita landholdings of
familes inside cooperatives with those who had not joined is
therefore misleading if taken to indicate a move by richer
peasants into the cooperatives [Gordon 1981]. In addition, the
apparent fall in the proportion of peasant familes inside
cooperatives in 1963-64 [Table:69] does not simply reveal a
setback to the cooperative movement, for the total number of
cooperator families was still rising [Table:70], and at a rate
rather faster than the total agricultural labour force (5.).

The French colonial plantations formed the basis for the
50-odd state farms that existed in 1960, and these rapidly
expanded their labour force during the Five Year Plan until by
1965 they employed nearly 70,000 [Tables:69 and 73]. This compares with a total agricultural labour force of 5.6 m., of
which nearly 90% was in the collective sector [Table:72]. The
legal status of state farms was similar to that of state
industrial enterprises. There is no output data that separates
the three sectors.

Although the initial collectivisation drive was extremely rapid, with most delta peasants joining in under a year,
the early cooperatives were of the so-called lower-level (bac
thap) type. Primarily because it could not follow Leninist

112

principles of distribution solely according to work done, such a cooperative was viewed as less Socialist than the so-called higher-level (**bac cao**) type and from the earliest days there was pressure for lower-level cooperatives to 'advance' to higher-level status (6.). This trend entailed a greater centralisation of management power in the cooperatives, since a greater proportion of collective output was subject to the cooperative's direct control. The other dominant trend also sought to increase the volume of resources subject to the cooperative's control by amalgamating cooperatives. The average size of a cooperative therefore rose steadily over the period both in terms of labour and cultivated acreage [Table:71].

The basic institutional model for North Vietnamese collectives was therefore the agricultural producer cooperative (**hop tac xa san xuat nong nghiep**) and this was drawn directly from Soviet experience. The two basic types of cooperative - the lower and higher level versions - also followed Soviet models [Wadekin 1982:63 et seq.]. In the lower level cooperative peasants in principle retain a claim to a share of output based upon the amount of land and other non-labour resources they have contributed to it. Such a cooperative is rather similar in form to the production collectives (**tap doan san xuat**) used in the early stages of the Mekong delta's collectivisation after national reunification in 1975-76. In the higher-level cooperative, distribution to factors of production is in principle solely on the basis of labour performed for the collective. The cooperative may use some of its output for other purposes, such as accumulation and social welfare payments, but members no longer retain any right to a return for the land and other resources they contributed. This means that the cooperative has, again in principle, greater economic power.

These cooperatives were intended to act as the main agent for the Socialist Transformation of the peasantry who made up well over three-quarters of the DRV's population. The authorities laid down the norms to which they should have conformed in a variety of Party and legal documents, to most of which the foreign observer lacks access. A key document, however, was the basic Statute governing the formal operation of each cooperative that was meant to constitute its establishing document. This is available [Fforde 1984] and provides considerable insight into the basic framework of cooperative organisation. In addition, the Party and state supplied organisational norms intended for use within this basic framework. These dealt with the details of internal structure, relations between the cooperative's constituent elements, the role of the Party and mass organisations, the pattern of economic development and so on. These varied over time as perceptions of the difficulties facing the collectivised system changed. The overall trend was towards increasing centralisation of cooperative management within the enlarged cooperatives that the amalgamations created, and for pressure against peasants' attempts to extend and defend their 'own-account' activities. It is hard to understand the evolution of these policies in isolation from the precise detail of the cooperative system, and an outline of these shifts is therefore delayed until the next section.

The Statute for higher-level cooperatives reveals a number of key elements of their intended operational methods (7.). It provides the official definition of a cooperative's constituent elements: its two Management Committees; the Assembly of cooperators or cooperator representatives; the Brigades which had stable contractual relations with the cooperative; the specialised sub-units, usually teams; and the cooperators themselves, grouped into families (8.). In essence, the power centre of a cooperative was intended to be its Management Committee (**Ban quan tri**), whose Chairman, the cooperative's Manager (**Chu nhiem hop tac xa**) was held responsible for relations between the cooperative and higher levels. The Management Committee was vested with the collective's property-rights and thereby given considerable economic power. It was in principle elected by the cooperators through the Assembly, which also elected a Supervisory Committee (**Ban kiem tra**). In practice, the Secretary of the local Party Committee (**Bi thu chi bo Dang**) customarily held the post of Chairman of the Supervisory Committee. Only the Supervisory Committee could call extra-ordinary meetings of the Assembly and so easily dismiss Management cadres. The Statute viewed relations between these various groups as essentially harmonious, and gave no method for resolving conflicts that might arise. Relations were basically seen as governed by duties and rights: cooperators had the right to work for the cooperative, and correspondingly the duty to defend its assets against encroachments and attack.

By far the most important constituent elements of the cooperative were its brigades (**doi**), for they were responsible for organising collective work and delivering collective output to the Management Committee. They therefore acted, _inter alia_, as the first step in the chain of procurement, appropriating output in the name of the collective that would eventually end up in the hands of the state's trading organs for allocation to state employees and others. Although they were in principle allowed to elect their own leaders, provision was made for a Management Committee to appoint its own members to act as Brigade Heads. The simple rice-producing brigades of a cooperative operated relatively independently, usually subject to an agreement made with the Management Committee. This in effect allocated them usufruct to collective assets, mainly land and implements, 'in return' for delivery of all or part of their output to the cooperative. The brigades were responsible for the direct supervision of production. Beside these production brigades existed specialised units, usually known as teams (to) but also called groups (nhom) responsible for particular tasks such as insecticide spraying and so on.

The cooperative's formal relations with superior levels were simple but clear. It was the tax-unit, corporately responsible for deliveries to the state of rice and other products since taxation was almost exclusively in kind. Meeting state procurement targets was a duty. The cooperative was also given responsibility for supplying labour for infrastructural work such as dyke upkeep and maintaining the communications network. This was now called Socialist Duty-labour. The cooperative was also to assist with troop mobilisation. All these functions recall the duties placed upon the traditional commune by the Imperial dynasties. But as an important institutional element of the Democratic Republic the Statute also required cooperatives to participate actively in the Socialist Revolution. Here their primary duty was to develop the collective economy, but in addition cooperators were to educate those who remained outside the cooperatives so they would 'support the Revolution'. Thus the cooperatives were to become part of the system of education and propaganda aimed at creating solid ideological support for the Party and Revolution. Here the mass organisations for Women, Youth and others were of importance.

Whilst the present discussion is mainly concerned with the cooperatives' economic functions, their wider social role should not be underestimated. The recent experience of the appalling consequences of the loss of corporate support during the colonial period had heightened peasant appreciation of the value of collective social welfare provision. The Statute clearly laid out a cooperative's obligations in the fields of education, pensions, child-care, care of those unable to work, the families of war-dead and invalids and the provision of the general capacity for collective mutual assistance that peasants, with good reason, valued highly in such a poor and risky environment. Rising population and the uncertainties introduced by the unpredictability of state policy encouraged support for collective methods of insurance against risk. The literacy drive and the development of mass education were largely carried out through the DRV's new institutions of which the cooperatives were a key part. The DRV's educational achievements are certainly impressive, not least when the poverty of the area is recalled [Tables:145-7]. The cooperatives also made an important contribution to mass welfare through their activities in the organisation of primary health care facilities in the rural areas, and by 1965 most communes possessed dispensaries or midwiferies [Table:150]. Unfortunately the fate of these services was closely bound up with the availability of resources, and severe shortages and priority allocation to other sectors frequently starved them of good personnel and medical equipment.

The basic economic structure of a cooperative was the triadic interaction between the Management Committee, the simple production brigades and the cooperators themselves. Cleavages amongst these three levels reflected systematic differences in interests and economic power. Since the state maintained direct relations only with the Management Committee, which was therefore often referred to as 'the co-operative' in official writings, emasculation of it was an essential pre-requisite to use of the cooperative's institu-tions as a 'protective intermediary'. The brigades, on the other hand, were not only closer to cooperators, but were also naturally interested in maintaining and extending their rights over the collective property entrusted to them (9.). Thus there was a tendency to look for some form of alliance between brigades and cooperators. This would either effectively remove most economic power from the cooperative's Management Committee, or ensure that it never possessed any. In this way the supposed managerial organs of the cooperative could become nominalised and real economic power located at the level of the brigade and the cooperators. A basis for such an alliance could be found in an expansion of the private plots beyond the statutary '5%' limit and support from cooperators for the production brigades against attempts by an active Management Committee to reduce their power.

The confrontational relationship between the brigades and the cooperators on the one hand and the cooperative's Manage-ment Committee on the other is at the root of much official policy towards the Agrarian Question as it evolved in North Vietnam after collectivisation. The focus of attempts to deal with perceived difficulties was almost always upon the need to improve cooperative management, and thereby ensure that co-operatives functioned as real economic units and agents for the Socialist Revolution - rather than as precisely the opposite, and a means for keeping the state at arms length. This largely explains the initial sense of artificiality that sometimes arises when the foreign observer first confronts North Vietnamese writings on the subject aimed at domestic consumption. The primary focus of policy was to get coopera-tives to function in accordance with the prescribed norms laid down by the Party and derived, it was maintained, from the correct Line and 'Mac Le-nin'.

The first major movement to improve cooperative management dates from 1963 [Dinh Thu Cuc 1977], and stressed the use of contracts as a means for controlling the production brigades [Nguyen Chi Thanh 1969]. At this time cooperatives were still extremely small, with only a few dozen families (10.), and labour management within the brigades not yet as complicated a task as it was later to become. It is of note that the pres-cribed relationship between brigades and Management Committees should have taken the form of 'contracts', for this points up the sense that social relations needed to be defined in terms of duty and responsibility. There was very little suggestion that these contracts should have resulted from competitive bargaining, or reflected the different interests and opportunities facing the two contracting parties.

These simple contracts developed into the so-called 'Three-point contracts' which were an important element of the New Management System introduced from the early 1970s. This Management System represented an attempt to deal with the problems of the collectivised system by still further increasing the formal powers of the cooperative's central management to exercise a detailed and fine control over economic activity within it. 'Three-point contracts' stipulated: (I) the brigade's planned output and the inputs (both labour (II) and non-labour (III)) that it would use to meet that target. It was therefore a simple example of the idea discussed in Chapter 2 that planners could use an assumed stable relationship between inputs and outputs as a basis for using direct control over input allocation to generate required output levels.

In principle, the cooperative's labour and non-labour resources were contracted out to the production brigades in stipulated amounts, and the idea was that this would then result in some corresponding level of production and delivery of output back to the Management Committee. This presupposed that the Committee was in control of the cooperative's means of production. The idea that the brigades should deliver contracted output levels to the Committee meant that there had to be some method of organising income distribution for work done throughout the cooperative. This was to be based upon the system of labour norms used to relate inputs to output when establishing the Three-point Contracts. Records of work done provided the normative basis for a brigade's workforce to obtain access to part of its own output for consumption purposes. This utilised a system of work-points and labour norms. A cooperator carrying out a particular task was set a norm, in other words a particular physical target (e.g. so many square metres to weed). If he or she met that norm, they received an allocation of work-points that varied according to such conditions as the quality of norm-fulfillment, the severity or skill of the work involved, and the category of labourer to which they belonged. The basic unit of remuneration was therefore the value of the work-point, which was not usually known until the Management had calculated the cooperative's net income after the harvest and deductions for deliveries to the state, administrative expenses, and payments to the social welfare and accumulation funds.

In principle, the general system of economic management offered by the producer cooperatives could be progressive. Control over resources was concentrated in the hands of the central Management Committee, which thereby acquired sources of surplus mobilisation and a means for directly allocating labour into valuable local infrastructural projects such as land-levelling and work on the hydraulic system. But the principles governing the cooperative's internal organisation stressed the Socialist value of <u>collective</u> production, which meant that the production brigades had to be allocated responsibility for the direct control of labour. This was fundamentally less efficient than family-based production. In addition, a factor making things worse were the unfavourable incentives facing participants in the collective when compared with those on the free market. Administered supply of resources, in any case limited by the industrial orientation of the overall development program, was wasteful; the essentially extractive view taken of agricultural surplus mobilisation further reduced the attraction of deliveries to the state. And once the aggravated shortage economy became entrenched supplies from the state were far from buoyant. The free-market offered a ready and profitable outlet for effort on the cooperators' own account, generating both cash incomes needed for such important events as weddings and a continual sense that the most advantageous outlet for those mobile resources under the cooperator's control was not usually the collective. The available micro-level evidence suggests beyond much doubt that cooperators' involvement in own-account activities was basically constrained by pressure from cadres to participate in the Socialist economy in accordance with higher level prescriptions [<u>Fforde</u> 1982]. At times, however, cooperative cadres could raise cooperator interest in collective activity by making own-account activity conditional upon such participation.

6.4 <u>Policy response: towards the New Management System</u>

Chapter 1 emphasised the importance that the Communist leadership attached to the validity of 'Mac Le-nin' and the likely problems that arose from the need for such new ideas to compete with others, even if covertly. As an area dominated by the deep-rooted problems of a subsistence agriculture long characterised by population saturation, the Agrarian Question was of great importance. The closure of the southern border to migrants and the continual pressure upon the intensive subsistence margin in the North meant that yields had to rise rapidly if the government was to avoid a crisis. Aid imports masked this, but it was still increasingly clear that rising import dependency was storing up considerable problems for the future. The new institutional forms had therefore to satisfy certain simple criteria if the Communist leaders were to retain any popular respect for 'Mac Le-nin'. Yields had to rise and subsistence had to be ensured for those deemed worthy of it - most importantly war-invalids and the families of war-dead. Since experience showed early that an unadapted collective system, within which the '5%' plots were strictly limited, was extremely inefficient, meeting the objective of higher yields meant adapting the collective system in some way, and thereby raising its operational efficiency. Thus the combination of a toleration of excess own-account activity with a perpetuation of certain elements of the collective system met basic goals. For some cooperatives, increasing centralisation was a way of increasing the efficiency of relatively unadapted systems. In others, a high degree of adaptation and nominalisation of collective structures permitted the more efficient family-based economy to develop further.

The 1961 5th Plenum

During the First Five Year Plan the main thrust of official policy aimed at increasing the economic rights of cooperatives' central management organs. The important 5th Plenum of 1961 on the role of agriculture during the First Five Year Plan asserted this quite clearly. The main problem with the cooperative movement was that it was 'not yet firmly established' [TWD 1963:7]; this meant the following:

1. Cooperative management was weak. Planning of production and organisation of collective labour was insufficient and financial controls confused (lung tung), resulting in waste and corruption.

2. People were not properly carrying out the general policy on cooperativisation, especially with regard to Socialist principles of income distribution and popular education.

3. Technical improvements to implements were very weak; cultivation methods were incorrect and inadequate. Cooperatives' material circumstances were poor and the value of shares contributed by cooperators still very low [id.:8].

The Plenum presented four main goals for the development of agriculture during the Five Year Plan: adequate supplies of food for the population; sufficient supplies of raw materials to industry and of exports; ensuring proper supplies of labour for the development of both agriculture and industry; creation of a large-scale market for industry [id.:12]. It put forward specific targets for 1965: 9.5 tonnes of staples of which 7 m. tonnes should be rice; a rice yield of 2.4 tonnes per ha.; an increase in the total cultivated area of 550,000 ha.; an area equivalent to 10% of the cultivated area to be devoted to industrial crops; 1.8 m. draught animals and 8-8.5 m. pigs [id.:16-21]. These targets were missed by very large margins (11.).

The Plenum's main emphasis was upon the need to reinforce

and strengthen the agricultural cooperatives. To this end, it advocated their expansion to the village (thon) level of around 150-200 families (ho) [id.:36]. Cooperatives 'had to have a plan that was correctly coordinated with the state plan...that was executed well and in good time' [id.:40]. They had to use their labour rationally, utilising the 'Three-contract' system with work-groups and raising the number of days worked [ibid.]. The grass-roots unit responsible for this was the commune's Party committee, which had to 'manage closely the cooperative's Party cell and go right down to the cooperative level' [id.:49].

Chapter 3 discussed the gathering problems with the entire development strategy that came to the fore in the distributional crisis of the closing years of the First Five Year Plan. Out of this appears to have come a reluctant acceptance of import dependency and a degree of ideological adaptation to the day-to-day realities of aggravated shortage, though without any fundamental change in the overall policy stance. But during the late 1960s the sharp decline in per capita domestic staples output (see Table 6.1 above) and rising procurement pressure appear to have precipitated some form of policy crisis. This is known in the West as the 1968-69 'Three-contracts Controversy' (12.). Most commentators view this as a debate about agrarian policy. There are reasons for doubting whether the debate was even primarily about agrarian issues, although it was couched in terms of difficulties with the collectivised system (13.).

A single province in the North (Vinh Phu) was severely criticised for allowing its cooperatives to sign production contracts with cooperators that were very similar to the familiar Three-point Contracts that long-established policy had encouraged them to sign with brigades. It is possible that this behaviour was becoming increasingly common as collective production came under increasing pressure from rising free market prices and state procurement demands, and the effects of US bombing. As large-scale food imports from the Soviet Union started to come in during 1968 the authorities had announced a 'New Food Policy' that sought - abortively - to abolish the free-market in staples. By effectively enlarging own-account activities, direct contracting with cooperators would have permitted greater economic efficiency. But it is also possible that the decision to condemn such contracting was simply a top-level political manoeuvre. In the absence of more direct evidence from the grass-roots firm conclusions cannot be drawn. But it is likely that this episode committed top policy-makers to methods of cooperative management that sought to centralise economic power and control in the hands of the cooperative's Management Committee.

The New Management System

In the very early 1970s official policy continued to follow this logic on to its conclusion, and the authorities began to introduce a more detailed and comprehensive management model in a number of experimental cooperatives. The Thai Binh Conference of 1974 presented this as a coherent model, and, various cooperatives' experiences with it, known as the 'New Management System', have been studied in some detail [Fforde 1982; Nguyen Xuan Lai 1977]. From 1974 it was the established norm by which to evaluate cooperative managements. In 1976, after national reunification, the top leadership confirmed its validity and applicability throughout the Socialist Republic. It was effectively abandoned during the economic crisis of the late 1970s and replaced by the so-called 'output contract' ('khoan san pham') system [Fforde forthcoming:Ch.12].

The New Management System had three key elements: unification of economic activity, of management and of distribution at the level of the cooperative. This entailed establishing the Management Committee's control over the cooperative and its sub-units. In cooperatives where the Committees lacked real power it therefore involved the creation of mechanisms for reducing the effective autonomy of the production brigades and curbing cooperator own-account activities. The management system operated as an integrated package, so that enhanced control over output distribution, for example, both resulted from and facilitated better control over labour.

Prescribed methods of remuneration did not greatly change; the Three-point contracts were now supplemented by formal penalty-bonus systems operating on brigades as a whole. The central management of such a cooperative sought to dominate the previously autarkic rice-producing brigades by such measures as land reallocation. This helped to ensure that the work-point was of constant value throughout the cooperative, and facilitated close supervision of material output by the enlarged accounting office. In addition, specialised brigades were set up to supply the rice-producing brigades with such essential inputs as fertiliser, seeds, ploughing and harrowing services and so on. This cut at their power by increasing their dependence upon the cooperative. By monitoring inter-brigade transactions (e.g. supply and delivery of manure) the Management improved their control of output and economic activity generally. Specialised brigades were also established outside cultivation, both in the artisanal and light industrial sideline activities (nganh nghe) and in livestock (chan nuoi). There was great pressure for cooperatives to establish collective pig-herds. The idea was to raise fertiliser availability by rearing more pigs, and furthermore to increase supplies to agriculture as a payment in return for the higher mobilised surplus of pork. This hoped-for virtuous circle was a major feature of the New Management System.

The attempt to introduce the new system in cooperatives that had previously operated with largely nominalised structures revealed both the existence of such structures and the basic goal of the system. This reflected at root the desire to control the rural economy by integrating it into an overall planning framework. Once implemented, the New Management System was an extremely powerful tool for directing economic activity. Cooperators' own-account activities on the private-plots, which would in any case no longer extend beyond the Statutary limit of 5% of the cooperative's land, came under great pressure. The family economy was given responsibility for delivering to the cooperative stipulated amounts of such goods as pork and manure. Cooperators had also to meet their collective labour duties, which reduced the time available for own-account activities. In a show-piece cooperative that possessed well above-average supplies of machinery and other produced inputs there could be quite substantial benefits to going along with such 'reforms' to the cooperative's management system. In others, however, the attack on both the brigades and the cooperators' own-account activities met considerable resistance. The decline in the DRV collective pig-herd between 1973 and 1975 reveals the non-viability of that element of the policy (see footnote 3.). But the mid-1970s saw the Party strongly committed to the New Management System, and so the political economy of the delta areas remained dominated by the struggle between 'reformist' Management Teams pushed by higher-level concern and local interests entrenched in the autarkic brigades and the family economy of individual co-operators.

Certain cooperatives, perhaps a substantial minority, modified the New Management System to take account of the balance of incentives facing cooperators. In such cooperatives collective output of paddy was often used as a way of buying pork or manure from cooperators, with the implicit understanding that it would be sold on the free market [Fforde 1982:Ch.9]. This allowed the cooperative to meet its duty to supply pork to the state and cooperators to exploit their Statutary right to sell on the free market. Although this right in principle only extended to their own produce, it was a right denied to the cooperative. But to use such strategies the cooperative Management had to have some control over the distribution of collective output. In other 'active' co-operatives there were instances of excess '5%' land being effectively rented out to cooperators [Fforde 1982:Chs 8 and 11].

It seems that the New Management System's dense management structure could require, according to some sources, over 100 cadres [The Dat 1981:230]. But whilst the existence of conflicts is clear, the aggregate picture is hard to establish.

Such conflicts at the micro level involved the production of misleading reports as an inherent part of the nominalisation strategy. But it has been estimated that the great majority of cooperatives were acting as protective intermediaries in the mid 1970s, and perhaps 75-80% had an only nominal existence [Fforde 1982:132-3]. They functioned primarily as a means of maintaining local interests in opposition to higher levels, with real economic power shared between the production brigades and the cooperators, who concentrated their activities upon their private plots as much as possible. The collective production that occurred within the brigades was largely independent of the central management organs of the cooperative, and allowed the commune to preserve its Socialist credentials and thereby insure against higher-level intervention.

6.5 Conclusions: the North Vietnamese 'Agrarian Question' on the eve of National Reunification

By the mid 1970s the 'Agrarian Question' in North Vietnam had many aspects. On one side, the widespread adaptation of neo-Stalinist models of itself represented a major defeat for official policy and, more profoundly, for Marxism-Leninism. Daily reality showed that policy was unimplementable. Any discussion of the nature of the Vietnamese Socialist Revolution had to take account of this, but the top leadership's public pronouncements continued to maintain that the prescribed institutional models were the reality of rural life and a concrete expression of the way forward. This was profoundly misleading. Peasants' unwillingness to go along with neo-Stalinist models revealed one element of their unsuitability to North Vietnamese conditions. On the other side, however, experience showed that adaptions of these institutions tended to raise their economic efficiency. Such behaviour was constrained both by higher-level pressure for the preservation of Socialist institutions and the need to defend local interests. The well-established patterns of systemic conflicts had created social structures that had two main sources of built-in economic inefficiency: first, the need to retain wasteful local institutions as a protection against outside interference; second, the inherently inefficient nature of agricultural collectives themselves coupled with the state's bias against accumulation in the economically attractive non-Socialist areas of the rural economy.

This meant that North Vietnamese agriculture confronted two main difficulties. First, the deepening population problem meant that economic growth was of great importance. In a poor area this would have to come from a highly efficient use of the limited resources available, coupled with the maintenance of corporate institutions as a means of reducing risk and encouraging farmers to adopt new techniques and investigate

123

strategies of product diversification in order to move away from subsistence cultivation. In developing such a strategy the autonomous pattern of institutional development away from the neo-Stalinist models had already shown the likely optimal path, which would involve a blending of family-based control of much - but not all - of the production process with extensive use of market relations in order to provide an efficient incentives structure. This would likely be under-written by a preservation of communal institutions to finance local social welfare and valued infrastructural investment.

But the second main problem was the role to be played by the state in the development and implementation of such a strategy. Here the importance placed by the DRV leadership upon the validity of 'Mac Le-nin' and the legacy of the years spent attempting to implement the unimplementable was a major difficulty. Furthermore, the institutions of the DRV themselves created considerable obstacles for reformers. State industry was starved of resources and accustomed to obtaining them through the state trading organs with little regard paid to their social cost. The aggravated shortage economy gave incentives for its preservation to those who had managed to secure access to the low-price goods circulating within the state distributional system. Rural cadres supported in a nominalised cooperative by their cooperators because of their willingness to turn a blind eye to illegal behaviour would loose much of their power if that behaviour became legal.

The Agrarian Question on the eve of National Reunification was not, therefore, easy to resolve. Possible improvements were not difficult to envisage, but getting them accepted, and then implemented, would have required overcoming obstacles at most levels of DRV society.

Footnotes

1. See Lam Quang Huyen (1964) for a rare regional study stressing the attractions of a policy that defined priority areas of rice cultivation in order to maximise state procurement. He gives data showing that per capita staples outputs in the early 1960s varied throughout delta provinces from a maximum of 365 kg (Hai-duong) to a minimum of 268 (Thanh-Hoa) [op.cit:25]. He saw cooperative success very much in terms of surplus mobilisation.

2. For an argument quoting official Party Reports and provincial data see Dinh Thu Cuc (1977); for comments on excess private-plot - '5%' - land in individual cooperatives see Pham Tran Thinh (1976) and Tran Dinh Thien (1976). See also The Data (1981) pp.202-3 on 'land abandonment'.

3. During the First Five Year Plan official policy stressed the positive role of the private pig-herd [TWD 1963:18]; by the early 1970s policy stressed the development of collective herds. Data supplied to one of the authors by

Hanoi University in 1979 gave the information in the table -
'DRV Pig-herd...' - below.
    4. Data from EPU (n/d) vol. 2 p.72 - unfootnoted table.
    5. It is important to realise that the family (ho) was the
unit of rural population registration. It typically consisted
of a husband and wife with their children. Micro data used in
Fforde (1982) suggested that it might typically contain around
4.8 people. As such, it was not the same as other, perhaps

DRV Pig-herd, thousands

	Total	A: Collective	B: Private
1965	4790.8	272.5	4518.3 (94.3%)
1973	6304.1	704.5	5599.6 (88.8%)
1974	6303.6	646.5	5657.1 (89.7%)
1975	6599.4	638.6	5970.8 (90.3%)

more natural, kinship organisations, especially the ill-
defined but socially extremely important household (gia dinh).
Between 1960 and 1965 the total number of families reportedly
rose from 2.80 m. to 3.12 m. (+11.4%) at a time when the
collective labour force rose from 4.93 m. to 5.25 m (+6.4%),
implying a fall in the average number of family workers from
1.76 to 1.68 [Tables: 69, 70 and 73]. Since the rural population was growing over the same period from 14.70 m. to 16.79
m. [Table:8], an increase of 14.2%, this implies that the
underlying nature of the family was changing as the cooperatives became more firmly established. The reader should perhaps note that, as in the case of the terminology for rural
population concentrations (commune, village and hamlet), this
convention for translation of the Vietnamese words is not
universally accepted.
    6. The most basic difference between the so-called 'lower-
level' cooperative and the 'higher-level' form is the presence
of some form of remuneration to the land or other non-labour
inputs brought into the cooperative by the cooperator. In the
more Socialist 'higher-level' form the only reward to factors
of production in principle is the payment to cooperators for
work done. See Luu Quang Hoa (1967) for an example of the
arguments for increases in the average size of cooperatives,
based upon a sample of cooperatives from Ninh-binh and a
simple classification of them into 'good', 'average' and 'bad'
[op.cit.:34].
    7. For further details see Fforde (1985).
    8. I.e. the ho - see footnote 5 above.
    9. Many brigades could not practically be 'entrusted' with
land, since they already occupied and largely controlled it.
This was because they drew their population from distinct
administrative-geographical areas of the commune, whose populations had originally brought into the collective the land

they possessed by the time Land Reform and the Correction of Errors had finished. Typically, this was scattered around the commune. Thus a brigade's land was also likely to be scattered, which was known as 'near land, far land; good land, bad land' ('dat gan, dat xa; dat tot, dat xau').

10. The early cooperatives drew their populations from the sub-village hamlets (xom); as cooperatives grew in size, these maintained their underlying importance by becoming the basis for the brigades of the larger amalgamated cooperatives now based upon the commune's villages (thon or lang) or even the commune itself. In the mid 1970s, micro-level studies used in Fforde (1982) showed that a typical commune might have a population of around 5,000, with perhaps a dozen hamlets in two or three villages. A hamlet would therefore have around 400 inhabitants.

11. These targets compare with the following reported outcomes (targets in brackets): 5.6 m. (9.5) tonnes of staples of which 4.5 m. tonnes (7) were rice; rice yield of 1.9 (2.4) tonnes per ha.; total cultivated area rose by 226,000 ha. 1961-65 (550,000 ha.); 6.4% of the cultivated area devoted to industrial crops (10%); 4.8 (8-8.5) m. pigs [Tables 75, 77, 80 and 92]. Note that the data in Table 92 on draught power shows a buffalo and oxen herd over 2.3 m. in 1960, suggesting some problem in data comparability since the target was set at 1.8 m.

12. See Gordon (1972), Honey (1969) and Turner (1975) pp. 205 et seq.

13. This entire episode is subject to considerable uncertainty because of the difficulties of separating out the very real economic policy questions from its wider political dimension. The stakes may have been very high, since it appeared as a direct conflict between the General-Secretary, Le Duan, and the one-time General-Secretary, Truong Chinh. Ho Chi Minh, the undisputed 'Father of the Revolution' died in September 1969. The 1968 Tet offensive, whilst precipitating U.S. President Johnson's fall from political power, also destroyed much of the Southern fighting forces and must also have created severe political tensions.

Chapter 7

CONCLUSIONS: THE LIMITS OF NATIONAL LIBERATION

The Limits of National Liberation and the changing nature of binding constraints

This study has attempted to bring out the deep-rooted structural problems of the North Vietnamese economy. In so doing, it has concentrated upon systemic issues. It therefore may appear to downplay, or possibly even ignore, the real direct costs imposed by the wars, as well as the deep poverty of the region. This is not the authors' intention. But it is an analytical understanding of the socio-economic effects of the DRV's institutions that is important, in order to appreciate fully how the society operated within those constraints.

The analysis has taken a strong position in favour of a view of the DRV economy that sees it as having been dominated by 'aggravated shortage': a structural combination of the chronic shortages familiar from developed centrally-planned economies with an extensive development of market-oriented activities. This concept, whilst valuable, remains theoretically rather weak: no effort has been made to develop any more general implications that it might have. Furthermore, whilst the evidence presented tends to confirm the analysis, there remains a substantial body of unutilised materials that might be used to support different or even contradictory conclusions. One of the authors' main hopes is that the study will stimulate further research.

The prospects for development in a reunified Vietnam

By the end of 1975 the constraints facing socio-economic development in North Vietnam were quite different from those that had confronted the DRV in the late 1950s. For the finally reunified nation the future now looked somewhat brighter. In the Mekong delta the country possessed an area of relatively low population density capable of generating large levels of mobilised food surpluses both relatively easily and at far

127

lower economic cost than the over-populated North. The
southern population, settled in relatively scattered and non-
corporate villages, appeared to have less ability to resist
extractive policies. This meant that the basic constraint of a
low supply elasticity of procured consumption goods that had
bedevelled the DRV's neo-Stalinist development programme was
no longer present. The export potential of the South was also
far better than the North. The reopening of the southern
border meant too that the long-run trend towards an easing of
the pressure on the intensive subsistence margin in the North
by out-migration could re-establish itself.

A united Vietnam was in fact far better suited to the neo-
Stalinist development model. Rapid industrialisation based
upon the DRV's institutions was possible in a way that it had
not been for the North alone. Had the Communist leadership
been able to start again from scratch, rapid forced
industrialisation along the lines expected for the First Five
Year Plan would probably have been successful. Extractive
policies aimed at mobilising food and other economic surpluses
would have been far more capable of feeding the growing urban
population and inflationary pressures much less intense.
Complementary input suppliers would have had less incentive to
divert mobile resources from the Socialist sectors; the
consequences of such behaviour would in any case have been
less severe.

But by 1975 the constraints facing short-run output gains
in the Socialist sectors were quite different from those of
the late 1950s. The leadership could not return to a 'tabula
rasa', but had instead to operate with and through the organs
and institutions of the DRV state as they had developed over
the two decades since the Liberation of Hanoi in 1954. It was
the nature of these organisations in their practical day-to-
day operation that constituted the real limits of national
liberation after 1975. The economic inefficiency and waste
that had come to characterise DRV society profoundly
constrained the national energies freed by the final end of
the prolonged National Liberation struggle. State industry and
employment had become deeply dependent upon the state's
ability to secure access to economic resources largely
regardless of cost; dependency upon aid imports was a major
part of this. The chronic fiscal deficit helped support the
extensive market-oriented activities typical of aggravated
shortage. This meant that the DRV's central economic
management organs could not effectively control resource
allocation within the Socialist sectors, so that inputs to
many priority producers could not be guaranteed. Higher
supplies of resources to the central economic management
system would not, therefore, lead to sharp output gains. The
effects of aggravated shortage, and the systemic diversion of
complementary inputs away from the planned sectors meant that
the level of current inputs to the state distributional system

was no longer the most important constraint upon output growth there. Put baldly, therefore, any extra resources supplied by the South would largely be wasted. *waste*

Post-reunification problems

This study does not cover the post-reunification period, and can therefore only point generally to the broad implications for post-war development of the troubled state of the DRV's economy. It is perhaps valuable to point out, however, that the necessary and inevitable reforms to the DRV's economic management system posed deep and essentially political problems. For a historic nation with long experience of the problems of nation-state management, this was to be expected. These issues covered the nature and timing of the South's Socialist Transformation. This was closely bound up with the relationship between the very real difficulties caused by Northern over-population, over-manning in state industry and the bloated DRV bureaucracy, and the development of some means by which the richer South could ease the acute poverty of the North without propping up its wasteful economic system. It is perhaps useful to view this in terms of the ability to create a tax-base that could finance such valid welfare expenditure without acting as a support for the inefficient and ineffective neo-Stalinist administrative supply system.

Immediately after the fall of Saigon in 1975 there were extensive short-term population movements between North and South. Knowledge of the realities of the Northern economy spread rapidly, most especially amongst the Mekong Delta peasantry and ex-members of the Southern resistance (the National Liberation Front - NLF). Throughout the country, people became aware of the daily realities of life in both North and South before 1975. People realised, if they had not previously done so, that the young Northern soldiers (bo doi) who had fought so well in the South came from cooperativised communes that spent much of their time avoiding the edicts of the central Party/State apparatus. Yet memories of the blood spilt during the wars, most of which had been Vietnamese, surely increased the value attached by many to a political - and therefore non-violent - solution to the inevitable problems posed by reunification. Transition to peacetime economic development required some way of adapting the chronically wasteful Socialist organisations of the North towards greater economic efficiency. Without such changes, those institutions would themselves remain the most important binding constraint upon economic growth in the Socialist Republic.

Vietnamese economic management in the years immediately after reunification remained steeped in the methods and thinking appropriate to the day-to-day realities of aggravated shortage and the corresponding behaviour of neo-Stalinist institutions. One important characteristic of the system was the extent to which illegal economic behaviour had become normal and accepted. The continual struggle against the free market made senior cadres feel that administrative measures were the only effective way of acquiring the resources needed to run installed industrial capacity, for that was how they had to confront suppliers - especially workers - on a daily basis. This way of thinking suggested that if only more inputs could be found, and concentrated upon priority areas, then the system could be made to work. Confronted with the economic resources of the Mekong, their natural response was therefore to apply the same extractive techniques as before. But the economic mechanism that in practice controlled these supplies was not an effectively operating neo-Stalinist system that would channel resources into priority sectors in accordance with the Plan. Instead, it was something quite different, run by people who were accustomed to diverting resources acquired on behalf of the state into activities more consistent with their own 'local' interests. The hoped-for economic growth therefore did not materialise. The resource flows generated by the imposition of duties to supply did not end up creating adequate output gains in the Socialist sectors. Instead, the state's economic management system would show itself unable to use effectively the sharp increase in the volume of resources available to it. Thus those who worked for the state, who supplied economic inputs to it in some other way, faced, not only a continual pressure to supply on terms that were not in accordance with their immediate material incentives, but also the knowledge that any resources actually supplied were likely to be used extremely wastefully, and frequently diverted back onto the free market in accordance with the interests of those who now had direct control over them.

North Vietnamese experience and Socialism

This study is in many ways too close to the detailed realities and systemic socio-economic problems of North Vietnam for it readily to suggest generalisable conclusions about the nature and validity of Socialism in developing countries. But it contains a number of implicit conclusions regarding alternative and more effective policies, and these should perhaps be made more explicit.

In North Vietnam socio-economic conditions were in many ways extreme. First, the level of pre-Revolutionary economic development was minimal, and high population densities meant that both the potential and the actual economic surpluses were very low. Second, the area's population had a long and sophisticated historical experience with centralised administrative systems. Third, the state possessed a rather effective monopoly over foreign economic contacts, which enabled it both to insulate the domestic economy from world markets and to control, in the first instance, imports - most especially of aid. Once they had moved further down the distributional network, of course, such control was far weaker. Fourth, the state lacked any corresponding degree of control over domestic resource allocation; crucial factors here were the fiscal deficit and the lack of rigid internal Party discipline. Fifth, the state possessed, in the sources of aid that financed the initial development programme, a slackening of the basic constraint of the poverty that dominated the region. Finally, despite such an unfavourable context, the planning model adopted was extremely ambitious, aiming at direct administrative control over modern industry and state farms, and also over the distribution of most economically important goods.

Although these conditions seem rather unlikely to have been met in any other country, the study nevertheless suggests a number of general implications. First, it does not imply that the neo-Stalinist model will necessarily result in 'aggravated shortage'. Such an outcome could be prevented by such measures as: effective use of the security forces and better fiscal discipline leading to smaller differentials between state and 'outside' prices. The latter might depend upon restraint in the growth of 'non-productive' state employment and other ways of maintaining fiscal balance. Second, it does suggest that, under certain conditions, the neo-Stalinist model can break down and market relations become widespread and illegal activity 'normal'. Under such circumstances, the system's fundamental 'laws of motion' quite contradict the basic assumptions of the neo-Stalinist model. Planners end up having to view output as constrained in the short-term by their inability to supply adequate levels of complementary inputs. They feel that these are a priority requirement of the national economy because installed capacity in state industry cannot be utilised fully. They therefore argue that extra supplies to the state's trading organs must be found from somewhere, and that their economic cost is rather unimportant. But additional inputs supplied through the state distributional system are unlikely to lead to anticipated output gains. The two main reasons for this are, first, the diversion of resources (especially consumer goods) towards more locally profitable outlets; and second, the effects of aggravated shortage upon the supply of other complementary inputs, most especially labour. Since the economic system will not be operating with stable relationships between inputs and output levels, the planners' simple Leontefian model will not work.

The major conclusion that comes from this is to do with the importance to the effective management of such an economy of understanding both the nature and the intensity of the economic incentives that operate to determine economic behaviour. It is clear that the DRV's neo-Stalinist institutions had considerable practical freedom to respond to economic incentives; it is also clear that the DRV state in no way controlled or determined those incentives - rather, it contributed to them in a multitude of ways both directly and indirectly. We would argue that this is always the case: economic agents within a planned system always have some scope to respond to a pattern of incentives that the state does not totally control. There is always choice. It follows that economic management is likely to be more effective if it recognises this point, and more economically efficient if it attempts to create and encourage appropriate incentive structures. This means that local and individual interests have to be identified and appreciated.

PART II: STATISTICAL APPENDIX

Introduction

This Statistical Appendix presents data from an important collection of statistics published during 1978 by the Statistical Offfice (**Tong cuc Thong ke**) in Hanoi. According to the printer's note inside the back cover, 5,000 copies were produced. The collection, entitled '<u>The</u> <u>Economic</u> <u>and</u> <u>Cultural</u> <u>development</u> <u>of</u> <u>Socialist</u> <u>North</u> <u>Vietnam</u> <u>1960-75</u>' ('**Tinh hinh phat trien Kinh te va Van hoa mien bac xa hoi chu nghia Viet nam 1960-75**'), was given to one of the authors in 1980 by the Statistical Office during a visit to Hanoi. There has been some difficulty in translating technical terms into English, for two main reasons. First, there are not always accepted conventional translations; second, it is often more valuable to attempt to find translations that convey to the reader the sense of the original Vietnamese. Certain Dictionaries tend to give the ordinary rather than the technical sense of the word. The co-author responsible for translating the tables has tried to convey the latter, helped by a familiarity with the North Vietnamese economic literature. Since this work has been somewhat isolated there remains a possibility of errors in translation. Although every effort has been made to avoid this the reader should be aware of the possibility. The reader should also bear in mind that Vietnamese words, here as elsewhere in the book, have been written without the proper diacritical and other marks that indicate different vowels, consonants and tones.

The Appendix reproduces the tables in the same order and with the same numbers as in the original; all footnotes have been included, and supplementary footnotes added where appropriate. We include below translations of the Preface (**Loi noi dau**) and Annotation (**Chu Thich**).

The book contains a number of diagrams; these have been omitted. The book uses the convention that a decimal point is marked by a comma; we have replaced this by the convention that a decimal point is marked by a full stop.

133

SUPPLEMENTARY TABLE

Principal ('planned') products at the time of the First Five
Year Plan (1961-65)

Electricity generated
Clean coal
Cast iron
Tin bars
Chrome ore
Zinc ore
Metal-working machines
Electric motors
Generators
Transformers
Diesel motors
Steam engines
Drawn machines
Water-irrigation pumps
'Agricultural product transformers'
Wood-working machines
Construction machines
Tractors
Narrow-gauge vehicles
Rolling stock (1m rail)
Tugboats (tau keo)
Motorboats (ca-no)
Steel barges
Bicycles
Improved agricultural implements
Ordinary agricultural implements
Apatite Ore
Phosphate fertiliser
? Crystal Phosphate (or Phosphor glass ?)(Phan lan thuy tinh)
Superphosphate
Apatite powder
'Chile-water phosphate' (?! - Phan lan nuoc ot)
Sulphuric Acid
Soda
Insecticides of all types
Zinc powder
Car tyres and inners of all types
Bicycle tyres of all types
Bicycle inners of all types
Acid batteries (ac-qui) of all types
Standard batteries
Antibiotics
Oxy-acetylene
Cement
Fire-proof tiles

134

Roof tiles
Concrete (**Be-tong**)
Untreated wood
Sawn wood
High quality wood
'Glued' wood
Paper of all types
  of which: Writing paper
Matches
Cloth of all types
Silk of all types
Netting/gauze
Cotton thread
Cotton blankets
? 'Hygenic warm clothes' (**Quan ao ret ve sinh**)
Face towels
Under clothes '**Xuan thu**'
Socks and stockings
Leather shoes
Cloth shoes
Sleeping mats
Gloves
Porcelain, bowls, plates,
teapots and cups
Whole milled rice
Potatoes and manioc flour
Sugar of all types
  of which: beet sugar
Sea salt
Caught fish
  of which: sea fish
Fish sauce
Meat of all types
  of which: pork
Tea of all types
Tobacco (boxes)
White alcohol
Beer
Aluminum Wares
Electric lights
Thermos flasks
Laundry and toilet soap
Toothpaste
Pens of all types
Pencils of all types
Radios of all types
Vegetable oil
Fuel Oil (**Dau cam** - Sic)
Enamel ware

Source: EFU 1962:198-200.

TRANSLATIONS FROM 'THE ECONOMIC AND CULTURAL DEVELOPMENT OF SOCIALIST NORTH VIETNAM 1960-75'

PREFACE

The General Statistical Office, in publishing this statistical collection 'The economic and cultural development of Socialist North Vietnam 1960-75', introduces to readers the profound changes that occurred in the national economy of the North from the IIIrd Party Congress to the day of total victory of the struggle against the United States to save the country.

Through its statistical tables, this book presents relatively adequately and systematically the results of the implementation of the line and policy of our Party and State with regard to economic development and the improvement of the people's livelihood. This occurred under conditions where the North had simultaneously to construct socialism when subject to the destructive attacks of US imperialism, whilst at the same time concentrating human and material efforts for the task of liberating the South and uniting the Motherland.

In this book there are a number of principal general indicators available continuously for the period 1960-75; a number of different indicators are also presented.

This is the first time since the country was re-united and the Socialist Republic of Vietnam came into being that the General Statistical Office has published such a book. It aims to serve broadly and effectively those readers carrying out economic research, studying and mobilising and inspiring the people in enthusiastic production emulation.

We very much want to receive readers' judgements and contributions regarding the contents and presentation of the collection, so that those published in the future can be improved.

The General Statistical Office

ANNOTATION

1. This book has based itself upon Decision No.37-CP (13-3-74) of the Government Council when establishing the constituent branches of the national economy and industry.

2. In each diagram that differs with regard to the range of calculation this is noted concretely for each diagram.

3. We use the following symbols:

-     = No occurrence.

...   = Occurrence, but no data available.

0.0   = Smaller than 0.1

4. Relative numbers (indices of development or structure) are calculated from the original unrounded data.

Hanoi 1978

NATURAL RESOURCES AND GEOGRAPHY

Table 1: Areas and use of land

	Area (*) (thousand ha.)	Percentage
TOTAL	15,840	100.0
Land used for agriculture.	2,402	15.2
Land that could be used in agriculture.	1,329	8.4
Forest and forest land.	10,620	67.0
Other land.	1,489	9.4

(*) Preliminary 1974 data from the Land Management Dept. of the Ministry of Agriculture.

Table 2: Major deltas

Red and Thai Binh River	1,500	thousand ha.
Thanh - Nghe - Tinh	680	" "
Binh - Tri - Thien	200	" "

Table 3: Major rivers

River	Length (km) A:Total; B:Inside the DRV		Surface area (sq. km) A:Total; B:Inside the DRV	
Da	983	543	52503	26395
Hong	1140	500	61627	21787
Ma	486	426	28123	25170
Ca	514	379	27699	18853
Chay	360	306	6522	4599
Cau	290	290	6013	6013
Lo	464	277	39037	22625
Day	241	241	5800	5870(*)
Ky Cung	230	230	6398	6398
Gam	295	210	17062	9641
Luc Nam	178	178	3048	3048
Thuong	156	156	3647	3647
Gianh	155	155	5058	5058
Ben Hai	66	66	758	758

(*) Sic.

Table 4: Peaks of high mountains

Peak (province)	Height(m.)
Phang xi Pang (Hoang Lien Son)	3,143
Pu Ta Leng (Lai Chau)	3,096
Pu Luong (Hoang Lien Son)	2,985
Lang Cung (Hoang Lien Son)	2,913
Sa Phin (Hoang Lien Son)	2,874
Pu Khao Luong (Hoang Lien Son)	2,810
Pu Xai Lai Leng (Nghe Tinh)	2,711
Pu Nam Nhe (Lai Chau)	2,534
Tay Can Linh (Ha Tuyen)	2,431

Table 5: Average yearly temperatures, C. deg

Station	Average over many years	1973	1974	1975
Lang Son	21.4	21.6	20.9	21.2
Lai Chau	23.2	23.1	22.7	22.9
Thai Nguyen	23.2	23.5	22.9	23.1
Ha Noi	23.5	24.0	23.2	23.5
Phu Lien	23.0	23.5	22.8	22.9
Thanh Hoa	23.6	24.0	23.2	23.4
Vinh	24.0	24.2	23.7	23.8
Dong Hoi	24.4	25.1	24.1	24.4

Table 6: Average yearly rainfall, mm

Station	Average over many years	1973	1974	1975
Lang Son	1395	1599	1535	1357
Lai Chau	1983	2009	2073	2045
Thai Nguyen	2002	2763	1593	1723
Ha Noi	1678	1945	1527	1978
Phu Lien	1753	2635	1415	1842
Thanh Hoa	1739	2402	1950	1996
Vinh	1891	3042	1528	1682
Dong Hoi	2149	1929	1689	2207

Table 7: Average yearly level of humidity, %

Station	Average over many years	1973	1974	1975
Lang Son	81	82	81	82
Lai Chau	84	83	81	82
Thai Nguyen	82	82	81	83
Ha Noi	84	82	82	82
Phu Lien	85	84	84	84
Thanh Hoa	85	85	91	85
Vinh	82	85	83	84
Dong Hoi	84	81	82	82

POPULATION AND LABOUR

Table 8: Average yearly population

		1960	1965	1974	1975
(numbers - million)					
TOTAL		16.10	18.63	23.94	24.55
of which - a) men	men	7.78	8.98	11.59	11.87
	women	8.32	9.65	12.35	12.68
b) urban	urban	1.40	1.84	2.51	2.65
	rural	14.70	16.79	21.43	21.90
(structure - percentage shares)					
TOTAL		100.0	100.0	100.0	100.0
of which - a) men	men	48.3	48.2	48.4	48.4
	women	51.7	51.8	51.6	51.6
b) urban	urban	8.7	9.9	10.5	10.8
	rural	91.3	90.1	89.5	89.2

Table 9: Population by ethnic group (based upon materials from the 1-4-1974 census)

Thousands	Total	Of which: Men	Women
TOTAL	23,787.4	11,638.0	12,129.4
Kinh	20,106.0	9,835.3	10,270.7
Tay	759.3	368.8	390.5
Thai	639.6	313.7	325.9
Muong	606.6	288.4	318.2
Nung	478.4	231.7	246.7
Meo	349.7	171.7	178.0
Dao	290.8	144.2	126.6
Hoa	257.7	132.6	125.1
San diu	57.5	28.3	29.2
Cao lan	41.9	20.1	21.8
Kho mu	31.0	15.3	15.7
Tho	27.0	13.0	14.0
San chi	25.8	12.6	13.2
Giay	25.8	12.7	13.1
Lao	11.4	6.7	4.7
Ha nhi	8.9	4.4	4.5
Xinh mun	7.6	3.8	3.8
Van kieu	7.2	3.7	3.5
Sa chi	5.5	2.7	2.8
Phu la	4.4	2.1	2.3
La hu	4.2	2.1	2.1
Other minorities	28.2	14.4	13.8
Foreign residents	12.9	9.7	3.2

Table 10: Population of working age

	1960	1965	1975
TOTAL - thousands	7,497	8,272	10,952
of which : a) men	3,659	4,093	5,324
women	3,838	4,179	5,628
b) urban	937	1,092	1,676
rural	6,560	7,180	9,276

Table 10: Cont.

(structure - percentage shares)

TOTAL			100.0	100.0	100.0
of which :	a)	men	48.8	49.5	48.6
		women	51.2	50.5	51.4
	b)	urban	12.5	13.2	15.3
		rural	87.5	86.8	84.7

Table 11: Social labour in branches of the national economy ✳

	1960	1965	1975
TOTAL	100.0	100.0	100.0
MATERIAL PRODUCTION of which -	96.6	94.2	89.3
Industry	7.0	8.3	10.6
Basic construction	1.7	3.3	7.5
Agriculture and forestry	83.0	78.6	64.7
Trade and materials supply	3.0	2.3	3.1
Transport and communications	1.2	1.7	2.2
Other material production	0.7	0.0	1.2
NON-MATERIAL PRODUCTION of which -	3.4	5.8	10.7
Credit and State insurance	0.1	0.1	0.3
Social and other services	0.6	1.5	1.8
Scientific research, education, culture, sport and exercise, medicine, society (sic : xa hoi)	1.3	2.5	6.2
State management, Party, collectives.	1.4	1.7	2.4

Table 12: Numbers of workers and functionaries in the branches of the national economy

A Thousands	1960	1965	1975
TOTAL	482.5	971.0	1,753.4
MATERIAL PRODUCTION of which –	350.5	730.4	1,148.9
Industry	124.1	259.6	405.0
Basic construction	114.2	210.4	327.3
Agriculture and forestry	17.7	83.1	139.2
Trade and materials supply	74.0	100.2	167.3
Transport and communications	20.5	75.5	106.2
Other material production	–	1.6	3.9
NON-MATERIAL PRODUCTION of which –	132.0	240.6	604.5
Credit and State insurance	7.0	9.2	16.1
Social and other services	4.4	27.8	65.0
Scientific research, education, culture, sport and exercise, medicine, society (sic : 'xa hoi')	49.7	118.2	372.2
State management, Party, collectives.	70.9	85.4	151.2

B Index numbers, 1960=100	1965	1975
TOTAL	201.2	363.4
MATERIAL PRODUCTION of which –	208.4	327.8
Industry	209.2	326.3
Basic construction	184.2	286.6
Agriculture and forestry	469.5	786.4
Trade and materials supply	135.4	226.1
Transport and communications	368.3	518.0
Other material production	100.0	243.7

Table 12: Cont.

NON-MATERIAL PRODUCTION of which -	182.3	457.9
Credit and State insurance	141.5	230.0
Social and other services	631.8	14.84(*)
Scientific research, education, culture, sport and exercise, medicine, society (sic : 'xa hoi')	237.8	748.9
State management, Party, collectives.	120.5	214.2

(*) i.e. an increase of 14.84 times.

Table 13: Numbers of workers and functionaries distributed according to the level of management

(thousands, index numbers to base 1960 in brackets)

Year	Total,	Of which: Centrally	Regionally
1960	482.5 (100.0)	257.6 (100.0)	224.9 (100.0)
1961	637.0 (132.0)	350.4 (1?3.1)(1.)	286.6 (130.7)
1962	689.4 (142.9)	373.3 (141.8)	316.1 (144.2)
1963	747.6 (154.9)	408.9 (155.3)	338.7 (154.5)
1964	828.0 (171.6)	439.0 (166.7)	389.0 (177.4)
1965	971.0 (201.2)	498.3 (189.2)	472.7 (215.6)
1966	1,118.1 (231.7)	538.4 (204.5)	579.7 (264.5)
1967	1,223.6 (253.6)	565.3 (214.7)	658.3 (300.3)
1968	1,275.8 (264.4)	578.7 (219.8)	697.1 (318.0)
1969	1,390.4 (288.2)	589.7 (224.0)	800.7 (365.3)
1970	1,430.6 (296.5)	681.8 (258.9)	748.8 (341.6)
1971	1,429.8 (296.3)	686.8 (260.8)	743.0 (339.0)
1972	1,478.7 (306.5)	713.9 (271.1)	764.8 (358.9)
1973	1,553.5 (322.0)	752.8 (285.9)	800.7 (365.3)
1974	1,673.2 (346.8)	805.7 (305.9)	867.5 (395.8)
1975	1,753.4 (363.4)	852.5 (323.8)	900.9 (411.0)

(1.) Sic. Table in original is unreadable.

*
central /
regl
mgmt

145

Table 14: Scientific-technical and economic management cadres

(thousands - multiple increase over 1960 in brackets)

Year :	1960	1965	1975
TOTAL	18.4	102.2(x5.55)	429.5(x23.3)
of which - State sector	16.8	93.3(x5.55)	394.2(x23.5)
Collective sector	1.6	8.9(x5.56)	35.3(x22.0)

University education and above -

	1960	1965	1975
Total	4.0	21.6(x5.40)	128.8(x32.2)
of which - State sector	4.0	21.6(x5.38)	128.0(x32.0)
Collective sector	-	-	0.8

Middle specialist schools -

	1960	1965	1975
Total	14.4	80.6(x5.60)	300.7(x20.9)
of which - State sector	12.8	71.7(x5.60)	266.2(x20.8)
Collective sector	1.6	8.9(x5.56)	34.5(x21.6)

Table 15: Technical workers

(thousands - multiple increase over 1960 in brackets)

Year :	1960	1965	1975
Total	130.1	325.3(x2.50)	757.4(x5.82)
Of which -			
State sector	105.9	265.2(x2.50)	607.4(x5.74)
a) Central	69.2	171.8(x2.48)	340.0(x4.91)
b) Regional	36.7	93.4(x2.54)	267.4(x7.43)
Collective sector	24.2	60.1(x2.48)	150.0(x6.20)

FIXED AND CIRCULATING CAPITAL

Table 16: Indicators of the development of fixed and
circulating capital in the sphere of material production

Year	Fixed capital (a.)		Circulating capital (b.)	
	Total	State sector	Total	State sector
1960	100.0	100.0	100.0	100.0
1965	205.4	202.7	223.3	240.9
1968	299.8	294.8	300.5	323.1
1974	501.3	498.3	364.7	389.6
1975	512.1	525.7	376.1	397.2

(a.) - Beginning of year data, calculated according to installation costs (nguyen gia ban dau hien hanh). Bridges and
roads of the road system are excluded.
(b.) Preliminary data.

Table 17: Fixed capital in material production by branch (a.)

A. Index numbers	1960	1965	1974	1975
TOTAL	100.0	205.4	501.3	512.1
Industry	100.0	209.7	458.3	481.1
Basic construction	100.0	278.3	x12.9	x16.0
Agriculture and forestry	100.0	272.3	710.7	715.3
Trade and material supply	100.0	250.4	793.8	650.3
Transport and communications	100.0	138.4	281.4	281.7

B. Structure	1960	1965	1974	1975
Industry	36.9	37.6	33.7	34.6
Basic construction	2.8	3.8	7.3	8.9
Agriculture and forestry	23.0	30.5	32.6	32.1
Trade and material supply	5.3	5.5	8.5	6.8
Transport and communications	32.0	21.6	17.9	17.6
TOTAL	100.0	100.0	100.0	100.0

(a.) Beginning of year data based upon installation costs and prices in force (nguyen gia ban dau, gia hien hanh).

Table 18: Circulating capital in material production by branch (a.)

A. Index numbers	1960	1965	1974	1975
TOTAL				
Industry	100.0	223.3	364.7	376.1
Basic construction	100.0	247.4	397.1	416.0
Agriculture and forestry	100.0	112.7	500.2	518.4
Trade and material supply	100.0	160.8	345.3	349.1
Transport and communications	100.0	40.5	154.0	191.9

The Limits of National Liberation

Table 18: Cont.

B. Structure	1960	1965	1974	1975
Industry	8.9	9.8	9.7	9.8
Basic construction	21.5	39.7	29.4	29.6
Agriculture and forestry	17.9	14.3	13.0	13.4
Trade and material supply	49.8	35.9	47.1	46.2
Transport and communications	1.9	0.3	0.8	1.0
TOTAL	100.0	100.0	100.0	100.0

(a.) Preliminary data.

TOTAL SOCIAL PRODUCT AND NATIONAL INCOME

* Table 19: Indicators of the development of Total Social
Product and National Income

Year	Total Social Product	National Income
1960	100.0	100.0
1965	154.8	136.0
1970	163.6	187.6
1974	216.9	180.3
1975	232.6	188.7

Table 20: Distribution of Total Social Product

	1960	1965	1974	1975
TOTAL	100.0	100.0	100.0	100.0
A: Distribution by economic sectors:				
Socialist Economy : State and Joint	66.6	90.1	87.7	91.7
State-Private	38.4	45.5	47.5	51.7
Cooperatives	28.2	44.6	40.2	40.0
Private Economy	33.4	9.9	12.3	8.3

Table 20: Cont.

Year	1960	1965	1974	1975
B: Distribution by economic branch:				
Industry	32.7	40.5	38.4	41.4
Basic construction	9.7	10.8	13.2	13.9
Agriculture and forestry	34.5	29.9	32.7	29.0
Trade and material supply	13.4	11.0	9.3	9.1
Transport and communications	2.7	2.7	3.3	3.4
Other material production	7.0	5.1	3.1	3.2

Table 21: Distribution of Produced National Income

Year	1960	1965	1974	1975
TOTAL	100.0	100.0	100.0	100.0
A: Distribution by economic sectors:				
Socialist Economy	62.7	88.9	83.7	90.1
: State and Joint State-Private	33.1	37.2	33.0	38.0
Cooperatives	29.6	51.7	50.7	52.1
Private Economy	37.3	11.1	16.3	9.9
B: Distribution by economic branch:				
Industry	18.6	23.1	24.2	27.9
Basic construction	4.6	6.7	8.4	9.2
Agriculture and forestry	42.7	39.8	45.7	40.4
Trade and material supply	20.3	18.4	13.3	13.7
Transport and communications	2.7	2.5	2.6	2.7
Other material production	11.1	9.5	5.8	6.1

Table 22: The use of National Income

	1960	1965	1974	1975
A. Index Numbers				
Use of National Income	100.0	150.4	163.4	257.1
of which –				
Accumulation	100.0	157.4	269.7	246.7
Consumption	100.0	141.1	249.5	260.3
B. Structure				
Use of National Income	100.0	100.0	100.0	100.0
of which –				
Accumulation	23.5	25.1	24.0	22.5
Consumption	76.5	71.7	75.1	77.5

Table 23: Accumulation

Year	1960	1965	1974	1975
A. Index Numbers				
TOTAL	100.0	167.4	269.7	246.7
of which:				
Fixed Capital	100.0	175.7	232.1	316.6
Circulating Capital and Stocks	100.0	159.6	305.2	180.8
B. Structure				
TOTAL	100.0	100.0	100.0	100.0
of which:				
Fixed Capital	48.5	50.8	41.7	62.2
Circulating Capital and Stocks	51.5	49.2	58.3	37.8

Table 24: Consumption

Year	1960	1965	1974	1975
A. Index Numbers				
TOTAL	100.0	141.1	249.5	260.3
Individual consumption by the population	100.0	130.2	214.5	223.6
Consumption by medical, cultural, educational and service organs	100.0	195.4	353.0	364.1
Consumption by administrative, security and defence organs	100.0	278.8	731.7	768.8
B. Structure (ie %)				
TOTAL	100.0	100.0	100.0	100.0
Individual consumption by the population	90.8	84.5	78.1	78.0
Consumption by medical, cultural, educational and service organs	3.2	4.3	4.5	4.5
Consumption by administrative, security and defence organs	6.0	11.2	17.4	17.5

Statistical Appendix Section V

FINANCE AND CREDIT

Table 25: Receipts and outlays of the State budget

	1960	1965	1974	1975
A. Index numbers				
Budgetary receipts	100.0	127.7	213.9	258.4
Budgetary outlays	100.0	125.4	205.8	260.5
B. Structure				
Total receipts	100.0	100.0	100.0	100.0
of which:				
Receipts from the State economy	81.4	86.5	84.4	87.5
Receipts from collective and private organisations	15.8	11.5	8.9	8.0
Other receipts	2.8	2.0	6.7	4.5
Total outlays	100.0	100.0	100.0	100.0
Accumulation	59.4	56.7	42.3	39.6
of which: capital invested in basic construction	50.6	43.3	33.6	34.3
Consumption	40.6	43.3	57.7	60.4
of which:				
Education (dao tao)	3.0	2.7	2.9	3.0
Scientific Research	0.3	0.6	0.5	0.4
Medicine, culture, society	5.6	4.5	10.0	9.1

154

Table 26: The structure of cash receipts by the banking sector

	1960	1965	1974	1975
Total receipts	100.0	100.0	100.0	100.0
of which:				
Receipts from the sale of goods	76.1	76.2	72.1	73.7
Receipts from services	3.9	3.5	3.5	3.6
Financial receipts	5.1	3.1	3.3	3.1
[of which: taxes	4.2	2.3	2.2	2.1]
Receipts from savings deposits	8.1	9.6	4.0	13.3
Other sources	6.8	7.6	17.1	6.3

Table 27: The structure of cash outlays by the banking sector

	1960	1965	1974	1975
Total outlays	100.0	100.0	100.0	100.0
of which:				
Wages and similar	29.8	42.4	37.4	36.9
Administrative expenses	6.7	7.0	3.9	3.7
Purchases	38.5	17.9	11.1	11.6
Repayments of deposits	2.7	11.9	...	8.5
Repayments of savings deposits	6.7	8.1	13.5	14.4

Table 28: Long-term loans by the banking sector
(year-end balances outstanding)

m. dong	1960	1965	1974	1975
Total	44.7	226.6	610.3	625.5
of which:				
Agricultural cooperatives	24.2	138.6	306.4	294.7
Fish cooperatives	4.8	49.7	105.0	107.1
Salt cooperatives	0.4	9.0	10.6	9.3
Artisanal and light industrial cooperatives	1.1	3.1	13.5	14.3
Transport cooperatives	0.2	6.3	21.6	22.0
Purchase and sale cooperatives	-	-	0.2	0.1

Table 29: Short-term loans by the banking sector
(year-end balances outstanding)

m. dong	1960	1965	1974	1975
Total	664.4	1517.8	2701.2	3689.9
of which:				
State and joint State-private	634.6	1450.2	2349.7	3345.8
Cooperatives	29.3	67.1	350.6	342.7
Other organisations and private sector	0.5	0.5	0.9	1.4

INDUSTRY

A. GENERAL INDICATORS

Table 30: Some principal indicators of the development of
industry

(index numbers)

Year	Labour	Value of fixed capital	Value of total output
1960	100.0	100.0	100.0
1961	104.6	113.9	114.4
1962	109.6	132.8	143.4
1963	113.4	156.5	155.5
1964	121.7	181.8	173.5
1965	127.0	215.8	189.4
1966	124.4	251.8	184.0
1967	122.2	275.8	159.8
1968	121.8	298.2	169.3
1969	125.6	323.7	184.6
1970	137.8	348.1	200.4
1971	153.9	372.9	232.3
1972	151.4	395.6	206.1
1973	156.2	416.7	241.6
1974	171.6	437.5	291.4
1975	178.0	448.2	336.2

Note: The indicators for labour and the value of fixed capital
are yearly averages. The indicator for the value of total
output is at fixed 1970 prices.

157

Table 31: Some principal indicators of the development of
State and Joint State-Private industry (index numbers)

Year	Number of enter-prises(*)	Productive industrial employees	Value of fixed assets	Value of total output
1960	100.0	100.0	100.0	100.0
1961	107.7	116.2	114.9	124.8
1962	108.6	138.7	137.3	163.1
1963	111.5	155.6	164.9	181.7
1964	111.2	188.7	192.3	212.8
1965	111.9	193.8	229.1	240.8
1966	126.3	202.7	266.0	231.1
1967	118.5	216.4	290.1	194.6
1968	127.3	227.7	311.5	215.5
1969	133.6	240.8	334.4	236.4
1970	130.9	250.4	358.6	259.6
1971	132.3	265.2	383.2	305.0
1972	130.6	255.5	405.5	261.7
1973	130.1	271.0	426.4	303.5
1974	128.2	296.5	450.7	376.2
1975	131.9	312.4	465.4	439.0

(*) End-year data. Note: for definitions see Table 30.

Table 32: Some principal indicators of the development of
artisanal and light industry (index numbers)

Year	Labour	Value of fixed capital	Value of total output
1960	100.0	100.0	100.0
1961	101.3	104.0	101.4
1962	101.3	88.0	118.1
1963	101.4	74.0	121.6
1964	102.7	78.9	121.9
1965	108.0	84.3	121.7
1966	102.3	111.0	122.0
1967	95.4	134.6	114.3
1968	91.7	167.6	108.6
1969	92.8	218.8	116.4
1970	105.8	245.1	122.4
1971	122.2	271.5	136.2
1972	121.8	298.2	132.4
1973	123.6	321.1	158.4
1974	136.1	304.1	178.6
1975	138.5	272.8	200.8

Note: for definitions see Table 30.

Table 33: Some principal indicators of the development of
central industry (index numbers)

Year	Number of enterprises(*)	Productive industrial employees	Value of fixed assets	Value of total output
1960	100.0	100.0	100.0	100.0
1961	95.6	116.4	114.5	125.9
1962	104.9	140.3	137.4	168.8
1963	104.9	156.8	166.7	188.5
1964	101.0	176.9	194.8	222.7
1965	101.0	187.2	230.5	251.0
1966	115.3	183.6	263.2	232.5
1967	127.6	181.9	279.8	175.3
1968	127.6	186.7	291.9	193.6
1969	136.5	194.7	306.5	212.6
1970	132.0	200.2	322.5	232.7
1971	142.4	219.1	338.4	279.6
1972	149.8	213.9	356.0	226.9
1973	150.7	233.2	370.9	261.4
1974	152.2	259.4	389.5	343.0
1975	155.2	275.7	404.0	411.2

Note: for definitions see Table 30.

Table 34: Some principal indicators of the development of
regional industry (index numbers)

	1960	1965	1974	1975
A. All regional industry				
Labour	100.0	117.0	157.1	160.6
Value of fixed assets	100.0	136.3	706.6	686.9
Value of total output	100.0	148.0	257.0	287.0

B. State and Joint State-private industry				
	1960	1965	1974	1975
Number of enterprises (end year)	100.0	114.6	122.1	126.1
Productive industrial employees	100.0	205.7	362.1	377.5
Value of fixed assets	100.0	240.6	x12.6	x12.8
Value of total output	100.0	216.9	451.4	507.3

Note: for definitions see Table 30.

B. ENTERPRISES

Table 35: State industrial enterprises, Joint State-Private (JSP) industrial enterprises, and specialised artisanal and light industrial cooperatives

Units	State and JSP enterprises	Of which:		Specialised industrial cooperatives
	Total	Central	Regional	
1960	1012	203	809	...
1961	1090	194	896	2760
1962	1099	213	886	2698
1963	1128	213	915	2409
1964	1125	205	920	2639
1965	1132	205	927	2529
1966	1278	234	1044	2376
1967	1199	259	940	2278
1968	1288	259	1029	2182
1969	1352	277	1075	2305
1970	1325	268	1057	2471
1971	1339	289	1050	2647
1972	1322	304	1018	2518
1973	1317	306	1011	2522
1974	1297	309	988	2586
1975	1335	315	1020	2377

Table 36: State industrial and Joint State-Private (JSP) enterprises according to Group and Branch (units)

	1960	1965	1974	1975
Total	1012	1132	1297	1355
of which: Group A	519	595	770	797
Group B	493	537	527	538
Industrial branches:				
Power, mineral extraction and energy	58	58	52	49
Metallurgy	19	11	5	5
Manufacture and repair of metal equipment and machines	159	148	282	291
Chemicals	50	65	71	72

Cont.

160

Table 36: Cont.

Construction materials, pottery, porcelain, glass, wood and forest products, cellulose and paper	352	429	480	506
Staples and food	245	272	233	236
Textiles, leather and clothing	76	64	80	79
Printing and cultural products	33	50	52	55
Other industry	20	35	42	42

C. LABOUR

Table 37: Industrial labour according to economic branch

	All industry:			Small and artisanal industry:		
	Total	Of which: State & JSP (a.)	Small & light (b.)	Total	Of which: Collec -tive	Indi- vid.
1960	515.0	113.9	401.1	305.8	218.1	87.7
1961	538.9	132.4	406.5	293.8	246.8	47.0
1962	564.5	158.0	406.5	293.8	246.8	47.0
1963	584.2	177.3	406.9	299.4	246.4	53.0
1964	626.9	215.0	411.9	271.8	223.6	48.2
1965	654.0	220.9	433.1	283.8	227.5	56.3
1966	641.2(*)	230.6	410.3	282.3	241.2	41.1
1967	629.1	246.5	382.6	260.1	223.1	37.0
1968	627.1	259.4	367.7	245.5	213.7	31.8
1969	646.7	274.3	372.4	260.8	225.9	34.9
1970	709.8	285.2	424.6	309.8	259.0	50.8
1971	792.4	302.1	490.3	372.0	300.5	71.5
1972	779.7	291.0	488.7	370.0	304.8	65.2
1973	804.3	308.7	495.6	382.1	306.1	76.0
1974	883.5	337.7	545.8	419.3	352.9	66.4
1975	911.4	355.8	555.6	433.7	369.4	64.3

(a.) The average number of industrial employees (**nhan vien**) in State and JSP enterprises.
(b.) Including workers in specialist artisanal and light industrial cooperatives, artisanal production groups and other collective forms such as: agricultural producer cooperatives also participating in artisanal industrial work.
(*) Sic. Total does not equal row sum in original.

The Limits of National Liberation

Table 38: Productive industrial employees, production workers
in State and JSP enterprises according to level of management

(thousands)

	Productive industrial employees Total	Of which: Central	Local	Productive industrial workers Total	Of which: Central	Local
1960	113.9	72.9	41.0	98.6	61.7	36.9
1961	132.4	84.8	47.6	113.2	70.8	42.4
1962	158.0	102.2	55.8	135.0	84.8	50.2
1963	177.3	114.3	63.0	151.0	95.3	55.7
1964	215.0	128.9	86.1	183.4	107.9	75.5
1965	220.9	136.4	84.5	186.5(*)	113.3	73.3
1966	230.9	133.9	97.0	190.7	109.5	81.2
1967	246.5	132.6	113.9	201.1	106.8	94.3
1968	259.4	136.1	123.3	209.0(*)	109.8	99.1
1969	274.3	141.9	132.4	222.0	114.5	107.5
1970	285.2	146.0	139.2	238.4	121.5	116.9
1971	302.1	159.7	142.4	254.1	134.6	119.5
1972	291.0	155.9	135.1	240.2	126.0	114.2
1973	308.7	170.0	138.7	252.8	137.1	115.7
1974	337.7	189.0	148.7	277.8	153.0	124.8
1975	355.8	201.0	154.8	297.5	166.3	131.2

(*) Sic. Total does not equal row sum in original.

Table 39: Production employees in State and JSP industry
(thousands)

	1960	1965	1974	1975
Total	113.9	220.9	337.7	355.8(*)
of which: Group A	74.7	134.6	205.8	222.6
Group B	39.2	86.3	131.9	133.2
Industrial branches:				
Power, mineral extraction and energy	19.0	28.0	36.3	38.1
Metallurgy	5.8	12.1	11.1	12.6
Manufacture and repair of metal equipment and machines	13.1	32.7	73.3	75.1
Chemicals	4.7	12.8	23.2	27.0
Construction materials, pottery, porcelain, glass, wood and forest products, cellulose and paper	41.5	79.1	96.6	102.3

162

The Limits of National Liberation

Table 39: Cont.

Staples and food	9.8	21.1	40.6	42.0
Textiles, leather and clothing	15.8	26.4	44.3	46.7
Printing and cultural products	2.3	5.3	7.9	8.1
Other industry	1.9	3.4	4.4	4.0

(*) Sic. Total does not equal column sum in original.

Table 40: Production workers in State and JSP industry

(thousands)

	1960	1965	1974	1975
Total	98.6	186.5	277.8(*)	297.5
of which: Group A	64.6	114.2	152.7	183.5
Group B	34.0	72.3	125.1	114.0

Industrial branches:

	1960	1965	1974	1975
Power, mineral extraction and energy	15.6	23.3	28.3	31.9
Metallurgy	5.1	9.9	8.6	9.8
Manufacture and repair of metal equipment and machines	10.7	25.8	57.6	59.4
Chemicals	3.9	10.1	19.0	22.5
Construction materials, pottery, porcelain, glass, wood and forest products, cellulose and paper	37.0	70.1	81.5	87.5
Staples and food	8.2	17.6	33.5	35.1
Textiles, leather and clothing	14.7	22.8	39.8	41.6
Printing and cultural products	1.8	4.3	6.4	6.6
Other industry	1.6	2.6	3.6	3.1

(*) Sic. Total does not equal column sum in original.

Table 41: <u>Specialised</u> <u>labour</u> <u>in</u> <u>small</u> <u>and</u> <u>artisanal</u> <u>industry</u>
<u>according</u> <u>to</u> <u>the</u> <u>form</u> <u>of</u> <u>production</u>

(data for 1-7 each year, excluding fish, salt and wood)

(thousands)

	Total	Of which: Specia- lised coopera- tives	Produc- tion Teams	Other collec- tive forms	Indivi- dual
1960	305.8	71.6	92.2	54.3	87.7
1961	293.8	136.4	21.0	89.4	47.0
1963	299.4	151.7	15.9	78.8	53.0
1964	271.8	132.2	17.1	74.3	48.2
1965	283.8	132.4	31.8	63.3	56.3
1966	282.3	139.5	19.0	82.7	41.1
1967	260.1	133.1	10.9	79.1	37.0
1968	245.5	130.3	17.9	65.5	31.8
1969	260.8	130.1	15.9	79.9	34.9
1970	309.8	138.2	18.1	102.7	50.8
1971	372.0	153.3	21.8	125.4	71.5
1972	370.0	154.1	31.9	118.8	65.2
1973	382.1	162.9	21.0	122.2	76.0
1974	419.3	169.0	23.3	160.6	66.4
1975	433.7	178.1	21.1	170.2	64.3

Note: 1962 omitted from original table.

Table 42: <u>Labour</u> <u>in</u> <u>fisheries,</u> <u>salt-making</u> <u>and</u> <u>wood</u>
<u>exploitation</u> (thousands)

	1965	1971	1973	1974	1975
TOTAL	149.3	118.3	113.5	126.4	121.9
Sea fishing	59.1	55.0	54.8	56.8	56.3
River fishing	22.3	15.0	11.5	13.2	11.8
Salt-making	39.9	29.1	29.3	32.0	32.6
Wood exploitation	28.0	19.2	17.9	24.4	21.2

D. OUTPUT

Table 43: The value of total industrial output

(at fixed 1970 prices, million dong)

	1965	1974	1975
TOTAL	2352.7	3619.5	4175.4
According to economic branch: State and JSP	1665.1	2612.6	3043.5
Small and artisanal	687.6	1006.9	1131.9
According to management level: Central	1193.4	1625.1	1948.3
Regional	1159.3	0994.4(*)	2227.1
According to Group: Group A	998.0	1554.3	1813.8
Group B	1354.7	2065.2	2361.6
According to Group:			
Power, mineral extraction and energy	211.2	211.4	278.6
Metallurgy	63.2	55.9	62.3
Manufacture and repair of metal equipment and machines	309.4	698.8	801.9
Chemicals	165.7	346.5	432.9
Construction materials, pottery, porcelain, glass, wood and forest products, cellulose and paper	531.6	710.4	765.8
Staples and food	600.8	965.2	1108.9
Textiles, leather and clothing	380.6	502.3	579.3
Printing and cultural products	28.5	57.2	69.1
Other industry	61.7	71.8	76.6

(*) Sic. Probably in error for 1944.4.

165

Table 44: Index numbers of the development of the value of
Total Industrial Output

(1960 = 100)

	1965	1974	1975
TOTAL	189.4	376.2	336.2
According to economic branch: State and JSP	240.8	376.2	439.0
Small and artisanal	121.7	178.6	200.8
According to management level: Central	251.0	343.0	411.2
Regional	148.0	257.0	287.0
According to Group:			
Group A	241.5	376.2	439.0
Group B	162.9	248.5	284.2
According to Group:			
Power, mineral extraction and energy	219.6	219.9	289.7
Metallurgy	820.8	805.3	897.6
Manufacture and repair of metal equipment and machines	244.5	548.6	629.6
Chemicals	484.1	X10.0	X13.7
Construction materials, pottery, porcelain, glass, wood and forest products, cellulose and paper	183.2	244.5	263.6
Staples and food	176.6	282.2	324.2
Textiles, leather and clothing	115.6	151.9	175.2
Printing and cultural products	159.5	320.0	387.0
Other industry	198.1	230.6	246.1

Table 45: The structure of Total Industrial Output

	1960	1961	1974	1975
TOTAL	100.0	100.0	100.0	100.0
According to economic branch: State	52.4	66.8	(72.2	(72.9
JSP	4.9	6.0	(	(
Collective	37.7	23.7	25.5	24.8
Individual	4.6	3.5	2.3	2.3
Capitalist	0.4	-	-	-
According to management level: Central	40.2	53.3	44.9	46.7
Regional	59.8	46.7	55.1	53.3
According to Group:				
Group A	33.7	42.9	42.9	43.4
Group B	66.3	57.1	57.1	56.6
According to Group:				
Power, mineral extraction and energy	6.2	7.1	5.9	6.7
Metallurgy	0.8	3.7	1.6	1.5
Manufacture and repair of metal equipment and machines	10.9	14.1	19.3	19.2
Chemicals	3.7	9.5	9.6	10.4
Construction materials, pottery, porcelain, glass, wood and forest products, cellulose and paper	22.6	21.9	19.5	18.3
Staples and food	24.9	23.2	26.6	26.6
Textiles, leather and clothing	26.3	16.1	13.9	13.9
Printing and cultural products	1.8	1.5	1.6	1.6
Other industry	2.8	2.9	2.0	1.8

Note: 1960 and 1965 calculated at fixed 1959 prices; 1973 - 75 calculated at fixed 1970 prices.

Table 46: Output of the principle products of industry

	1960	1965	1974	1975
Electricity (m. kWhr)	255.3	633.6	1025.1	1339.9
of which: Hydro	-	9.8	345.2	410.9
Thermo	...	617.6	574.2	816.1
Dry coal (m. tonnes)	2.6	4.2	3.7	5.2
of which: coking coal				
(thousand tonnes)	737	957	633	851
Cast Iron (thous. tonnes)	7.4	127.8	97.3	95.1
Chrome Ore (id.)	19.4	13.1	9.3	10.4
Tin bars (tonnes)	473	436	230	263
Metal-working machines				
(units)	799	1866	1232	1695
of which:				
Lathes	243	297	361	678
Drills	477	202	400	489
Planes	58	30	50	130
Diesel Generators (units)	-	1115	1330	2705
Electric Motors				
(thous. kWhr)	-	16.6	12.8	32.5
Electric Transformers				
(units)	488	5712	9452	10069
Tugs, motor-boats	-	532	318	472
inc. small motorised craft	22	88	115	90
Steam engines (id.)	440	112	504	...
Car trailers	165	256	713	990
Water pumps (irrigation)				
(units)	71	1915	510	500
'Bong Sen' Tractors (id.)	-	-	400	810
Threshers (id.)	2771	1932	762	1162
Rice grinders and				
millers (id.)	-	1154	454	613
Poultry feed crushers (id.)	-	202	301	265
Film Projectors (id.)	47	48	70	104
Bicycles (thousands)	23.1	70.6	32.0	60.4
Ploughs, all types (id.)	281.0	135.5	150.3	169.4
Harrows, all types (id.)	13.0	90.0	155.8	133.1
Grass rakes, advanced				
types (id.)	-	250.5	175.9	248.1
Advanced vehicles (id.)	-	59.6	49.4	65.2
Spades, hoes and				
shovels.	778	1250	569	1267

Table 46: Cont.

	1960	1965	1974	1975
Chemical fertiliser (thous. tonnes)	51.4	144.4	344.1	423.0
of which:				
Superphosphate	–	87.2	182.1	204.0
Crude Apatite Ore (id.)	490.0	680.1	151.4	279.0
Insecticides (tonnes)	45	3676	4006	4683
of which:				
666 Powder	–	1569	3686	3760
Merchandise Sulphuric Acid (id.)	–	4688	2683	3500
Soda (NaOH) 100% (id.)	–	1842	1623	1703
Car tyres and inner tubes (thousand sets)	–	29.0	40.0	42.8
Bicycle tyres (thousands)	88.0	779.6	2003.0	2872.0
Bicycle inner tubes (thousands)	31.9	254.9	1309.4	2002.0
Acetylene (Hoi han) (thousand cubic metres)	115.5	491.6	1349.6	...
Batteries (1.5 volt equivalent, millions)	–	19.1	31.5	36.2
Drugs in tubes, all types, (million tubes)	55.8	198.5	268.9	301.5
of which:				
Antibiotics	–	11.0	24.2	22.0
Pills (billion)	0.43	1.35	2.95	3.23
of which:				
Antibiotics	–	0.30	0.16	0.18
Drugs in liquid form (thousand litres)	–	1684	3900	4183
Bagged cement (thousand tonnes)	408	574	350	371
Fire-proof bricks (id.)	4.6	5.0	7.4	7.5
Building bricks (bn.)	0.80	1.56	1.92	1.91
Roof tiles (id.)	0.12	0.22	0.57	0.60
Fibre-cement tiles (thousand tonnes)	200.8	588.3	405.2	664.0
Lime (id.)	202.0	585.2	965.0	970.7
of which:				
Fertiliser	...	179.6	136.2	134.9
Stones, all types (million cubic metres)	0.22	2.04	4.01	4.13
Glass (thousand tonnes)	3.2	9.5	16.6	19.4
Electric light bulbs (thousand units)	–	866	1557	1728
Thermos flasks (id.)	–	204	208	228

Table 46: Cont.

Household porcelain (million units)	44.7	53.4	65.5	82.3
Unprocessed round wood thous. cubic metres)	753.2	1089.2	812.6	836.8
Sawn wood (id.)	230.3	219.2	218.8	245.2
Firewood (id.)	304.8	543.9	382.3	333.3
Bamboo, vau (million plants)	14.6	17.5	15.5	17.2
Building bamboo (nua hang) (id.)	86.9	105.5	78.5	64.3
Paper bamboo (nua giay) (thou. tonnes)	–	76.4	53.1	58.9
Paper and cardboard, all types (id.)	5.6	23.9	19.7	21.3
of which: Writing paper	1.8	10.9	4.7	6.1
Matches (million boxes)	182.7	154.0	158.4	168.8
Rush mats for interior use (thou. pairs)	2660	2638	3385	3931
Salt (thou. tonnes)	119.1	157.0	231.5	222.4
Sea fish (id.)	94.5	93.6	83.2	94.0
Fresh water fish (id.)	–	8.5	3.5	3.8
Fish sauce (m. litres)	37.5	39.4	29.3	34.5
Sauce (id.)	–	4.3	22.6	20.0
Sugar, honey (thou. tonnes)	32.2	41.7	15.4	19.6
of which: Pure sugar	1.3	16.5	9.3	13.4
White spirit (equi. 100 deg.; million litres)	3.7	5.9	8.6	11.9
Beer (id.)	3.2	11.1	28.5	25.9
Cigarettes (million packets)	73.4	165.5	287.6	261.0
Tea, all types (tonnes)	2203	3951	8789	10210
Ground rice (thou. tonnes)	217.5	398.1	521.1	648.6
Taste powder (tonnes)	–	21	133	157
Whole thread (thousand tonnes)	10.4	12.7	11.5	13.0
Semi-finished cloth (million metres)	89.7	100.3	95.8	105.2
Gauze (id.)	19.5	25.4	38.2	45.5
Artificial silk (id.)	5.5	6.9	3.4	3.9
Real silk (id.)	1.5	0.04	0.3	0.3
Sown clothing (million units)	4.4	7.9	17.2	19.1
Knitted woollens, all types, (tonnes)	36.5	133.2	122.0	132.0

Table 46: Cont.

Woven woollen carpets (id.)	–	80.5	217.0	241.0
Woollen carpets (thou. square metres)	1.1	14.6	81.4	98.2
Stiff leather (tonnes)	822	357	153	116
Supple leather (thou. 'frames' – bia)	1705	1465	1471	1669
Leather shoes and sandles (thou. pairs)	67	887	298	182
Typographical printing paper (13x9 equivalent, million sheets)	1892	5005	15175	15089
Pencils (million units)	11.4	38.1	14.6	23.2
Pens (thou. units)	377	1212	2079	2461
Laundry soap (tonnes)	1834	6378	7520	8656
Scented soap (id.)	114	788	657	782
Toothpaste (million tubes)	1.6	5.2	14.3	20.3
Enamelled steel items (thou. units)	1291	4730	1824	2153

Table 47: A number of industrial products, calculated on a per capita basis

	1960	1965	1974	1975
Electricity generated, (kWh)	15.9	34.0	42.8	54.6
Clean coal (kg)	161.2	225.3	153.0	210.7
Cast Iron (id.)	0.5	6.9	4.1	3.9
Bicycles (per thousand)	1.4	3.8	1.3	2.5
Cement (kg)	25.3	30.8	14.6	15.1
Unprocessed round wood (cubic metres)	0.045	0.060	0.034	0.034
Cardboard and paper (kg)	0.35	1.28	0.82	0.87
Matches (boxes)	11.4	8.3	6.6	6.9
Sleeping mats	0.33	0.28	0.28	0.32
Cloth and Silk (metres)	6.0	5.8	4.3	4.4
Salt (kg)	7.3	8.4	9.7	9.1
Sea fish (id.)	5.6	5.0	3.5	3.9
Fish and ordinary sauce (litre)	2.3	2.3	2.5	2.3
Sugar and honey (kg)	2.0	2.2	0.6	0.8
Beer (litre)	0.2	0.6	1.2	1.1
Cigarettes (packets)	4.6	8.9	12.0	10.6
Laundry soap (kg)	0.30	0.31	0.31	0.35

E. INDIVIDUAL BRANCHES

Table 48: Some general indicators of the development of the
heavy and energy industries

	1960	1965	1974	1975
Number of enterprises at end year (thou.) of which:	58	58	52	49
Central	19	22	26	24
Regional	39	36	26	25
Average number of productive industrial employees (thou.) of which:	19.0	28.0	36.3	38.1
Central	18.3	26.6	35.1	37.0
Regional	0.7	1.4	1.2	1.1
Average number of productive industrial workers (thou.) of which:	15.6	23.3	28.3	31.9
Central	15.0	22.1	27.4	31.1
Regional	0.6	1.2	0.9	0.8
Growth of the value of total output (index no.) of which:	100.0	219.6	219.9	289.7
State and JSP	100.0	217.9	226.8	298.6
:Central -	100.0	213.0	222.7	294.7
:Regional -	100.0	696.8	617.2	618.7
Light and artisanal industry	100.0	250.5	54.3	75.2
Electricity production (million kWh) of which:	255.3	633.6	1025.1	1339.9
Central	253.2	627.5	997.5	1309.5
Regional	2.1	6.1	27.6	30.4
Clean Coal output (thou. tonnes) of which:	2595.5	496.9 (*)	3664.4	5171.1
Central	2575.0	470.0	3590.0	5060.9
Regional	20.5	126.9	74.4	110.2

(*) Sic. Total does not equal column sum in original.

Table 49: Some general indicators of the development of manufacturing industry

	1960	1965	1974	1975
Number of enterprises at end year (thou.)	159	148	282	291
of which:				
Central	47	33	85	85
Regional	112	115	197	206
Average number of productive industrial employees (thou.)(*)	13.1	32.7	73.3	75.1
of which:				
Central	9.1	18.6	44.3	44.1
Regional	4.0	14.1	29.0	31.0
Average number of productive industrial workers (thou.)(*)	10.7	25.8	57.6	59.4
of which:				
Central	7.2	14.3	33.7	34.1
Regional	3.5	11.5	23.9	25.3
Growth of the value of total output (index no.)	100.0	244.5	548.6	629.6
of which:				
State and JSP	100.0	330.3	762.8	878.5
:Central -	100.0	350.1	775.9	891.7
:Regional -	100.0	282.7	745.1	861.8
Light and arti-sanal industry	100.0	131.8	266.0	301.6

(*) Belonging to State and JSP enterprises

Table 50: Some general indicators of the development of the chemical industry

	1960	1965	1974	1975
Number of enterprises at end year (thou.)	50	65	71	72
of which:				
Central	14	17	22	24
Regional	36	48	49	48

Table 50: Cont.

Average number of productive industrial employees (thou.)(*) of which:	4.7	12.8	23.2	27.1
Central	3.9	8.9	13.7	16.8
Regional	0.8	3.9	9.5	10.3
Average number of productive industrial workers (thou.)(*) of which:	3.9	10.1	19.0	22.5
Central	3.1	6.9	11.1	13.9
Regional	0.8	3.2	7.9	8.6
Growth of the value of total output (index no.) of which:	100.0	484.1	x10.0	x13.7
State and JSP	100.0	462.0	965.5	x11.9
:Central -	100.0	441.9	858.6	x11.2
:Regional -	100.0	594.5	x17.5	x19.7
Light and arti-sanal industry	100.0	884.8	x16.8	x20.8

(*) Belonging to State and JSP enterprises

Table 51: Some general indicators of the development of the basic construction, pottery, porcelain, glass, wood, forestry products, cellulose and paper industries

	1960	1965	1974	1975
Number of enterprises at end year (thou.) of which:	352	429	480	506
Central	53	57	86	91
Regional	299	372	394	415
Average number of productive industrial employees (thou.)(*) of which:	41.5	79.1	96.6	102.3
Central	16.2	31.6	34.7	38.0
Regional	25.3	47.5	61.9	64.3

Table 51: Cont.

Average number of productive industrial workers (thou.)(*)	37.0	70.1	81.5	87.5
of which:				
Central	14.2	27.9	29.1	32.1
Regional	22.8	42.2	52.4	55.4
Growth of the value of total output (index no.)	100.0	183.2	244.5	263.6
of which:				
State and JSP	100.0	199.6	225.9	248.3
:Central -	100.0	221.9	208.6	240.0
:Regional -	100.0	171.4	248.8	260.4
Light and artisanal industry	100.0	163.8	265.5	281.0

(*) Belonging to State and JSP enterprises

Table 52: Some general indicators of the development of the food and staples industries

	1960	1965	1974	1975
Number of enterprises at end year (thou.)	245	272	233	236
of which:				
Central	38	44	45	45
Regional	207	228	188	191
Average number of productive industrial employees (thou.)	9.8	21.1	40.6	42.0
of which:				
Central	5.5	13.2	15.8	17.1
Regional	4.3	7.9	24.8	24.9
Average number of productive industrial workers (thou.)	8.2	17.6	33.5	35.1
of which:				
Central	4.3	10.7	13.0	14.2
Regional	3.9	6.9	20.5	20.9

Table 52: Cont.

Growth of the value of total output (index no.)	100.0	176.6	282.2	324.2
of which:				
State and JSP	100.0	214.4	371.7	424.1
:Central –	100.0	213.1	293.7	349.7
:Regional –	100.0	216.0	470.2	518.6
Light and arti-sanal industry	100.0	109.0	126.8	150.0

(*) Belonging to State and JSP enterprises

Table 53: Some general indicators of the development of the textile, leather, clothing and dyeing industries

	1960	1965	1974	1975
Number of enterprises at end year (thou.)	76	64	80	79
of which:				
Central	15	11	20	21
Regional	61	53	60	58
Average number of productive industrial employees (thou.)(*)	15.8	26.4	44.2	46.7
of which:				
Central	13.3	21.4	28.1	29.2
Regional	2.5	5.0	16.1	17.5
Average number of productive industrial workers (*)	14.7	22.8	39.3	41.6
of which:				
Central	12.4	18.4	25.2	26.2
Regional	2.3	4.4	14.1	15.4
Growth of the value of total output (index no.)	100.0	115.6	151.9	175.2
of which:				
State and JSP	100.0	162.3	220.3	250.4
:Central –	100.0	157.8	181.9	204.3
:Regional –	100.0	190.1	468.6	547.0
Light and arti-sanal industry	100.0	85.0	107.1	125.8

(*) Belonging to State and JSP enterprises

BASIC CONSTRUCTION

Table 54: A number of general indicators for the construction
branch

	Actual capital investment (m. dong)(a.)		Average number of registered workers (thousands)
	Total	Of which: Assembly	
1960	669.7	387.2	114.2
1961	726.1	415.1	144.4
1962	732.9	414.5	136.2
1963	690.3	379.4	139.6
1964	790.4	473.4	157.8
1965	959.1	568.0	210.4
1966	1055.4	562.8	226.9
1967	1037.9	448.4	211.1
1968	1044.8	440.2	197.8
1969	1027.8	428.2	188.0
1970	1065.5	516.6	199.0
1971	1225.9	646.2	220.3
1972	1280.3	705.0	238.8
1973	1625.7	899.1	263.2
1974	1822.7	1014.0	304.8
1975	2049.8	1066.4	327.3

(a) This does not count capital invested in basic
construction, in air defence works and in wartime evacuation
during the years of the anti-American struggle.

Table 55: Average numbers of officials and workers in the
construction branch

		1960	1965	1974	1975
		(thousands)			
TOTAL		114.2	210.4	304.8	327.3
	Central	101.1	149.6	186.1	199.7
	Regional	13.1	60.8	118.7	127.6
		(development - index numbers)			
	Total	100.0	184.2	266.9	286.6
	Central	100.0	148.0	184.0	197.5
	Regional	100.0	464.1	906.1	974.0
		(structure - %)			
	Total	100.0	100.0	100.0	100.0
	Central	88.5	71.1	61.0	61.0
	Regional	11.5	28.9	39.0	39.0

Table 56: Actual volume of capital invested in basic
construction distributed according to form of investment

A: Capital invested (m. dong)

	Total:	Of which Assembly	Equipment	Other work
1960	669.7	387.2	232.2	50.3
1961	726.1	415.1	264.2	46.8
1962	732.9	414.5	275.5	42.9
1963	690.3	379.4	269.8	41.1
1964	790.4	473.4	256.4	60.6
1965	959.1	568.0	345.1	46.0
1966	1055.4	562.8	475.7	16.9
1967	1037.9	448.4	554.0	35.5
1968	1044.8	440.2	564.2	40.4
1969	1027.8	428.2	549.9	49.7
1970	1065.5	516.6	497.0	51.9
1971	1225.9	646.2	521.1	58.6
1972	1280.3	705.0	497.7	77.6
1973	1625.7	899.1	627.2	99.4
1974	1822.7	1014.0	685.7	123.0
1975	2049.8	1066.4	840.0	143.4

Table 56: cont

B: Structure (%)

	Assembly	Equipment	Other work
1960	57.8	34.7	7.5
1961	57.2	36.4	6.4
1962	56.5	37.6	5.9
1963	55.0	39.1	5.9
1964	59.9	32.4	7.7
1965	59.2	36.0	4.8
1966	53.3	45.1	1.6
1967	43.2	53.4	3.4
1968	42.1	54.0	3.9
1969	41.7	53.5	4.8
1970	48.5	46.6	4.9
1971	52.7	42.5	4.8
1972	55.1	38.9	6.0
1973	55.3	38.6	6.1
1974	55.6	37.7	6.7
1975	52.0	41.0	7.0

Table 57: The actual volume of capital invested in basic construction distributed according to level of management

A. Capital invested (m. dong)

	Central		Regional	
	Total	Construction and Assembly	Total	Construction and Assembly
1960	596.4	320.7	73.3	66.5
1961	641.1	349.9	85.0	65.2
1962	629.2	335.6	103.7	78.9
1963	587.1	300.8	103.2	78.6
1964	667.0	373.0	123.4	100.4
1965	803.7	449.0	155.4	119.0
1966	812.4	413.8	243.0	149.0
1967	751.7	291.6	286.2	156.8
1968	754.7	294.4	290.1	145.8
1969	718.4	276.1	309.4	152.1
1970	665.9	307.4	399.6	209.2
1971	857.7	407.7	368.2	238.5
1972	898.4	451.1	381.9	253.9
1973	1070.0	543.6	555.7	355.5
1974	1244.9	612.5	577.8	401.5
1975	1457.6	641.2	592.2	425.2

Table 57 cont.

B.Structure (%)

	Total		Construction and Assembly	
	Central	Regional	Central	Regional
1960	89.1	10.9	82.8	17.2
1961	88.3	11.7	77.6	22.4
1962	85.9	14.1	81.0	19.0
1963	85.0	15.0	79.3	20.7
1964	84.4	15.6	78.8	21.2
1965	83.8	16.2	79.0	21.0
1966	77.0	23.0	73.5	26.5
1967	72.4	27.6	65.0	35.0
1968	72.2	27.8	66.9	33.1
1969	69.9	30.1	64.5	35.5
1970	62.4	37.6	59.5	40.5
1971	69.9	30.1	63.0	37.0
1972	70.2	29.8	63.9	36.1
1973	65.8	34.2	60.5	39.5
1974	68.3	31.7	60.4	39.6
1975	71.1	28.9	60.1	39.9

Table 58: Capital invested in basic construction divided according to economic branch

	1960	1965	1974	1975
(volume of investment in m. dong)				
TOTAL	669.7	959.1	1822.7	2049.8(*)
Industry	256.7	363.9	641.6	761.7
Basic construction	51.6	23.2	140.5	116.2
Agriculture and forestry	69.0	171.6	321.6	319.5
Trade and material supply	46.0	55.1	104.1	96.4
Transport and communications	115.0	277.7	336.9	479.8
Credit and State Insurance	0.9	1.3	1.6	2.6
Public and other services	50.0	18.9	93.5	100.4
Scientific research, education, physical training, medical and social services	56.3	38.1	163.1	141.4
State management, Party and collectives	24.2	9.3	19.8	13.4

(*) Sic. Total does not equal column sum in original.

Table 58 cont:

	1960	1965	1974	1975
(index numbers of growth - %)				
TOTAL	100.0	143.2	272.2	306.1
Industry	100.0	141.8	249.9	296.7
Basic construction	100.0	45.0	272.3	225.2
Agriculture and forestry	100.0	248.7	466.1	463.0
Trade and material supply	100.0	119.8	226.3	209.6
Transport and communications	100.0	241.5	292.9	432.9
Credit and State Insurance	100.0	144.4	177.8	288.9
Communal and other services	100.0	37.8	187.0	200.8
Scientific research, education, physical training, medical services	100.0	67.7	289.7	251.2
State management, Party and collectives	100.0	38.4	81.8	55.4
(structure - %)				
TOTAL	100.0	100.0(*)	100.0	100.0
Industry	38.3	37.9	35.2	37.2
Basic construction	7.7	2.4	7.7	5.7
Agriculture and forestry	10.3	17.9	17.6	15.6
Trade and material supply	6.9	5.7	5.7	4.7
Transport and communications	17.2	28.9	18.6	24.3
Credit and State Insurance	0.1	0.1	0.1	0.1
Communal and other services	7.5	1.9	5.1	4.9
Scientific research, education, physical training, medical services	8.4	4.0	8.9	6.9
State management, Party and collectives	3.6	0.8	1.1	0.6

(*) Sic. Total does not equal column sum in original.

Table 59: Index numbers of the development of investment in basic construction managed by the State in branches of the national economy (1960 = 100)

	1965	1974	1975
TOTAL	134.8	208.7	244.4
By type of investment, of which:			
Construction and Assembly	140.0	191.0	199.9
Equipment	138.2	236.5	308.1
By economic branch:			
Industry	130.2	201.9	245.9
Basic construction	44.8	229.4	179.8
Agriculture and forestry	196.4	185.6	207.5
Trade and material supply	115.0	187.4	166.5
Transport and communications	231.7	255.4	406.9
Credit and State Insurance	144.4	177.8	288.9
Communal and other services	36.9	96.6	109.6
Culture, medical services, sport and physical education, social services	63.3	283.5	196.1
State management, Party and collectives	37.9	95.8	29.5

Table 60: Investment in basic construction managed by the State divided according to type of investment and economic branch

	1960	1965	1974	1975
TOTAL	100.0	100.0	100.0(*)	100.0(*)
By type of investment:				
Of which : Construction and Assembly	53.8	54.9	49.2	44.0
Equipment	37.9	38.3	43.0	47.8
By economic branch:				
Industry	41.7	40.3	40.3	41.9
Basic construction	8.5	2.8	9.3	6.2
Agriculture and forestry	9.7	14.1	8.6	8.2
Trade and material supply	7.7	6.6	6.9	5.3
Transport and communications	17.9	30.8	21.9	29.8
Communal and other services	6.0	1.6	2.8	2.7
Scientific research, education, culture, physical training, medical services	6.9	3.2	9.4	5.5
State management, Party and collectives	1.6	0.6	0.7	0.2

(*) Sic. Total does not equal column sum in original.

Table 61: Index numbers of the development of investment in basic construction managed locally in branches of the national economy

	1965	1974	1975
TOTAL	212.0	788.3	807.9
By type of investment Of which:			
Construction and Assembly	178.9	603.8	639.4
Equipment	541.7	2511.7	2381.7
By economic branch:			
Industry	497.5	1723.5	1858.0
Basic construction	50.0	2075.0	2133.3
Agriculture and forestry	515.9	1898.2	1768.1
Trade and material supply	100.0	813.6	900.0
Transport and communications	366.3	775.9	766.3
Communal and other services	40.0	408.3	424.1
Scientific research, education, culture, physical training, medical and social services	79.6	308.6	400.0
State management, Party and collectives	39.5	72.8	72.1

Table 62: Investment in basic construction managed locally divided according to type of investment and branch of the national economy

	1960	1965	1974	1975
TOTAL	100.0	100.0	100.0	100.0
By type of investment Of which: Construction				
and Assembly	90.7	76.6	69.5	71.8
Equipment	8.2	20.9	26.1	24.1
By economic branch:				
Industry	11.1	25.9	24.2	25.4
Basic construction	1.6	0.4	4.3	4.3
Agriculture and forestry	15.4	37.5	37.1	33.7
Trade and material supply	0.0	1.4	3.1	3.4
Transport and communications	11.3	19.6	11.1	10.7
Communal and other services	19.8	3.7	10.2	10.4

Table 62: Cont.

Scientific research, education, physical training, culture, social and medical services	20.7	7.8	8.1	10.3
State management, Party and collectives	20.1	3.7	1.9	1.8

Table 63: Capital invested in basic construction in industry (m. dong)

	1960	1965	1974	1975
TOTAL	256.7	363.9	641.6	761.7
According to Group: Group A	193.7	318.5	490.4	574.9
Group B	63.0	45.4	151.2	186.8
According to Branch:				
Energy, extraction and transformation of fuels	57.1	123.2	163.6	162.3
Metallurgy	35.3	70.3	33.7	92.7
Manufacture and repair of machinery, equipment and metal products	15.2	30.6	102.3	120.4
Chemicals	39.7	53.1	80.5	67.3
Construction materials inc. pottery, porcelain, glass, wood, forestry products, cellulose and paper	64.7	40.7	141.5	165.0
Staples and food	17.8	30.8	66.2	57.9
Cloth, leather, clothing and dyeing	7.5	5.8	34.2	65.1
Printing and production of cultural objects	2.0	1.4	4.4	9.6
Other industry	17.4	8.0	15.2	21.4

Table 64: Investment in basic construction in agriculture

(m.dong)	1960	1965	1974	1975
TOTAL	69.0(*)	158.8(*)	281.8(*)	271.0(*)
Of which:				
Irrigation	16.2	91.6	79.9	76.8
Dykes, barrages and ditches	9.7	12.3	61.6	53.7
Tractor stations and teams	1.7	2.0	6.8	7.4
State farms and other installations	36.5	25.0	77.4	88.8

(*) Sic. Total does not equal column sum in original.

Table 65: Investment in basic construction in transport

(m. dong)

	1960	1965	1974	1975
TOTAL	105.7	267.3	300.1	479.7(*)
Divided according to level of management: Central	97.5	237.7	236.0	416.4
Regional	8.2	29.6	64.1	63.3
Divided according to branch: Railways	46.2	68.7	83.4	91.4
Roads	39.6	173.7	130.4	117.2
Waterways	19.9	24.9	86.3	264.1

(*) Sic. Total does not equal column sum in original.

Table 66: Value of new (moi tang) fixed capital according to level of management

(m. dong)

	Total	Of which: Central	Local
1960	507.5	456.6	50.9
1961	501.5	425.8	75.7
1962	626.2	536.4	89.8
1963	609.0	531.9	77.1
1964	595.9	490.3	105.6
1965	581.2	448.7	132.5
1966	589.6	387.1	202.5
1967	549.5	340.5	209.0
1968	763.0	525.7	237.3
1969	612.3	422.5	189.8
1970	739.7	453.2	286.5
1971	712.2	477.4	234.8
1972	667.9	446.8	221.1
1973	1039.1(*)	683.6	255.5
1974	1138.5	751.8	386.7
1975	1135.1	753.6	381.5

(*) Sic. Total does not equal row sum in original.

AGRICULTURE

Table 67: Land use in agricultural production in 1974
(according to preliminary figures of the Ministry of
Agriculture)

	Area (thousand ha.)	% of total
TOTAL	2402	100.0
Land used for yearly crops:	1960	81.6
Rice area	1163	48.4
Triple harvest -	3	0.1
Double harvest -	833	34.7
Single harvest -	327	13.6
Rice and crop (mau) area	226	9.4
Land used for crops (mau) and short-term industrial crops	296	12.3
Area specialising in vegetables	17	0.7
Other cultivated areas	258	10.7
Land used for long-term crops:	149	6.2
Long-term industrial crops	63	2.6
Fruits	23	1.0
Other crops	63	2.6
Natural pasture:	192	8.0
Ponds, lakes, bog, streams (song cut) and pools (thung dau)	101	4.2

The Limits of National Liberation

Table 68: Some general indicators of agricultural development

	1960	1965	1974	1975
Cooperator families as a % of all peasant families	85.8	90.1	95.2	95.6
Higher-level cooperator families as a % of all cooperator families	14.5	72.1	97.3	97.4
State farms (including those set up locally) - no.	56	59	115	115
Independent tractor stations - no.	23	75	134	122
Agricultural coops - no.	40422	31651	17902	17000
Workers of an age to work - thousands	5759	5897	5654	5758
Investment by the State (m. dong)	69.0	158.8	281.8	271.0
Value of agricultural, forestry and other material output of the peasantry (m. dong)	2633	3222	3525	3452
Of which: Agriculture	2327	2864	3193	3036
Of which: cultivation	1840	2208	2556	2301
livestock	487	656	637	735
Staples output (thousands of tonnes, paddy equivalent)	4698	5562	6277	5491
Staples supplied to the State (thousand tonnes)	878	1125	1017	796
Pigs of 2 months age and older (thousands)	3806	4791	6406	6596
Pigs supplied to the State (thousand tonnes)	44.7	60.3	90.9	109.6

Table 69: Agricultural Cooperativisation

(percentages)

| | Cooperator families compared with total number of working peasant families | Cultivated area of cooperative compared with total cultivated area of working peasantry | Higher-level cooperatives compared with all cooperatives: | | |
			A. Cooperatives	B. Cooperator families	C. Cultivated area
1960	85.8	68.4	10.8	14.5	15.5
1961	88.9	70.9	25.3	34.4	34.2
1962	86.3	69.1	33.7	43.2	43.7
1963	85.1	68.1	34.5	46.1	45.5
1964	84.7	75.6	43.3	53.7	51.7
1965	90.1	80.3	60.1	72.1	67.8
1966	92.7	89.1	69.7	86.0	84.8
1967	94.1	90.9	75.9	86.5	86.0
1968	94.8	92.2	80.5	92.9	90.8
1969	95.1	92.4	83.6	94.3	91.6
1970	95.5	94.6	84.6	96.2	92.3
1971	95.9	95.0	84.2	95.9	92.1
1972	95.7	94.9	86.9	96.1	92.4
1973	94.8	94.7	87.4	96.3	92.5
1974	95.2	95.0	89.5	97.3	93.0
1975	95.6	95.2	90.1	97.4	93.2

Table 70: Cooperatives and cooperators

| | Agricultural cooperatives (*) | | | Cooperator families (thousands) | | |
	Total	Of which: Higher-level	Lower level	Total	Of which: Higher-level	Lower level
1960	40422	4346	36076	2404.7	346.0	2058.7
1961	31827	8043	23784	2512.2	863.5	1648.7
1962	29746	10017	19729	2517.9	1087.1	1430.8
1963	30592	10569	20023	2522.9	1164.0	1358.9
1964	32378	14013	18365	2591.3	1393.6	1197.7

Table 70: Cont.

1965	31651	19035	12616	2810.8	2026.5	784.3
1966	26811	18681	8130	2915.3	2507.2	408.1
1967	23624	17921	5703	2989.6	2586.2	403.4
1968	22162(+)	17839	4223	3049.8	2836.0	213.8
1969	20725	17323	3402	3083.8	2907.0	176.8
1970	19924	16860	3064	3114.5	2997.3	117.2
1971	19739	16623	3116	3166.9	3036.6	130.3
1972	19564	16994	2570	3200.8	3076.8	124.0
1973	18336	16027	2309	3227.1	3133.6	93.5
1974	17902	16032	1870	3294.8	3207.3	87.5
1975	17000	15319	1681	3383.6	3297.2	86.4

(*) For 1960-69, based upon annual survey of 1/9; for 1970-75, based upon annual survey of 1/8.
(+) Sic. Total does not equal row sum in original.

Table 71: The size of agricultural cooperatives
(average per cooperative)

	1960	1965	1974	1975
Cooperator families (ho)	68	85	156	199
Workers of working age	125	170	247	337
Cultivated (canh tac) area	33	49	89	115
Value of fixed assets (*)	3.9	24.8	87.5	230.6

(*) Thousand dong, based upon a yearly sample of between 400 and 2,500 cooperatives.

Table 72(*): Workers in agriculture (of working age, thousands)

| | Total | Of which: | | |
		State sector	Collective sector	Individual sector
1960	5563.0(+)	11.3	4931.5	816.2
1965	5897.1	68.4	5251.7	577.0
1968	4928.0	78.1	4668.2	181.7
1969	4980.0	80.8	4654.0	245.2
1970	4909.7	87.3	4599.3	223.1
1971	5165.2	84.6	4843.7	236.9
1972	5269.1	92.2	4914.4	262.5
1973	5367.4	92.9	4960.7	313.8
1974	5654.1	102.4	5243.1	308.6
1975	5757.6	102.8	5338.5	316.3

(*) Table 73 in original.
(+) Sic. Total does not equal row sum in original.

<u>Table</u> 73 <u>(1.)</u>: <u>The</u> <u>value</u> <u>of</u> <u>the</u> <u>output</u> <u>of</u> <u>agriculture,</u>
<u>forestry</u> <u>and</u> <u>other</u> <u>material</u> <u>sectors</u> (*)

(calculated at 1970 prices, in m. dong)

	Total	Of which: Agriculture Total	Of which: Cultivation	Livestock	Forestry (2.)	Other material output of the peasantry
1960	2632.6	2327.1	1840.0	487.1	2.9	302.6
1961	2776.3	2438.9	1978.4	460.5	4.9	332.5
1962	2964.8	2599.2	2060.2	539.0	8.3	357.3
1963	2910.6	2542.0	1983.1	558.9	9.5	359.1
1964	3119.4	2739.1	2142.6	596.5	10.7	369.6
1965	3222.5	2863.7	2208.1	655.6	14.8	344.0
1966	3112.5	2751.2	2133.6	617.6	13.8	347.5
1967	3164.8	2816.1	2221.6	594.5	13.8	334.9
1968	2916.1	2559.4	1977.0	582.4	16.3	340.4
1969	2997.2	2633.0	2009.1	623.9	25.3	338.9
1970	3208.4	2850.4	2299.1	551.3	24.6	333.4
1971	3075.9	2753.0	2169.8	583.2	22.2	300.7
1972	3413.6	3092.9	2478.6	614.3	23.5	297.2
1973	3265.7	2937.6(+)	2270.5	666.1	29.3	299.8
1974	3524.8	3192.8	2555.5	637.3	28.6	303.4
1975	3452.4	3036.4	2301.5	734.9	35.3	380.7

(*) Data only includes the value of material output of the peasantry.
1. Table 72 in original.
2. **Trong cay gay rung.**
(+) Sic. Total does not equal row sum in original.

Table 74: Capital invested by the State in agriculture and loans by the State to agricultural cooperatives and peasants (m. dong)

	Capital invested by the State in Agriculture	State loans to agricultural cooperatives (*)		
		A. Long-term		B. Short-term loans outstanding at end of year
		Yearly Loans	Amount outstanding at end of year	
1960	69.0	18.1	26.0	1.5
1961	109.1	54.4	56.0	22.7
1962	149.5	26.2	65.6	26.0
1963	162.7	47.5	94.7	34.7
1964	177.2	51.6	115.0	30.8
1965	158.8	64.9	144.3	41.0
1966	184.7	117.1	231.2	31.7
1967	158.6	114.1	294.6	7.5
1968	133.2	100.5	347.8	6.2
1969	178.9	112.0	407.8	4.8
1970	171.5	61.8	406.9	109.5
1971	172.5	63.0	392.2	235.7
1972	239.7	59.0	360.3	247.1
1973	267.0	56.0	333.8	273.4
1974	281.8	59.8	306.4	270.1
1975	271.0	66.7	297.4	270.7

(*) Including loan funds and **tiep von** (?capital contributions) contributed by the State Bank to credit cooperatives.

Table 75: State agricultural water-works fully brought into use

	Number of works	Area served (capacity, thousand ha.)		Area served (real output, thousand ha.)	
		A. Supply	B. Drainage	A. Supply	B. Drainage
TOTAL	1333	1090.2	545.0	736.1	278.7
WATER-WORKS DIRECTLY SERVING AGRICULTURE:					
Total	1262	1081.6	544.7	729.4	277.6
A. Large-scale	95	766.0	413.8	555.0	201.9
Of which:					
Lakes	11	48.1	-	23.4	-
Dykes	11	164.0	36.3	111.1	30.4
Ditches	19	246.4	260.9	196.9	65.2

Table 75: Cont.

Electric pumping stations	54	307.5	116.6	223.6	106.3
B. Independent	928	286.5	130.9	151.8	75.7
Of which:					
Lakes	228	65.5	4.4	33.0	1.9
Dykes	221	33.8	-	27.1	-
Ditches	187	94.2	44.9	32.6	24.7
Electric pumping stations	292	93.0	81.6	59.1	49.1
Oil-fired pumping stations outside the system	239	29.1	-	22.6	-
HYDROELECTRIC SCHEMES TIED TO IRRIGATION	71	8.6	0.3	6.7	1.1

Data from 31/12/75. (*) Only including water-works in the system or independent.

Table 76: Electricity and machines serving agriculture (excluding State farms)

	Units	1973	1974	1975
Electricity distributed to agriculture	M. KwHr	110.1	101.4	148.5
Engines	Numbers	29773(*)	31721	32591
	Thou. kW	517.7	548.6	576.6
Of which:				
Electric motors	Numbers	7935	9281	9883
	Thou. kW	189.8	209.6	267.4
Diesels	Numbers	21686	22298	22586
	Thou. kW	326.8	337.5	357.9
Steam engines	Numbers	109	142	122
	Thou. kW	1.1	1.5	1.3
Trucks and vans (1.)	Numbers	116	161	169
Tractors a. Actual units	Numbers	3671	3942	4198
b. In standard tractors	"	10134	13409	14197

Table 76: Cont.

Work machines				
Hand ploughs	Numbers	1462	1652	2103
Tractor-drawn ploughs	"	3536	3557	3636
Tractor-drawn harrows	"	3334	3335	3365
Water pumps	"	21384	23263	23094
Threshers	"	8296	8923	9237
Mills	"	9019	9110	9058
Grinders	"	1928	1942	1927
Powered insecticide sprays	"	4025	5318	6161

(1.) Sic: O to van tai.
(*) Sic. Total does not equal column sum in original.

Table 77: Crop areas (*)

(thousand ha.)

	Annuals: Total (+)	Of which: Staples	Veg. & Beans	Ind.'l Crops	Perennials: Total	Of which: Ind.'l crops	Fruits
1960	2840.5	2625.4	93.6	120.2	18.6	17.7	0.9
1961	3107.6	2881.8	98.6	124.3	28.9	27.3	1.6
1962	3186.9	2921.3	106.6	151.1	39.4	37.1	2.3
1963	3248.7	2949.6	124.2	162.5	42.7	39.9	2.8
1964	3372.8	3075.5	124.0	162.1	38.2	36.2	2.0
1965	3333.3	3012.3	131.2	179.6	39.4	37.5	1.9
1966	3329.1	3013.5	136.6	170.6	34.9	33.1	1.8
1967	3153.1	2847.7	141.2	157.4	35.8	33.9	1.9
1968	2942.3	2660.6	140.9	136.9	37.9	35.9	2.0
1969	2967.0	2674.7	150.0	137.4	40.5	38.3	2.2
1970	3028.1	2723.7	153.8	144.7	38.4	36.3	2.1
1971	2873.4	2580.5	144.7	140.9	40.8	38.4	2.4
1972	3000.2	2697.7	156.5	137.2	43.6	40.8	2.8
1973	2845.8	2588.6	151.4	128.3	44.3	40.7	3.6
1974	3037.1	2747.9	153.0	128.8	44.1	39.5	4.6
1975	3017.6	2714.9	152.2	135.7	49.1	43.2	5.9

(*) Before 1965 data was inadequate, so, in order to have a basis for comparison, the series for yearly crops excludes pharmaceuticals, livestock feeds and green fertiliser for each province; the series for perennials excludes green tea (tea with two leaves), betel, camellia and a number of economic plants for each province; the fruit area excludes the centrally grown areas of State farms.
(+) Sic. Totals do not equal row sums in original.

Table 78: Staples output in paddy equivalent

	Staples output (thousand tonnes)	Percentage of rice in	
		A. Staples output	B. Staples area
1960	4698.1	88.9	86.4
1961	5201.4	84.5	82.9
1962	5173.3	84.8	82.4
1963	5013.3	82.0	80.0
1964	5514.9	80.0	79.1
1965	5562.0	81.7	79.6
1966	5099.9	80.9	79.2
1967	5397.8	79.5	76.9
1968	4628.6	80.0	77.9
1969	4708.9	83.0	80.4
1970	5278.9	84.4	81.2
1971	4920.9	83.8	80.1
1972	5742.2	85.7	81.3
1973	5190.4	86.1	81.6
1974	6276.6	87.4	82.6
1975	5490.6	87.0	82.9

Table 79: Sown rice area (thousand ha.)

	All rice	Of which: Spring and Cham rice	Autumn rice	Main harvest rice
1960	2268.1	853.5	55.6	1359.0
1961	2390.3	906.5	98.0	1385.8
1962	2406.4	930.7	95.9	1379.8
1963	2360.5	909.2	94.3	1357.0
1964	2433.8	946.8	94.5	1392.5
1965	2397.6	965.7	77.4	1354.5
1966	2386.3	959.3	91.3	1335.7
1967	2190.5	880.0	65.4	1245.1
1968	2079.5	885.4	49.8	1144.3
1969	2151.2	894.6	39.5	1217.1
1970	2213.2	899.8	48.3	1265.1
1971	2066.3	939.7	33.3	1093.3
1972	2194.6	951.3	31.1	1212.2
1973	2088.7	963.6	26.2	1098.9
1974	2268.8	944.0	28.4	1296.4
1975	2250.8	994.2	26.7	1229.9

Table 80: Rice yields (100 kg. (ta) per ha.)

	Average harvest	Spring and Cham rice	Autumn rice	Main harvest rice	Yearly rice yield on 1 ha. of field with two harvests
1960	18.42	13.61	17.30	21.48	35.90
1961	18.38	18.83	13.05	18.46	...
1962	18.23	17.37	13.36	19.16	...
1963	17.42	16.43	12.11	18.45	...
1964	18.18	18.74	12.73	18.16	...
1965	18.96	18.86	13.99	19.32	39.10
1966	17.29	15.22	14.43	18.98	34.01
1967	19.59	18.94	9.84	20.56	39.51
1968	17.82	18.27	10.11	17.81	37.77
1969	18.16	17.82	11.78	18.62	38.60
1970	20.14	19.79	11.30	20.73	43.11
1971	19.95	23.33	8.10	17.42	42.82
1972	22.43	23.66	10.56	21.78	47.19
1973	21.39	22.33	8.78	20.88	44.35
1974	24.18	27.33	12.43	22.14	51.73
1975	21.22	21.18	13.48	21.42	44.93

Table 81: Rice production (thousand tonnes)

	All rice	Of which: Spring and Cham rice	Autumn rice	Main harvest rice
1960	4177.2	1162.1	96.1	2919.0
1961	4393.0	1707.1	127.9	2558.0
1962	4387.8	1616.4	128.2	2643.2
1963	4112.4	1493.9	114.2	2504.3
1964	4424.5	1774.7	120.4	2529.4
1965	4546.9(*)	1821.2	108.3	2617.5
1966	4126.3	1459.7	131.8	2534.8
1967	4291.4	1666.8	64.4	2560.2
1968	3705.9	1617.4	50.4	2038.1
1969	3907.4	1594.5	46.4	2266.5
1970	4457.6	1780.5	54.6	2622.5
1971	4123.0	2192.5	25.4	1905.1
1972	4924.4	2250.6	32.8	2641.0
1973	4468.8	2151.7	23.0	2294.1
1974	5486.0	2580.3	35.3	2870.4
1975	4776.1	2105.8	36.0	2634.3

(*) Sic. Total does not equal row sum in original.

Table 82: Area of crops (1.) and staples (thousand ha.)

	Total	Of which: Maize	Sweet Potatoes	Manioc	Water and taro potatoes	Dong rieng (2.)	Other cereals
1960	357.3(*)	197.6	122.8	36.8	...	...	...
1961	491.5(*)	229.2	180.4	81.7	...	...	...
1962	515.3(*)	226.1	176.9	112.0	...	...	...
1963	589.2	237.8	189.3	122.6	17.9	21.3	0.3
1964	641.7	242.3	230.2	126.6	21.1	21.3	0.2
1965	614.7	240.7	220.0	111.3	20.4	18.9	3.4
1966	627.2	238.0	229.0	119.9	19.9	17.9	2.5
1967	657.2	234.4	263.8	123.7	16.9	16.3	2.1
1968	581.0	213.0	235.5	98.2	14.4	15.5	4.4
1969	523.5	197.8	208.7	84.4	15.1	13.9	3.6
1970	510.5	205.2	189.0	86.6	12.2	12.7	4.8
1971	514.2	205.4	184.4	94.0	10.3	14.6	5.5
1972	503.1	208.4	167.4	93.9	11.2	13.7	8.5
1973	469.9	195.2	155.4	78.9	11.5	13.8	15.1
1974	479.1(*)	214.0	147.3	86.1	10.6	13.6	7.1
1975	464.1	204.1	140.3	85.3	9.2	15.6	9.6

1. **Cay hoa mau.** 2. Phrynium parvillorum and galingale.
(*) Sic. Total does not equal row sum in original.

Table 83: Yields of crops (1.) and staples (100 kg. (ta) per ha.)

	General Average	Of which: Maize grain	Sweet potatoes	Manioc	Water and taro potatoes	Dong rieng (2.)
1960	14.58	11.13	46.79	89.06	...	...
1961	16.45	11.35	45.06	85.31	...	...
1962	15.24	11.52	51.44	67.00	...	...
1963	15.29	9.17	54.03	72.73	132.1	126.4
1964	17.00	11.51	51.44	72.86	115.2	142.2
1965	16.51	11.43	54.03	71.66	88.1	106.5
1966	15.52	9.29	54.15	67.17	76.9	108.9
1967	16.83	11.03	56.09	71.09	80.4	102.3
1968	15.88	9.49	50.78	71.91	148.8	134.6
1969	15.31	9.52	49.08	70.61	108.5	137.8
1970	16.08	10.99	49.91	73.63	121.4	136.5
1971	15.52	9.87	48.32	73.94	117.8	117.3
1972	16.25	10.56	57.10	80.03	101.8	125.0
1973	15.37	10.00	48.45	79.35	101.7	124.7
1974	16.53	10.88	49.66	87.93	104.7	137.2
1975	15.40	10.09	46.28	78.55	105.9	125.6

1. **Cay hoa mau.** 2. Phrynium parvillorum and galingale.

Table 84: Output of crops and staples (thousand tonnes)

	Total (paddy equi't)	Of which: Maize	Sweet potatoes (1.)	Manioc	Water and taro potatoes (1.)	Dong rieng (1.) (2.)	Other cereals (dry grain)
1960	521.0	220.0	574.7	328.2	...	...	...
1961	808.4	260.1	947.9	697.0	...	...	...
1962	785.5	260.5	823.9	751.1	...	...	...
1963	900.9	218.2	852.9	891.4	236.4	270.0	0.1
1964	1090.4	279.0	1184.4	922.4	243.1	302.3	0.0
1965	1015.1	275.0	1193.9	800.6	179.3	201.4	1.6
1966	973.6	221.0	1239.9	805.6	152.8	195.4	1.1
1967	1106.4	258.5	1479.6	879.5	135.6	166.9	1.0
1968	922.7	202.1	1196.0	706.4	214.9	208.7	1.7
1969	801.5	188.4	1024.3	595.8	164.9	191.6	1.3
1970	821.3	225.4	943.4	643.1	147.6	173.7	3.5
1971	797.9	202.9	899.5	695.3	121.9	171.7	4.7
1972	817.8	220.5	855.5	751.5	113.6	170.7	4.6
1973	721.6	195.1	752.9	626.2	128.9	165.2	6.7
1974	790.6	232.8	731.5	750.2	111.1	186.9	4.5
1975	714.5	206.0	649.3	670.0	97.0	196.0	9.4

1. Fresh tubers.   2. Phrynium parvillorum and galingale.

Table 85: Vegetables and beans (areas in thousands of ha.; yields in 100 kg. (ta) per ha.; output in thousands of tonnes)

	All vegetables:			All beans (excluding soya):		
	Area	Yield	Output	Area	Yield	Output
1960	31.0	...	...	62.6	2.32	14.5
1961	40.1	...	...	58.5	2.99	16.9
1962	17.6	...	...	59.0	2.9	17.2
1963	61.8	...	...	62.4	2.21	13.8
1964	68.0	...	...	56.0	3.15	17.6
1965	74.0	108.2	800.6	57.2	2.88	16.5
1966	86.3	96.1	829.0	50.3	2.88	11.5
1967	93.4	110.5	1032.0	47.8	2.87	13.7
1968	96.5	117.4	1133.4	44.4	2.94	13.0
1969	107.0	104.5	1117.6	43.0	2.63	11.3
1970	112.5	133.6	1504.2	41.2	2.75	11.3
1971	105.4	127.3	1341.8	39.9	2.84	11.2
1972	116.8	128.0	1495.6	39.7	2.86	11.4
1973	115.9	119.2	1382.6	35.5	2.84	10.1
1974	115.1	132.4	1524.2	37.9	3.21	12.2
1975	115.5	126.6	1452.3	36.7	2.92	10.7

Table 86: Jute and Hemp (areas in ha.; yields in 100 kg. (ta)
per ha.; output in tonnes)

	Jute: Area	Yield	Output	Hemp: Area	Yield	Output
1960	8331	17.32	14427	602	5.81	353
1961	6573	15.02	9876	704	5.44	383
1962	9893	12.99	12851	1053	4.74	499
1963	11364	14.11	16063	1774	3.51	623
1964	13438	9.10	12226	3301	2.50	826
1965	13450	16.21	21809	3958	2.60	1033
1966	11652	14.07	16393	3504	2.72	954
1967	11056	14.63	16178	2707	2.75	745
1968	11339	12.35	14005	1757	2.88	507
1969	12827	16.05	20593	1113	3.89	433
1970	11450	18.10	20728	546	4.65	184
1971	9243	15.97	14764	531	4.65	247
1972	9579	23.12	22195	483	4.92	238
1973	9983	21.79	21751	550	3.98	219
1974	11117	25.04	27847	398	5.00	199
1975	12232	19.38	24349	374	4.43	166

Table 87: Rushes and sugar cane (areas in thousands of ha.
(except rushes - ha.); yields in 100 kg. (ta) per ha.; output
in thousands of tonnes)

	Rushes: Area	Yield	Output	Sugar cane: Area	Yield	Output
1960	3764	45.07	16965	10.8	423.2	456.6
1961	3883	45.94	17839	12.1	399.3	484.8
1962	5774	43.19	24939	18.0	363.2	653.9
1963	6895	38.32	26421	20.8	341.3	710.9
1964	7468	45.45	33943	19.3	346.7	669.9
1965	8120	49.79	40431	19.4	388.7	752.4
1966	8159	45.72	36934	17.3	366.8	633.6
1967	7192	47.52	34174	14.8	360.9	535.7
1968	7491	40.27	30164	14.1	310.6	424.6
1969	8159	41.96	34233	14.2	336.6	479.4
1970	8443	46.83	39537	15.4	357.8	549.9
1971	9051	49.41	44724	15.1	325.3	505.4
1972	9420	48.15	45366	14.5	379.3	557.0
1973	8653	47.1	40771	13.6	350.2	475.6
1974	8606	56.01	48205	13.6	400.8	539.4
1975	9360	54.09	50637	13.5	377.1	510.3

The Limits of National Liberation

Table 88: Peanuts and soybeans (areas in thousands of ha.; yields in 100 kg. (ta) per ha.; output in thousands of tonnes)

	Peanuts: Area	Yield	Output	Soybeans: Area	Yield	Output
1960	30.8	8.86	27.3	26.6	4.31	11.5
1961	28.7	10.34	29.7	28.0	3.66	10.2
1962	38.8	8.76	34.0	25.2	3.83	9.6
1963	43.2	7.95	34.4	27.3	3.24	8.8
1964	46.1	8.91	41.1	24.2	3.66	8.8
1965	54.3	8.91	48.3	29.5	3.54	10.9
1966	50.3	7.83	39.6	33.4	2.78	9.3
1967	45.8	8.65	39.6	37.1	3.23	12.0
1968	36.6	7.49	27.4	29.7	2.98	8.9
1969	42.2	8.36	35.3	23.2	3.04	7.0
1970	47.3	8.61	40.7	20.9	3.52	7.4
1971	49.5	8.80	43.6	18.2	3.04	5.5
1972	49.6	9.04	44.9	16.1	3.40	5.5
1973	42.8	8.36	35.7	15.3	3.29	5.0
1974	40.3	9.58	38.6	16.8	3.87	6.5
1975	42.1	8.91	37.5	21.3	3.61	7.7

Table 89: Sesame and tobacco (areas in ha.; yields in 100 kg. (ta) per ha.; output in tonnes)

	Sesame: Area	Yield	Output	Tobacco: Area	Yield	Output
1960	11572	2.39	2768	2908	5.80	1687
1961	11304	2.30	2831	4410	5.99	2641
1962	15248	2.04	3112	7042	5.54	3901
1963	12497	2.03	2541	8008	5.29	4237
1964	11629	2.30	2681	8502	4.63	3939
1965	9334	2.37	2216	10798	5.22	5639
1966	8347	2.08	1738	11268	4.96	5588
1967	6411	2.28	1464	10026	5.11	5120
1968	7499	2.27	1703	8907	1.83	4305
1969	7319	2.22	1627	9181	4.74	4351
1970	7149	2.30	1645	11349	5.35	6082
1971	6815	2.21	1501	12067	5.27	6361
1972	6029	2.54	1533	12521	5.55	6976
1973	6884	2.15	1483	12278	5.02	6167
1974	8209	2.64	2174	12836	6.08	7810
1975	8277	2.37	1921	13847	4.52	6407

Table 90: Area of perennial industrial crops (ha.)

	Tea	Coffee	Lacquer	Rubber	Pepper
1960	8884	6405	1865	187	5
1961	10025	10791	2897	3249	9
1962	12740	14388	3216	6369	49
1963	14540	14807	3382	6725	49
1964	14951	11962	3404	5569	51
1965	16640	11962	3030	5569	51
1966	14147	11962	1093	5569	55
1967	15290	11962	754	5569	55
1968	17084	11965	934	5569	55
1969	18980	11962	1445	5569	61
1970	21006	9210	1306	4527	53
1971	22823	9415	1212	4707	61
1972	25891	8664	1172	4718	68
1973	27623	7201	1172	4381	72
1974	28070	5081	1236	4528	80
1975	30076	5180	1299	4529	86

Table 91: Output of perennial industrial crops (*) (tonnes)

	Tea	Coffee	Lacquer	Rubber	Pepper
1960	2799	256	567	2	0.9
1961	2640	676	661	1	0.8
1962	2410	910	525	1	0.9
1963	3900	866	500	2	0.9
1964	4457	1177	520	2	1.7
1965	4736	3949	525	2	11.3
1966	6803	3165	420	2	65.5
1967	7031	4385	199	13	77.0
1968	8107	2015	119	116	63.7
1969	6627	2441	112	432	26.2
1970	9054	3384	129	1011	43.0
1971	9711	2083	140	1819	66.0
1972	9652	2447	137	1836	9.3
1973	9950	1865	168	2505	49.5
1974	10327	1464	176	2878	47.6
1975	11820	697	148	3164	56.0

(*) Output calculated as follows: tea - dry leaf; coffee - beans; rubber - dry latex; pepper - dry seeds.

Table 92: Numbers of livestock and poultry (thousand head)

	Buffalo	Oxen	Pigs (a.)	Horses	Goats	Poultry (b.)
1960	1449.2	856.0	3806.0	39.4	48.8	20.4
1961	1434.5	761.9	3810.5	42.2	57.3	21.2
1962	1463.9	776.2	4423.4	45.8	60.7	21.6
1963	1508.3	696.2	4464.1	49.8	68.7	32.7
1964	1570.4	822.5	4561.1	56.1	99.0	23.3
1965	1611.4	813.8	4790.8	57.7	114.5	30.0
1966	1659.9	790.7	5100.6	60.4	121.0	27.2
1967	1644.1	755.3	5006.6	66.4	120.4	28.0
1968	1619.2	715.9	5265.8	84.8	113.2	28.8
1969	1654.6	716.8	5301.2	93.8	132.3	28.9
1970	1705.7	708.0	5380.8	102.3	134.2	30.4
1971	1729.1	690.5	5627.2	107.5	130.1	28.9
1972	1730.3	675.6	5728.9	113.3	143.8	33.7
1973	1768.9	654.5	6331.0	118.7	135.6	34.9
1974	1763.7	642.5	6406.4	124.1	138.7	33.8
1975	1798.5	657.2	6595.8	124.8	147.4	35.7

(a) Excluding pigs under two months. (b) Million animals.

Table 93: Main agricultural products supplied to the State

	Units	1960	1965	1974	1975
Staples (paddy equ't)	Thou. tonnes	878.3	1124.9	1013.6	787.2
Of which: Rice	"	834.3	1057.9	981.8	762.2
Fresh vegetables	"	-	95.3	125.8	128.8
Beans (excluding soya)	"	1446	4375	2070	1815
Jute (leaves: quy be)	Thou. tonnes	11.1	18.1	25.6	22.5
Rushes all types	"	12.2	25.7	39.8	43.8
Sugar cane all types	"	316.8	371.2	348.9	...
Shelled peanuts	"	10.3	25.3	20.2	17.4
Soybeans	"	3.8	3.0	1.2	1.6
Tobacco (dry leaves)	Tonnes	964	4771	6073	5763
Lao tobacco	"	1569	2032	806	714
Dry tea leaves	"	1693	3470	5903	6852
Coffee beans	"	211	3475	1947	914
Pepper corns	"	-	11	48	56
Beaf (live-wt. (1.))	Thou. tonnes	23.3	17.7	11.2	13.3
Pork (live-wt. (1.))	"	44.7	60.3	89.5	109.6
Poultry meat (live-wt. (1.)	Tonnes	2782	2571	3731	5477
Chicken and duck eggs	Million	...	23.2	108.9	106.3
Fresh fresh-water fish	Tonnes	2000	3618	4019	4832

(1.) Sic: Can hoi

DOMESTIC AND FOREIGN TRADE

Table 94: A number of general indicators on the development of State trade

	Average number of registered employees (thou.)	Points of sale	Total value of merchandise received in the country (a) (m. dong)	Total value of merchandise retail sales (m. dong)
1960	70.4	1897	983.0	739.6
1961	74.8	...	899.4	919.8
1962	74.4	...	1144.3	1024.9
1963	68.9	...	1171.3	1238.0
1964	76.4	3701	1422.2	1467.3
1965	87.0	5148	1547.2	1609.0
1966	105.7	5936	1462.9	1699.3
1967	106.8	6127	1587.3	1820.4
1968	107.6	5995	1586.2	1989.9
1969	114.9	5809	1644.3	2264.4
1970	118.6	5776	1652.3	2155.8
1971	114.4	5826	1955.9	2419.7
1972	116.1	6197	1966.0	2397.3
1973	119.0	5874	1979.0	2689.7
1974	124.2	6124	2232.2	2750.9
1975	130.5	6404	2429.8	3086.2

(a) Excluding purchases for export.

Table 95: The State retail trade network

	1965	1974	1975
A. Points of sale - numbers			
TOTAL	5148	6124	6404
Retail trade:	4577	5321	5504
Staples	1264	1141	1063
Other food	760	1100	1250
Indust'l goods & constr'n mat's	1722	1970	2074
Pharmaceuticals	508	750	745
Books	323	360	372
Public Restaurants	571	803	900
B. Index numbers (1964 = 100)			
TOTAL	139.1	165.5	173.0
Retail trade:	134.7	156.6	162.0
Staples	143.3	129.4	120.5
Other food	141.8	205.2	233.2
Indust'l goods & constr'n mat's	142.1	162.5	171.1
Pharmaceuticals	109.5	161.6	160.6
Books	106.3	118.4	122.4
Public restaurants	188.4	265.0	297.0
C. Structure - %			
TOTAL	100.0	100.0	100.0
Retail trade:	88.9	86.9	85.9
Staples	24.6	18.6	16.6
Other food	14.7	18.0	19.5
Indust'l goods & constr'n mat's	33.4	32.2	32.4
Pharmaceuticals	9.9	12.2	11.6
Books	6.3	5.9	5.8
Public restaurants	11.1	13.1	14.1

Table 96: Average number of registered employees (1.) in trade belonging to the systems of the Ministries of Domestic Trade and Staples and Food (thousands)

	1964	1965	1974	1975
TOTAL	57.6	64.6	101.4	103.9
Trade employees (2.)	50.5	57.1	84.1	85.6
Of which:				
Employees in trading activities	48.6	55.3	76.0	76.9
Of which:				
Employees in sales and direct activities	37.2	44.6	57.6	58.5
Employees in indirect activities	11.4	10.7	18.4	18.4
Employees outside trading activities	1.9	1.8	8.1	8.7
Employees in public restaurants	7.1	7.5	17.3	18.3

Table 96: Cont.

(index numbers)

TOTAL	100.0	112.2	176.0	180.4
Trade employees (2.)	100.0	113.1	166.5	169.5
Of which:				
Employees in trading activities	100.0	113.8	136.4	158.2
Of which:				
Employees in sales and direct activities	100.0	119.9	154.8	157.3
Employees in indirect activities	100.0	94.0	161.4	161.4
Employees outside trading activities	100.0	95.0	426.3	457.9
Employees in public restaurants	100.0	105.6	243.7	257.7

(structure - percentages)

TOTAL	100.0	100.0	100.0	100.0
Trade employees (2.)	87.7	88.4	82.9	82.4
Employees in public restaurants	12.3	11.6	17.1	17.6
Total employees in trade	100.0	100.0	100.0	100.0
Employees in trading activities	96.2	96.8	90.4	89.8
Of which:				
Employees in sales and direct activities	73.6	78.1	68.5	68.3
Employees in indirect activities	22.6	18.7	21.9	21.5
Employees outside trading activities	3.8	3.2	9.6	10.2

1. Cong nhan vien chuc. 2. Nhan vien.

Table 97: Numbers in petty trade and service activities (thousands)

	1960	1965	1974	1975
TOTAL	206.0	161.6	200.1	190.6
Trade and restaurants	185.0	107.6	119.8	112.4
Of which:				
People registered	143.2	47.6	50.1	62.1
People participating in some collective form	93.1	11.5	8.7	7.9
Service activities and repairs	21.0	54.0	80.3	78.2
Of which:				
People registered	14.3	26.9	52.3	64.6
People participating in some collective form	9.4	14.0	19.9	16.3

Table 97: Cont.

(index numbers)

	1960	1965	1974	1975
TOTAL	100.0	78.4	97.3	92.5
Trade and restaurants	100.0	58.2	64.8	60.8
Of which:				
People registered	100.0	33.2	35.0	43.4
People participating in some collective form	100.0	12.4	9.3	8.5
Service activities and repairs	100.0	257.1	382.4	372.4
Of which:				
People registered	100.0	188.1	365.7	451.7
People participating in some collective form	100.0	148.9	211.7	173.4

Table 98: Value of merchandise received by the trading branch in the country (m. dong)

	Total	Of which: Industrial goods (a)	Agricultural goods: Total	Of which: Staples	Food	Other
1960	983.0	625.5	357.5	235.1	...	122.4
1961	899.4	550.1	349.3	235.6	...	113.7
1962	1144.3	706.4	437.9	264.0	...	173.9
1963	1171.3	794.8	376.5	209.8	...	166.7
1964	1422.2	921.5	500.7	296.7	136.0	68.0
1965	1547.2	978.1	569.1	328.3	149.7	91.1
1966	1462.9	1045.4	417.5	186.5	140.5	90.5
1967	1587.3	1094.3	493.0	265.7	143.5	83.8
1968	1586.2	1166.8	419.4	187.3	154.2	77.9
1969	1644.3	1237.2	407.1	162.4	170.9	73.8
1970	1652.3	1259.1	393.2	164.1	176.6	52.5
1971	1955.9	1387.4	568.5	292.3	197.9	78.3
1972	1966.0	1267.5	698.5	420.4	210.7	67.4
1973	1979.0	1356.0	623.0	315.0	254.3	53.7
1974	2232.2	1599.4	632.8	311.9	273.3	47.6
1975	2429.8	1690.2	739.6	358.5	328.2	52.9

(a) Excluding books and newspapers

Table 99: Index numbers of the development and structure of the total value of goods received by the trading branch in the country

	Total	Of which: Industrial goods	Agricultural goods Total	Of which: Staples	Food and other

(index numbers of development - 1960 = 100)

	Total	Industrial goods	Agricultural Total	Staples	Food and other
1964	91.5	87.9	97.7	100.2	92.8
1965	157.4	156.4	159.2	139.6	196.7
1966	148.8	167.1	116.8	79.3	188.7
1967	161.5	174.9	137.9	113.0	185.7
1968	161.4	186.5	117.3	79.7	189.6
1969	167.3	197.8	113.9	69.1	199.9
1970	168.1	201.3	110.0	69.8	187.2
1971	199.0	221.8	159.0	124.3	225.7
1972	200.0	202.6	195.4	178.8	227.2
1973	201.3	216.8	174.3	134.0	251.6
1974	227.1	255.7	177.0	132.7	262.2
1975	247.2	270.2	206.9	152.5	311.3

(structure - percentages)

	Total	Industrial goods	Agricultural Total	Staples	Food and other
1960	100.0	63.6	36.4	23.9	12.5
1964	100.0	64.8	35.2	20.9	14.3
1965	100.0	63.2	36.8	21.2	15.6
1974	100.0(*)	71.7	28.8	14.0	14.4
1975	100.0(*)	69.5	30.4	14.8	15.6

(*) Sic. Total does not equal row sum in original.

Table 100: Principal industrial goods received in the country by the trading branch

	Unit	1972	1973	1974	1975
Fresh salt water fish	Thou. tonnes	...	14.3	13.8	13.2
Salt	"	...	123.4	198.8	194.8
Fish sauces	M. litres	30.9	41.0	53.6	52.4
Sugar of all types	Thou. tonnes	18.6	18.4	10.2	13.2
Tobacco cigarettes	M. packets	...	132.3	285.1	259.3
Cloth of all type	M. meters	71.0	71.8	76.8	80.0
Silk	"	4.5	5.0	5.6	8.7
Mosquito netting and crepe	"	19.4	23.8	43.4	50.5
Ready-made clothing	M. items	...	9.1	31.9	34.1
Rush mats	"	2.4	4.8	6.4	6.6

Table 100: Cont.

Bowls and plates of porcelain (su)	"	48.7	44.7	29.3	66.0
Laundry soap	Thou. tonnes	5.8	7.5	7.4	8.4
Matches	M. boxes	176.4	155.7	164.8	167.2
Writing paper	Thou. tonnes	...	4.5	9.9	8.8
Bicycles	Thou. items	...	70.6	30.0	60.7
Firewood	Thou. cu. m.	234.7	460.7	208.8	176.7
Than qua bang	Thou. tonnes	...	190.9	164.0	237.1
Coal	"	...	747.5	80.0	108.3
Round wood	Thou. cu. m.	...	95.5	16.4	21.0
Sawn wood	"	62.3	28.0	7.5	8.1
Bamboo tre	M. plants	12.5	16.8	11.4	10.1
Bamboo nua	"	56.1	52.4	21.8	13.6
Palm cabbage	M. tau	25.1	30.5	22.3	16.3
Bricks	M. units	343.5	441.9	545.8	555.6
Tiles	"	36.1	59.4	95.3	80.7
Cement	Thou. tonnes	...	126.8	19.4	44.3

Table 101: Principal agricultural goods received in the country by the trading branch

	Unit	1960	1965	1974	1975
Staples (paddy equ.'t)	Thou. tonnes	867.5	1105.5	1008.8	787.1
Of which Rice	"	833.9	1048.1	979.2	766.1
Pork (live-weight)	"	44.7	74.1	88.4	106.4
Beef (Oxen and Buffalo, live-weight)	"	22.8	16.8	9.8	11.9
Chickens, ducks, wild geese and geese	"	2.8	2.5	3.7	5.0
Chicken and duck eggs	M. eggs	-	25.0	107.0	94.4
Fresh fresh-water fish	Thou. tonnes	2.0	3.5	3.8	4.1
Fresh vegetables	"	-	94.3	125.8	128.8
Soybeans	"	3.8	3.0	1.2	1.5
Beans of all types	"	1.4	4.4	2.7	1.8
Peanuts	"	9.9	23.8	20.1	17.2
Sesame seeds	"	1.1	0.5	0.4	0.3
Pure tea	"	1.7	2.4	3.3	3.5
Of which received by domestic trading branch	"	1.7	1.2	0.4	0.6
Tobacco (dry leaves)	"	0.7	4.1	6.8	5.8
Of which received by domestic trading branch	"	0.7	4.1	0.4	0.6
Water-pipe tobacco	"	1.5	2.0	0.8	0.7
Hemp	"	0.3	0.3	0.1	0.1
Cottonseed	"	2.4	1.6	0.1	0.1
Jute (spathes - be)	"	11.1	18.1	25.6	22.5
Rushes	"	11.4	22.7	37.8	41.2

Table 102: Total retail sales of social trade divided
according to economic branch (m. dong)

	Total retail sales	Of which: Organised market Total	Of which: State	P'se/sale coops.	Unorganised market Total	Of which Private trade
1960	1634.6	1309.4	747.1	314.4	325.2	128.1
1961	1752.9	1433.1	929.4	312.5	319.8	113.1
1962	1930.6	1569.6	1041.5	328.4	361.0	111.5
1963	1832.7	1534.1	1302.5	110.2	298.6	126.6
1964	2189.1	1811.5	1532.8	222.5	377.6	216.7
1965	2434.1	2071.0	1675.0	333.0	363.1	205.0
1966	2647.4	2263.4	1749.3	479.1	384.0	208.0
1967	2857.5	2412.5	1874.4	528.1	445.0	254.0
1968	3051.2	2595.2	2039.9	547.3	456.0	255.0
1969	3335.5	2870.6	2292.6	569.5	464.9	258.2
1970	4043.7	2954.8	2249.2	570.0	1088.9	594.3
1971	4386.5	3262.1	2529.7	569.1	1124.4	596.4
1972	4587.0	3247.0	2496.0	641.8	1340.0	719.2
1973	5153.5	3657.7	2824.4	671.1	1495.8	826.6
1974	5194.0	3707.5	2873.5	711.3	1486.5	898.7
1975	5358.3	4016.7	3179.8	741.1	1341.6	883.4

Table 103: Indicators of the development and structure of
total retail sales of the social trading sector divided
according to economic branch(*)

	Total retail sales	Of which: Organised market Total	Of which: State	P'se/sale coops.	Unorganised market Total	Of which Private trade
		(index numbers of development - 1960 = 100)				
1961	107.2	109.4	124.4	99.4	98.3	88.3
1965	148.9	158.2	224.2	105.9	111.7	160.0
1966	162.0	172.9	234.1	152.4	118.1	162.4
1967	174.8	184.2	250.9	168.0	136.8	198.3
1968	186.7	198.2	273.0	174.1	140.2	199.1
1969	204.1	219.2	306.9	181.1	143.0	201.6
1970	247.4	225.7	301.1	181.3	334.8	463.9
1971	268.4	249.1	338.6	181.0	345.8	465.6
1972	280.1	248.0	334.1	204.1	412.0	561.4
1973	315.3	279.3	378.0	213.4	460.0	645.3
1974	317.7	283.	384.6	226.2	457.1	701.6
1975	327.8	306.8	425.6	235.7	412.5	689.6

(*) 1962-64 inclusive omitted in original.

Table 103: Cont.

(structure - percentages)

1960	100.0	80.1	45.7	19.2	19.9	7.8
1964	100.0	82.7	70.0	10.1	17.3	9.9
1965	100.0	85.1	68.8	13.7	14.9	8.4
1974	100.0	71.3	55.7	15.4	28.7	17.3
1975	100.0	75.0	59.6	13.8	25.0	16.4

Table 104: Total sales of the pure trading sector divided according to economic branch (m. dong)

	Total retail sales	Of which: Organised market Total	Of which: State	P'se/sale coops.	Unorganised market (private trade)
1960	1388.5	1260.4	772.1	310.4	128.1
1961	1463.1	1350.0	887.0	304.5	113.1
1962	1563.2	1451.7	975.0	319.0	111.5
1963	1478.1	1351.5	1169.4	97.5	126.6
1964	1841.2(*)	1624.4	1386.7	208.5	216.7
1965	2099.8	1894.8	1533.8	315.0	205.0
1966	2316.8	2108.8	1621.7	464.1	208.0
1967	2497.0	2243.0	1724.4	516.1	254.0
1968	2694.1	2439.1	1896.8	539.3	255.0
1969	2987.8	2729.6	2166.5	559.6	258.2
1970	3210.9	2616.6	2056.9	556.3	594.3
1971	3451.5	2855.1	2301.0	548.6	596.4
1972	3621.7	2902.5	2280.9	618.6	719.2
1973	4025.1	3198.5	2547.0	645.7	826.6
1974	4179.9	3281.3	2594.4	681.4	898.6
1975	4502.7	3619.3	2893.0	716.3	883.4

(*) Sic. Total does not equal row sum in original.

Table 105: Indicators of the development and structure of total retail sales of the pure trading sector divided according to economic branch(*)

	Total retail sales	Of which: Organised market Total	Of which: State	P'se/sale coops.	Unorganised market
(index numbers of development - 1961 = 100)					
1961	105.4	107.1	122.8	98.1	88.3
1965	151.2	150.3	212.4	101.5	160.0
1966	166.9	167.3	224.6	149.5	162.4
1967	179.8	178.0	238.8	166.3	198.3
1968	194.0	193.5	262.7	173.7	199.2
1969	215.2	216.6	300.0	180.3	201.6
1970	231.2	207.8	284.8	179.2	463.9
1971	248.6	226.5	318.7	176.7	465.6
1972	260.8	230.3	315.9	199.3	561.4
1973	289.9	253.8	352.8	208.0	645.3
1974	301.1	260.3	359.3	219.5	701.5
1975	324.3	287.2	400.6	230.8	689.6
(structure - percentages)					
1960	100.0	90.8	40.8	21.3	9.2
1964	100.0	88.2	75.3	11.3	11.8
1965	100.0	90.2	73.0	15.0	9.8
1974	100.0	78.5	62.0	16.3	21.5
1975	100.0	80.3	66.2	15.9	19.7

(*) 1962-64 inclusive omitted from original.

Table 106: Total retail sales of the public restaurant sector divided according to economic branch (m. dong)

	Total retail sales	Of which: Organised market Total	Of which: State	P'se/sale coops.	Unorganised market (private restaurants)
1960	101.5	41.5	17.5	4.0	60.0
1961	112.5	73.5	32.8	8.4	39.0
1962	168.3	101.3	49.9	9.4	67.0
1963	188.1	118.1	68.6	12.7	70.0
1964	172.6	121.6	80.6	14.0	51.0
1965	153.2	110.2	75.2	18.0	43.0
1966	142.6	104.6	77.6	15.0	38.0
1967	150.5	115.5	96.0	12.0	35.0

Table 106: Cont.

1968	146.1	106.1	93.1	8.0	40.0
1969	150.0	112.9	97.9	10.0	37.1
1970	335.1	114.8	98.9	13.8	220.3
1971	386.7	145.3	118.7	20.5	241.4
1972	475.3	140.9	116.4	23.2	334.4
1973	525.5	169.3	141.8	25.4	356.2
1974	503.1	188.9	156.5	29.8	314.2
1975	414.1	220.7	193.2	24.9	193.4

Table 107: Indicators of the development and structure of
total retail sales of the public restaurant sector divided
according to economic branch(*)

	Total retail sales	Of which: Organised market Total	Of which: State	P'se/sale coops	Unorganised market
(index numbers - 1960 = 100)					
1960	110.8	117.1	187.4	210.0	65.0
1965	150.9	265.5	429.7	450.0	71.7
1966	140.5	252.0	443.4	375.9	63.6
1967	148.3	278.3	578.6	300.0	58.3
1968	143.9	255.7	532.0	200.0	66.7
1969	147.8	272.0	559.1	250.0	61.8
1970	330.1	276.6	565.1	345.0	367.2
1971	381.0	350.1	678.3	512.5	402.3
1972	468.3	339.5	665.1	580.0	557.3
1973	517.7	408.0	810.3	635.0	593.7
1974	495.7	455.2	594.3	745.0	523.7
1975	403.0	531.8	x11	622.5	322.3
(structure - percentages)					
1960	100.0	40.9	17.2	3.9	59.1
1964	100.0	70.5	46.7	8.1	29.5
1965	100.0	71.9	49.1	11.7	29.1
1974	100.0	37.5	31.1	5.9	62.5
1975	100.0	53.3	46.7	6.0	46.2

(*) 1961-64 inclusive omitted from original.

Table 108: A number of principle commodities sold by State trading organisations and purchase/sale cooperatives

	Units	1960	1965	1974	1975
Staples (paddy equi.)	Thou.tonnes	468.1	683.5	1277.9	1193.1
Salt	"	53.8	145.3	147.0	147.8
Meat	"	26.5	43.4	58.8	70.0
Fish sauces	M. litres	15.0	36.4	55.7	56.7
Sugar, all types	Thou. tonnes	8.5	21.1	43.8	44.1
Tobacco cigarettes	M. packets	37.4	97.7	258.1	243.2
Water-pipe tobacco	Thou. tonnes	0.8	2.1	1.8	2.1
Cloth, all types	M. meters	55.1	83.2	132.0	123.4
Gauze, mosquito nets	"	10.1	16.4	30.7	29.5
Silk	"	2.8	4.0	6.9	8.4
Porcelain bowls & plates	M. items	30.7	39.8	35.3	50.6
Rush mats	"	3.6	4.2	5.9	5.6
Laundry soap	Thou. tonnes	2.1	6.8	14.7	17.3
Matches	M. boxes	82.9	127.5	152.8	160.0
Writing paper and student exercise books	Thou. tonnes	2.2	4.8	8.8	9.0
Bicycles	Thou. items	45.8	144.6	89.0	92.2
Firewood	Thou. cu m.	115.5	317.0	264.2	210.3
Coal (inc. qua bang coal)	Thou. tonnes	95.3	313.9	358.2	535.6
Non-cooking oil (1.)	"	8.3	20.5	54.6	62.5
Sawn wood	Thou. cu. m.	12.1	22.9	2.9	6.1
Bamboo (tre)	M. plants	5.2	8.9	9.9	9.2
Bamboo (nua)	"	29.2	36.8	24.0	15.8
Roofing leaves	M. leaves (tau)	7.5	20.7	17.8	21.9
Bricks	M. items	49.4	319.0	411.9	423.3
Tiles	"	6.9	35.2	69.8	72.5
Cement	Thou. tonnes	12.4	70.9	40.8	83.2

(1.) Dau hoa.

Table 109: Price indices for commodity retail sales of the social trading branch (1964=100)

	General Index	Of which: Staples and food	Other consumption items	Agricultural means of production
1965	99.8	99.4	100.0	100.0
1973	111.7	116.9	104.8	107.9
1974	120.4	134.0	106.3	110.3
1975	119.5	131.4	105.0	113.0

Table 109: Cont.

(previous year = 100)

1973	102.8	104.6	99.9	103.7
1974	105.3	108.8	101.3	101.7
1975	101.7	101.9	100.1	104.9

Table 110: Price indices for retail sales of State trade (1964=100)

	General Index	Of which: Staples and food	Other consumption items	Agricultural means of production
1965	98.5	98.6	99.0	99.7
1973	99.6	100.6	99.6	92.7
1974	100.2	100.7	100.6	92.7
1975	101.1	103.5	100.1	92.7

(previous year = 100)

1973	100.0	100.7	99.4	99.8
1974	100.5	100.0	101.1	100.0
1975	100.9	102.8	99.3	100.0

Table 111: Price indices of commodities in the unorganised market (1964=100)

	General Index	Of which: Staples and food	Other consumption items	Agricultural means of production
1965	101.4	100.4	109.5	100.1
1973	149.9	144.2	166.3	167.7
1974	202.6	209.0	174.0	188.2
1975	189.0	185.5	168.9	217.9

(previous year = 100)

1973	108.9	199.0	102.6	113.2
1974	116.2	120.1	102.0	105.7
1975	103.3	100.8	105.7	117.4

The Limits of National Liberation

Table 112: Total value of exports (a.) (m. dong)

	1960	1974	1975
TOTAL	232.5	412.4	486.7
Industrial goods	111.4	309.7	365.5
Artisanal (thu) industrial goods	57.2	69.7	79.8
Unprocessed agricultural output	63.9	33.0	41.4

(indicators of development - index numbers)

	1960	1974	1975
TOTAL	100.0	177.4	209.3
Industrial goods	100.0	278.0	328.1
Artisanal (thu) industrial goods	100.0	121.8	139.5
Unprocessed agricultural output	100.0	51.6	64.8

(structure - percentages)

	1960	1974	1975
TOTAL	100.0	100.0	100.0
Industrial goods	47.9	75.1	75.1
Artisanal (thu) industrial goods	24.6	16.9	16.4
Unprocessed agricultural output	27.5	8.0	8.5

(a.) In each group of industrial goods, artisanal industry includes agricultural and forestry products that have been industrially processed.

Table 113: Total value of imports (m. dong (a.))

	1960	1974	1975
TOTAL VALUE	380.6	1192.9	1455.1
Means of production	331.1	808.8	1014.2
Of which:			
Complete equipment	97.8	202.8	264.8
Machines and means of transport	56.7	173.0	148.4
Tools and spares	46.4	73.9	85.9
Raw materials, energy and materials	130.2	359.1	515.1
Means of consumption	49.5	384.1	440.9

Table 113: Cont.

(index numbers of development)

	1960	1974	1975
TOTAL VALUE	100.0	313.4	382.3
Means of production	100.0	244.3	306.3
Of which:			
Complete equipment	100.0	207.4	270.8
Machines and means of transport	100.0	304.9	259.8
Tools and spares	100.0	156.7	184.9
Raw materials, energy and materials	100.0	275.8	395.6
Means of consumption	100.0	776.0	890.7

(structure - percentages)

	1960	1974	1975
TOTAL VALUE	100.0	100.0	100.0
Means of production	87.0	67.8	69.7
Of which:			
Complete equipment	25.7	17.0	18.2
Machines and means of transport	14.9	14.5	10.2
Tools and spares	12.2	6.2	5.9
Raw materials, energy and materials	34.2	30.1	35.4
Means of consumption	13.0	32.2	30.3

(a.) See footnote (a.) to Table 112.

TRANSPORT AND COMMUNICATIONS

Table 114: Some general indicators of the development of
transport and communications

	Length of railways (a.) km.	Length of roads (b.) km.	Volume of merchandise carried m. tonne-km.	Passenger traffic m. person-km.
1960	778	9058	1192.9	1023.1
1961	778	9058	1259.1	1341.8
1962	778	10361	1321.7	1584.9
1963	778	10411	1601.4	1795.9
1964	927	10495	1722.6	1753.0
1965	927	12354	1569.1	1409.5
1966	927	27088	1413.1	666.0
1967	927	27872	1105.5	503.3
1968	987	34294	1286.4	739.2
1969	987	38661	1451.2	1716.4
1970	987	40527	1965.1	2303.3
1971	987	43375	2052.6	2567.4
1972	987	45604	1526.9	149960
1973	987	47003	2014.5	2326.6
1974	1157	51109	2874.8	3243.4
1975	1157	62779	3874.4	3587.4

(a.) Year-end; active (van doanh) lines only.
(b.) Year-end; from 1965 Type A rural roads also included.

Table 115: Average registered number of employees (1.) in the
transport branch divided according to level of management
(thousands)

	Total	Of which: Centrally managed: Total	Ministry of Transport	Regionally managed
1960	15.7	...	14.9	...
1961	29.4	19.9	17.3	9.5
1962	36.3	22.9	18.2	13.4
1963	48.4	30.3	19.4	18.1
1964	48.3	30.6	20.8	17.7
1965	65.1	34.3	24.0	30.8
1966	86.0	43.2	37.7	42.8
1967	108.0	55.8	49.2	52.2
1968	119.7	62.3	54.7	57.4
1969	115.2	60.4	55.9	54.8
1970	96.8	51.6	46.4	45.2
1971	84.8	44.1	41.2	40.7
1972	87.6	48.2	44.1	39.4
1973	91.4	52.1	47.7	39.3
1974	89.5	52.9	49.1	36.6
1975	89.3	52.2	...	37.1

Table 116: Surface communications

	1960	1965	1974	1975
		(km.)		
Railways				
Transportation	778	927	1157	1157
1 m. track	778	927	871	871
'Frame' track - 1 m. & 1.435 m.	-	-	241	241
1.435 m. track	-	-	45	45
Specialised track and track in stations	194	...	363	363
Tip-cart track	70	70	104	104
Roads	9058	12354	51109	62779
River routes	5442	...	6000	6000
Sea routes	937	937	937	937

(surface communications density - km. per thousand sq. km. of
land area)

	1960	1965	1974	1975
Density of transport railways	4.9	5.7	7.3	7.3
Density of roads	57.2	71.2	323.3	396.3

Table 117: Types of roads (km.)

	Total	Of which: A. Managed by the State Total	Of which: Tarmac	Stone	Minor (1.)	B. Type A rural roads
1960	9058	4747	747	1550	2450	–
1964	10495	5375	849	1881	2645	–
1965	12354	11282(*)	928	1823	2794	1072
1966	27088	11888	1200	2658	3152	15200
1967	27872	12672	1295	2766	3566	15200
1968	34294	13746	1528	3166	3063	20548
1969	38661	14319	2028	3734	6653	24342
1970	40527(*)	14319	2028	3734	6653	36208
1971	43375	15101	2878	4166	5367	28274
1972	45604	15140	3175	3778	5567	30464
1973	47003	15129	3312	3527	5665	31874
1974	51109(*)	19235	4296	8404	6515	35118
1975	62779	21687	4780	6358	7131	41092

1. Duong cap phoi.
(*) Sic. Total does not equal row sum in original.

Table 118: Means of transport (a.) (units)

	1960	1965	1974	1975
Railways:				
Locomotives	88	149	225	245
Freight rolling stock	1181	2322	3660	3625
Passenger rolling stock	199	312	564	641
Roads:				
Freight carriers	2769	8464	12606	12970
Trailers (Ro mooc)	179	1064	2778	3107
Passenger carriers	753	626	1498	1640
Rivers:				
Boats (1.), freight transports, tugs	74	184	560	604
Boats (1.), passenger transports	22	26	30	33
Barges	154	500	2042	2140
Boats (2.)	7223	5369	4932	...
Seaways:				
Tugs	2	6	6	6
Passenger and freight transports	5	5	211	221
Barges	4	15	10	10
Primitive means of transport:				
Buffalo and ox carts	1903	3709	6899	6321
Horse-drawn vehicles	874	492	736	931

(a.) Excluding military. 1. Ca no. 2. Thuyen.

Table 119: Volume of merchandise transported (thousand tonnes)

	1960	1965	1974	1975
TOTAL	12995	19849	31570	32075
Divided as follows:	(*)		(*)	
- According to economic branch:				
State and JSP	8123	12665	23746	24149
Cooperatives	1109	6407	7824	7926
Individual	3764	777	-	-
- According to transport sector:				
Railways	2915	4098	5840	5256
Roads	5008	9060	17202	17362
Rivers	4834	6416	7680	8528
Seaways	239	275	848	929
- According to level of management:				
Central	4673	7390	12832	12743
Regional	8323	12459	18738	19332
- According to scale:				
Inter-provincial	6752	10332	16166	16468
Intra-provincial	6244	9517	15404	15607
- According to technology:				
Mechanised	11887	11987	22746	24149
Primitive	1109	7862	7824	7926

(*) Sic. Total does not equal column sum in original.

Table 120: Indicators of the development of the volume of
merchandise transported (1960 = 100)

	1965	1974	1975
TOTAL	152.7	242.9	246.3
According to economic branch:			
State and JSP	155.9	292.3	297.3
Cooperatives	577.7	705.5	714.7
According to transport sector:			
Railways	140.6	200.3	180.3
Roads	180.9	343.4	346.7
Rivers	132.7	158.8	176.4
Seaways	115.1	354.8	388.7
According to level of management:			
Central	158.1	274.5	272.7
Regional	149.7	225.1	232.3
According to scale:			
Inter-provincial	153.0	239.4	243.9
Intra-provincial	152.4	246.7	249.9
According to technology:			
Mechanised	100.8	199.7	203.2
Primitive	708.9	705.5	714.7

Table 121: The structure of the volume of merchandise transported (percentage shares)

	1960	1965	1974	1975
TOTAL	100.0	100.0	100.0	100.0
Divided as follows:				
- According to economic branch:				
State and JSP	62.5	63.8	75.3	75.3
Cooperatives	8.5	32.3	24.7	24.7
Individual	29.0	3.9	-	-
- According to transport sector:				
Railways	22.4	20.6	18.3	16.4
Roads	38.5	45.7	54.4	54.1
Rivers	37.2	32.3	24.0	26.6
Seaways	1.9	1.4	3.3	2.9
- According to level of management:				
Central	36.0	37.2	40.6	39.7
Regional	64.0	62.8	59.4	60.3
- According to scale:				
Inter-provincial	52.0	52.1	51.2	51.3
Intra-provincial	48.0	47.9	48.8	48.7
- According to technology:				
Mechanised	91.5	60.4	75.2	75.3
Primitive	8.5	39.6	24.8	24.8

Table 122: Merchandise transport volume (m. tonne-km.)

	1960	1965	1974	1975
TOTAL	1192.9	1569.1	2874.8	3874.4
Divided as follows:	(*)			(*)
- According to economic branch:				
State and JSP	960.8	1307.2	2645.5	3629.4
Cooperatives	71.0	235.2	229.3	245.0
Individual	161.1	26.7	-	-
- According to transport sector:				
Railways	704.3	721.8	864.7	843.6
Roads	107.5	197.2	560.5	576.9
Rivers	313.5	550.4	879.8	1054.6
Seaways	67.6	99.7	569.8	1399.8
- According to level of management:				
Central	878.1	1070.1	2055.5	2985.6
Regional	314.8	499.0	819.3	888.8
- According to scale:				
Inter-provincial	978.1	1337.4	2485.9	3474.1
Intra-provincial	214.8	231.7	388.9	400.3
- According to technology:				
Mechanised	283.9	1270.4	2645.5	3629.4
Primitive	209.0	298.7	229.3	245.0

(*) Sic. Total does not equal column sum in original.

Table 123: Indicators of the volume of merchandise transport activity (1960=100)

	1965	1974	1975
TOTAL	131.5	240.9	324.8
According to economic branch:			
State and JSP	136.1	275.2	377.8
Cooperatives	331.2	322.9	345.1
According to transport sector:			
Railways	102.5	120.2	119.8
Roads	183.4	521.3	536.7
Rivers	175.6	280.6	336.4
Seaways	147.5	842.8	x20.7
According to level of management:			
Central	121.9	234.0	340.0
Regional	158.5	259.9	282.3
According to scale:			
Inter-provincial	136.7	254.1	355.2
Intra-provincial	107.9	180.6	186.4
According to technology:			
Mechanised	129.1	268.7	368.9
Primitive	142.9	109.7	117.2

Table 124: The structure of the volume of merchandise transport activity (percentage shares)

	1960	1965	1974	1975
TOTAL	100.0	100.0	100.0	100.0
Divided as follows:				
- According to economic branch:				
State and JSP	80.5	83.3	92.1	93.7
Cooperatives	6.0	15.0	7.9	6.3
Individual	13.5	1.7	-	-
- According to transport sector:				
Railways	59.0	46.0	30.1	21.8
Roads	9.0	12.6	19.5	14.9
Rivers	26.3	35.1	30.6	27.2
Seaways	5.7	6.3	19.8	36.1
- According to level of management:				
Central	73.6	68.2	71.5	77.1
Regional	26.4	31.8	28.5	22.9
- According to scale:				
Inter-provincial	82.0	85.2	86.4	89.7
Intra-provincial	18.0	14.8	13.6	10.3
- According to technology:				
Mechanised	82.5	81.0	92.0	93.6
Primitive	17.5	19.0	8.0	6.4

Table 125: Passengers carried (million)

	Total	Of which: Railways	Roads	Rivers	Seaways
1960	21.4	13.8	7.2	0.4	–
1961	29.4	18.6	10.1	0.7	–
1962	37.7	22.5	14.2	1.0	–
1963	42.1	24.0	16.9	1.2	–
1964	40.3	22.0	17.1	1.2	–
1965	34.0	15.7	17.3	1.0	–
1966	19.7	8.9	10.1	0.7	–
1967	8.9	3.7	4.7	0.5	–
1968	16.6	5.0	11.2	0.4	–
1969	31.0	13.3	16.7	1.0	–
1970	45.3	19.8	24.5	1.0	–
1971	54.4	20.1	33.1	1.2	–
1972	41.6	8.3	32.8	0.5	–
1973	49.2	14.5	33.6	1.1	–
1974	71.4	23.6	46.1	1.7	–
1975	76.2	25.2	49.3	1.7	0.02

Table 126: Indicators of the development and structure of passenger transport

	Total	Of which: Railways	Roads	Rivers
		(index numbers of development)		
1960	100.0	100.0	100.0	100.0
1961	137.4	134.8	140.3	175.0
1962	176.2	163.0	197.2	250.0
1963	196.7	173.9	234.7	300.0
1964	188.3	159.4	237.5	300.0
1965	158.3	113.8	240.3	250.0
1966	92.1	64.5	140.2	175.0
1967	41.6	26.8	65.3	125.0
1968	77.6	36.2	155.5	100.0
1969	144.8	96.4	231.9	250.0
1970	211.6	143.4	340.2	250.0
1971	254.2	145.7	459.7	300.0
1972	191.4	26.9	455.5	125.0
1973	229.9	105.1	466.7	275.0
1974	333.6	171.0	640.2	425.0
1975	356.1	182.6	684.7	425.0

Table 126: Cont.

(structure - percentages)

1960	100.0	64.5	33.6	1.9
1964	100.0	54.6	42.4	3.0
1965	100.0	46.2	50.9	2.9
1974	100.0	33.1	64.5	2.4
1975	100.0	33.1	64.8	2.1

Table 127: The volume of passenger transport activity (m. passenger-km.)

	Total	Of which: Railways	Roads	Rivers	Seaways
1960	1023.1(*)	622.9	372.9	27.5	-
1961	1341.8	832.1	468.9	40.8	-
1962	1584.9	1032.5	503.2	49.2	-
1963	1795.9	1155.2	582.9	57.8	-
1964	1753.0	1139.9	551.8	61.3	-
1965	1409.5	901.2	448.8	59.5	-
1966	940.0	534.4	357.3	48.3	-
1967	505.3	218.8	266.1	20.4	-
1968	739.2	354.9	366.2	18.1	-
1969	1716.4	1068.7	580.6	67.1	-
1970	2303.3	1466.2	779.6	57.5	-
1971	2567.4	1460.4	1038.4	68.6	-
1972	1499.6	583.6	887.2	28.8	-
1973	2326.6(*)	1168.5	1078.6	70.5	-
1974	3243.7	1825.5	1371.6	46.6	-
1975	3587.4	1987.9	1458.3	99.9	41.3

(*) Sic. Total does not equal row sum in original.

Table 128: Indicators of the development and structure of the volume of passenger transport activity

	Total	Of which: Railways	Roads	Rivers
		(index numbers of development)		
1960	100.0	100.0	100.0	100.0
1961	131.2	133.6	125.8	148.4
1962	154.9	165.8	135.0	178.9
1963	175.5	185.5	156.4	210.2
1964	171.3	183.0	148.1	222.9
1965	137.8	144.7	120.4	216.4

Table 128: Cont.

Year				
1966	91.9	85.8	95.8	175.6
1967	49.4	35.1	71.4	74.2
1968	72.3	57.5	98.3	65.8
1969	167.8	171.6	155.8	244.0
1970	225.1	235.4	209.2	207.6
1971	250.9	234.5	278.6	249.5
1972	146.6	93.7	238.0	104.7
1973	227.4	187.5	291.8	256.3
1974	317.8	293.0	368.0	169.4
1975	350.6	319.1	391.2	363.2

(structure - percentages)

Year				
1960	100.0	60.9	36.4	2.7
1964	100.0	65.0	31.5	3.5
1965	100.0	63.9	31.9	4.2
1974	100.0	56.2	42.2	1.6
1975	100.0(*)	55.4	40.7	2.8

(*) Sic. Total does not equal row sum in original.

Table 129: Some general indicators of the development of the postal and telegraphic services

	Average number of registered employees (thousands)	Length of telephone wire (thousand km.)	Receipts (m. dong)
1960	4.8	16.7	14.8
1961	5.3	22.3	17.9
1962	7.1	25.2	19.8
1963	7.5	27.1	22.2
1964	8.3	32.0	25.3
1965	10.4	36.6	27.4
1966	15.0	41.0	26.0
1967	19.0	46.5	28.6
1968	19.7	50.4	29.6
1969	19.1	49.7	28.3
1970	17.5	46.1	27.9
1971	14.5	48.9	29.4
1972	15.1	52.2	30.0
1973	16.1	48.6	31.3
1974	16.3	51.4	35.3
1975	16.9	53.1	42.9

Table 130: Telephone lines and equipment

	Length of telephone wire (thou. km. Total	Of which: Trunk & inter- province	Intra- province	Internal (1.)	Exch- anges (units)	Telephone equipment: Telephones Total (thousands)	Direct dial
1960	16.7	4.6	7.0	5.1	791	9.3	2.5
1964	32.0	5.5	11.6	14.9	1217	18.7	4.2
1965	36.6	6.2	12.9	17.5	1262	16.9	...
1966	41.0	6.0	14.4	20.6	1479	18.5	4.3
1967	46.5	6.2	16.7	23.6	1677	18.1	4.0
1968	50.4	6.0	16.0	28.4	1605	18.6	4.0
1969	49.7	6.9	17.7	25.1	1547	18.3	4.3
1970	46.1	9.4	15.9	20.8	1540	19.3	...
1971	48.9	9.1	17.2	22.6	1722	21.1	4.1
1972	52.2	10.4	18.4	23.4	1840	22.2	4.5
1973	48.6(*)	9.5	19.1	21.0	1884	23.3	5.4
1974	51.4	10.1	19.0	22.3	2131	27.0	5.9
1975	53.1	10.3	18.9	23.9	2168	26.7	6.0

1. Duong noi bat.
(*) Sic. Total does not equal row sum in original.

Table 131: Output and receipts of the postal and telegraphic services

		1960	1965	1974	1975
POSTS					
Mail	– million items	31.6	87.4	99.8	117.3
Parcels	– thousand items	32.6	204.4	374.4	497.8
Postal and telegraphic money transfers	– thousand items	356.0	909.0	476.5	490.4
Distribution of newspapers and journals	– thousand items	53.0	74.2	158.2	187.4
TELECOMMUNICATIONS					
Telegrams	– million	21.0	33.4	50.8	67.7
Long-distance telephones	– thousand units	3936	5394	6603	6581
: Of which – offical calls		3877	5303	6565	6540
Receipts	– m. dong	14.8	27.4	35.3	42.9
: Of which					
Posts		5.0	11.0	11.4	15.5
Telecommunications		8.4	15.0	21.6	24.7
Distribution of newspapers and journals		1.4	1.4	2.3	2.7

225

LIVING STANDARDS, CULTURE, EDUCATION AND HEALTH SERVICES

A. LIVING STANDARDS

Table 132: Indicators of the development of the average monthly pay (luong) of employees in different economic branches

(1960 = 100)

	1965	1971	1973	1974	1975
TOTAL	99.2	102.6	106.8	110.5	113.6
Material production:	98.8	104.4	110.0	114.6	118.1
Of which:					
Industry	100.1	102.0	107.6	111.8	117.3
Construction	98.4	108.3	116.8	112.6	125.0
Agriculture and forestry	104.9	112.6	115.9	119.4	121.3
Trade and material supply	102.6	107.4	110.4	113.2	115.2
Transport & communications	79.4	84.4	90.6	95.7	97.7
Non-material production:	100.9	98.4	99.6	101.6	103.8
Of which:					
Public services	78.2	83.2	89.1	92.3	95.0
Credit and State insurance	106.9	109.1	108.6	106.6	113.4
Scientific research, culture, sport and physical training, health and social services	102.0	83.6	98.3	100.2	102.4
State management, Party, collectives	97.6	98.7	100.8	102.8	103.8

Table 133: Indicators of the development and structure of the average per capita income (thu nhap) in employee households (gia dinh)

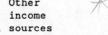

	Total	Of which: Pay of employees	Employee subsidies	Other pay	Scholar- ships, pensions, benefits (1.)	Other income sources
			(index numbers - 1960 = 100)			
1965	101.4	101.6	109.6	129.4	128.5	69.2
1971	112.6	111.0	116.1	51.6	457.7	152.9
1973	116.9	105.5	140.1	72.2	528.5	221.5
1974	124.5	117.1	137.7	30.2	514.3	236.6
1975	128.9	121.1	114.9	23.0	642.8	275.0
			(structure - percentages)			
1965	100.0	78.2	8.4	7.5	0.4	5.5
1971	100.0	76.9	8.2	2.7	1.3	10.9
1973	100.0	70.4	9.3	3.6	1.5	15.2
1974	100.0	73.3	8.6	1.4	1.4	15.3
1975	100.0	73.4	6.9	1.4	1.6	16.7

1. benefits to the infirm and wounded - tien thuong tat.

Table 134: Indicators of the development and structure of average monthly per capita expenses of employee households (gia dinh)

	Total	Of which: Food	Clothes	Purchases of other merchan- dise	Non-merchan- dise expenditure
			(index numbers - 1960 = 100)		
1965	103.2	112.1	89.5	59.2	118.4
1971	123.4	117.2	104.8	104.5	108.4
1973	118.5	118.8	113.3	128.4	103.3
1974	126.9	129.1	118.8	128.5	113.9
1975	132.8	136.7	116.7	125.6	127.3
			(structure - percentages)		
1965	100.0	75.5	6.0	8.6	9.9
1971	100.0	71.7	6.4	13.7	8.2
1973	100.0	69.7	6.6	16.2	7.5
1974	100.0	70.7	6.5	15.1	7.7
1975	100.0	71.5	6.1	14.1	8.3

Table 135: The proportion of total employee household (gia dinh) expenditures supplied by the State (as a percentage for each category)

	Total	Expenditure on: Food	Clothes	Purchases of other merchandise	Non-merchandise expenditure
1960	65.4	62.0	86.0	70.2	75.1
1961	68.1	68.7	88.3	76.8	43.9
1962	70.7	65.5	90.6	83.3	46.9
1963	72.9	68.2	97.9	86.0	75.1
1964	71.7	67.9	96.5	84.8	78.7
1965	76.4	73.4	96.4	86.0	78.4
1966	69.5	67.0	90.4	83.0	58.6
1967	70.2	65.2	92.5	80.2	91.5
1968	64.4	59.7	84.8	71.8	71.4
1969	67.1	63.7	88.3	86.5	70.4
1970	67.3	65.2	93.6	77.4	56.8
1971	69.7	69.2	94.9	82.4	62.6
1972	66.2	62.2	92.6	77.5	51.5
1973	65.6	63.9	91.4	74.9	49.7
1974	64.2	62.0	90.7	73.8	58.7
1975	64.8	63.6	89.4	72.5	56.9

Table 136: Indicators of the cost of living for employees

Base year:	1957	1959	1960	1965	1968	1971	1973	1974

Year of comparison:

	1957	1959	1960	1965	1968	1971	1973	1974
1957	100.00							
1959	93.80	100.00						
1960	98.40	104.80						
1961	111.90	119.20	113.70					
1962	117.40	124.40	118.70					
1963	123.50	131.50	125.40					
1964	123.40	131.40	125.30					
1965	125.20	133.00	127.00	100.00				
1966	134.60	142.97	136.52	107.50				
1967	143.18	152.90	145.23	114.36				
1968	146.44	156.38	148.54	116.97	100.00			
1969	144.53	154.34	146.60	115.44	98.70			
1970	140.80	150.35	142.81	112.46	96.15			
1971	136.57	145.83	138.52	109.08	93.26	100.00		
1972	142.03	151.66	144.06	113.40	96.99	104.00		
1973	146.23	156.15	148.32	116.80	99.86	107.08	100.00	
1974	153.54	163.96	155.73	122.64	104.85	112.43	105.00	100.00
1975	157.75	168.90	160.00	126.00	107.72	115.51	107.88	102.74

Table 137: Indicators of the development and structure of the average monthly income of cooperator households (gia dinh) in agricultural producer cooperatives

	Total	Of which: Income from the coop.	Income from the subsidiary economy	Other income
(indices of development - 1961 = 100)				
1965	113.4	113.6	116.5	97.5
1971	135.6	122.2	143.1	150.0
1973	147.9	127.7	155.5	186.6
1974	162.4	149.3	169.5	177.5
1975	161.4	143.3	173.8	169.2
(structure - percentages)				
1965	100.0	39.2	51.8	9.0
1971	100.0	35.3	53.2	11.5
1973	100.0	33.9	53.0	13.1
1974	100.0	36.0	52.6	11.4
1975	100.0	34.8	54.3	10.9

Table 138: Indicators of the development and structure of average per capita monthly expenses of cooperator households (gia dinh) in agricultural producer cooperatives

	Total	Of which: Food	Cloth-ing	Housing	Culture and Education	Health	Other
(indices of development - 1961 = 100)							
1965	111.7	108.6	88.6	102.2	113.6	80.6	134.9
1971	136.2	135.8	109.0	215.5	127.2	119.3	135.4
1973	154.4	138.9	123.8	264.4	154.5	125.8	216.8
1974	163.9	144.7	121.5	544.4	177.3	129.0	177.3
1975	165.2	142.5	122.7	642.2	263.6	125.8	158.7
(structure - percentages)							
1965	100.0	66.5	6.1	3.6	2.0	2.0	19.8
1971	100.0	68.2	6.2	6.3	1.8	2.4	15.1
1973	100.0	61.5	6.3	6.8	1.9	2.2	21.3
1974	100.0	62.0	6.9	12.4	2.1	2.2	14.4
1975	100.0	59.0	5.8	15.4	3.1	2.1	14.6

Table 139: Average yearly purchases of merchandise and sales of products by cooperators in agricultural producer cooperatives, per family (ho)

	Indices of development (1961 = 100)		Share of the State in the total:	
	Merchandise purchases	Product sales	Merchandise purchases	Product sales
1962	108.6	113.7	44.1	31.3
1963	117.7	117.7	42.8	27.8
1964	121.6	124.3	47.0	33.5
1965	124.6	131.5	50.8	38.8
1966	146.8	140.9	45.6	32.2
1967	164.0	168.3	41.3	27.1
1968	172.1	181.8	44.7	26.3
1969	182.9	174.6	46.8	26.6
1970	183.2	180.8	43.7	27.6
1971	176.4	172.7	47.5	30.7
1972	186.9	192.0	50.3	35.3
1973	201.8	204.3	44.4	32.0
1974	233.3	216.6	43.9	29.4
1975	225.1	228.5	46.3	30.3

B. CULTURE

Table 140: Books published

		1955-75	1960	1965	1975
TOTAL	Books	33893.0	1789.0	1887.0	1510.0
	Million impressions	539.5	29.7	22.4	42.5
Central					
	Books	24964.0	1509.0	1206.0	1054.0
	Million impressions	511.7	29.1	21.1	40.6
Regional					
	Books	8929.0	280.0	681.0	456.0
	Million impressions	27.8	0.6	1.3	1.9

Table 141: Public libraries

	1960	1965	1974	1975
Number of libraries	35	105	200	221
Of which managed centrally	2	2	3	3
Number of books (thousands)	1110.1	2555.7	4041.6	3840.1
Of which managed centrally	582.1	1307.8	857.0	869.0
Number of visits to read books in central libraries (thousands)	294.9	400.8	74.0	131.2

Table 142: Domestic film production

	1955-75	1960	1965	1974	1975
TOTAL					
No. of parts (1.)	1846	103	115	100	85
No. of films (2.)	3275	157	194	225	214
Of which:					
Fiction -					
No. of parts (1.)	66	4	2	7	5
No. of films (2.)	552	26	15	68	47
News films -					
No. of parts (1.)	1018	72	51	38	39
No. of films (2.)	1068	76	53	39	65
Documentaries -					
No. of parts (1.)	704	26	58	49	36
No. of films (2.)	1580	54	121	111	96
Cartoons -					
No. of parts (1.)	58	1	4	6	5
No. of films (2.)	75	1	5	7	6

1. So bo. 2. So cuon.

Table 143: Cinematography

	1960	1965	1974	1975
Cinematographic units (end-year)				
Total	240	344	505	516
Mobile teams	190	283	436	444
Fields (bai)	8	13	17	18
Theatres	42	48	52	54
Filmshows (thousands)	74.0	106.6	164.4	171.1
Audience visits (millions)	56.2	66.5	112.8	120.1

Table 144: Theatrical Art

	1960	1965	1974	1975
Specialised units	54	66	82	84
Of which - managed centrally	10	11	16	16
Activities of centrally managed units				
Performances	1414	1263	2492	1501
Audience (thousands)	3521	1628	4356	4187

C. EDUCATION

Table 145: Student and pupil numbers

	Total	Primary School	General School	Supplementary Schools	Middle and special Schools	Tertiary sector students
1959/60	3723.9	900.0	1522.3	1275.4	18.1	8.1
1960/61	4536.7	795.0	1899.6	1794.7	30.7	16.7
1961/62	4801.2	777.1	2268.9	1677.3	56.6	21.3
1962/63	4724.4	777.0	2571.0	1281.1	69.6	25.7
1963/64	4556.9	787.0	2599.7	1084.6	57.7	27.9
1964/65	4587.1	835.4	2673.9	1005.9	42.6	29.3
1965/66	4968.8	809.9	2934.9	1129.8	60.0	34.2
1966/67	5622.5	958.1	3325.8	1188.3	101.9	48.4
1967/68	6160.2	1087.9	3703.8	1191.8	118.5	58.2
1968/69	6513.2	1137.5	4100.0	1065.9	138.4	71.4
1969/70	6713.0	1251.4	4359.7	901.4	124.8	75.7
1970/71	6481.3	1208.8	4568.7	548.1	85.8	69.9
1971/72	6170.6	1058.0	4585.6	390.7	74.3	62.0
1972/73	6118.7	940.7	4680.5	386.1	57.6	53.8
1973/74	6287.2	876.7	4965.1	329.8	61.4	54.2
1974/75	6630.9	908.5	5151.5	445.6	69.8	55.5
1975/76	6796.9	908.6	5307.4	436.3	83.5	61.1

Table 146: Numbers studying per 10,000 head of population

	1960-61	1965-66	1974-75	1975-76
TOTAL	2818	2667	2769	2769
General schools	1180	1575	2151	2162
Tertiary and middle specialised schools	29	51	52	59

Table 147: The general schools - schools, classes, teachers and pupils according to level

	1960-61	1965-66	1971-72	1973-74	1974-75	1975-76
Schools:						
Total	7066	10294	11080	11563	11653	11832
Of which:						
Level I	6006	7018	6510	6538	6545	6598
Level II	989	2983	4228	4637	4714	4833
Level III	71	293	342	388	394	401

Table 147: Cont.

	1960–61	1965–66	1971–72	1973–74	1974–75	1975–76
Classes:						
Total	41447	71060	115557	124783	129447	132343
Of which:						
Level I	36458	55103	82678	85683	85336	86214
Level II	4455	14235	28795	34443	37922	39680
Level III	534	1722	4084	4657	6189	6449
Teachers:						
Total	44401	80488	141550	161224	168623	176611
Of which:						
Level I	36802	51901	87319	90931	91696	93071
Level II	6526	24207	46079	56781	61859	67809
Level III	1073	4380	8152	13512	15068	15731
Pupils (thousands):						
Total	1899.6	2934.9	4585.6	4965.1	5151.5	5307.4
Of which:						
Level I	1631.7	2180.5	3178.2	3212.4	3205.3	3232.3
Level II	241.8	675.8	1227.3	1498.4	1657.5	1772.8
Level III	26.1	78.6	180.1	254.3	288.7	302.3

Table 148: Specialised middle and tertiary schools in the country – numbers, teachers and students

	1960–61	1965–66	1971–72	1973–74	1974–75	1975–76
Middle Schools:						
Schools, branches and independent classes:	65	154	193	191	195	233
Teachers:	1631	3159	6389	6817	6618	6781
Pupils:	30677	60018	74281	61375	69813	83491
Of which:						
Long-term:	27459	41942	66934	56918	65651	76808
Attending special courses:	3218	5076	3979	3734	2999	3946
Attending in-service courses:	–	13000	3368	723	1163	2737
School-leavers:	6350	15606	13274	14993	20413	18339
Tertiary Education:						
Schools:	10	21	35	40	39	39
Branches and independent classes:	–	3	4	3	3	3
Teachers:	1260	3590	7738	8554	8658	8433

Table 148: Cont.

	1960-61	1965-66	1971-72	1973-74	1974-75	1975-76
Students:	16690	34208	61978	54150	55476	61102
Of which:						
Long-term:	13640	23906	48156	41371	42892	47642
Attending special courses:	650	2400	4078	3443	3002	3493
Attending in-service courses:	2400	7902	9744	9336	9582	9967
Graduates:	2836	7782	13242	11375	7364	9043

Table 149: Teachers and students at tertiary establishments during the academic year 1975-76

Establishment	Teachers Total	Of which: Women	TS(1.) PhTS	Students Total	Of which: Women
General Univ.	584	88	135	3060	662
Polytechnic (2.)	762	96	161	5789	535
School of Construction	398	40	57	2927	318
School of Mines and Geology	375	22	57	1800	122
School of Electr'l Mach'ry	167	12	6	1302	94
School of Light Industry	184	25	19	964	388
School of Roads and Railways	314	38	19	2712	210
School of Waterways	133	13	6	986	123
School of Information and Liason	120	20	7	793	124
School of Architecture	179	27	4	1228	741
School of Agriculture 1.	314	57	35	3005	1108
School of Agriculture 2.	137	33	9	1584	711
School of Agriculture 3.	105	21	5	761	331
School of Forestry	141	11	8	1150	152
School of Marine Products	124	15	2	792	169
School of Economics and Planning	363	55	42	3447	707
Central School of Trade	209	54	10	1680	445
School of Finance and Accounting	179	22	1	1238	540
School of Foreign Trade	103	20	2	748	346
Central School of Banking	29	3	1	644	97
No. 1 Teacher Training School	424	117	8	2245	1175
No. 2 Teacher Training School	510	145	58	3190	1797

Table 149: Cont.

Establishment	Teachers Total	Of which: Women	TS(1.) PhTS	Students Total	Of which: Women
Vinh Teacher Training School	250	45	24	2709	957
Viet Bac Teacher Training School	364	37	33	1959	905
Foreign Language Teacher Training School	336	116	5	2157	1454
Foreign Language School of the Ministry of Higher Education	265	104	6	1097	421
Hanoi Medical School	291	72	24	2383	1190
Hanoi School of Pharmacy	153	63	22	903	488
School of International Relations	...	...	...	60	8
School of Sport and Physical Training	85	17	3	610	87
Higher School of Aesthetics (3.)	40	7	–	147	11
School of Industrial Aesthetics(3.)	20	2	–	161	23
Hanoi School for In-service training	58	11	2	862	...
Hoa Binh Youth School	32	6	1	289	60
Thai Binh Medical School	102	34	2	1012	420
Viet Bac Medical School	154	66	–	1194	444
School of Music	...	...	...	77	12
Haiphong School for In-service training	45	6	1	466	78
Naval School	96	8	1	446	–
Tertiary-level classes in Construction (part-time study)	43	4	3	557	144
Tertiary-level classes in Hydrology	225	22	16	1929	241
Tertiary-level special classes in Meteorology	20	4	1	39	2

1. Holders of higher and lower level doctoral degrees i.e. **Tien si** and **Pho tien si.** 2. Literally, 'multi-branch University'. 3. **My thuat**; according to Bui Phung (1978) 'design' would perhaps be a better translation.

D. HEALTH SERVICES

Table 150: Preventative and curative installations

	1960	1965	1970	1971	1972	1973	1974	1975
Installations:								
Hospitals	65	252	440	431	430	437	441	442
Dispensaries	180	350	595	587	619	698	528	645
Sanatoria (1.)	6	16	73	94	89	92	85	93
Clinics and commune obstetric units (2.)	3298	5463	5692	5690	5699	5673	5591	5567
Beds (a):								
Total (thou.)	48.2	69.7	96.4	102.9	99.4	103.6	104.7	109.9
Of which:								
Hospitals	13.4	19.1	32.8	33.8	33.1	36.8	38.7	40.4
Dispensaries	5.6	8.9	8.5	8.7	9.0	9.7	6.9	8.8
Sanatoria (1.)	2.2	1.6	7.6	7.8	7.2	7.3	7.3	7.4
Clinics and commune obstetric units (2.)	23.9	38.2	44.2	45.1	45.9	46.4	47.5	48.4

(a) Including beds in hospitals, dispensaries, sanatoria
(including leprosy), clinics and commune obstetric units.
1. Vien dieu duong. 2. Tram y te, ho sinh xa.

Table 151: Health Service Staff

	1960	1965	1970	1971	1972	1973	1974	1975
MEDICAL STAFF:								
Doctors	409	1525	3806	4122	4989	5064	5513	5684
Medical assistants	1799	8043	18087	21366	20102	21156	21035	23906
Nurses and orderlies	29117	38928	48677	48427	45499	42345	43499	42354
Midwives	13159	14886	12190	41578	11266	10914	9552	8517
PHARMACISTS								
High-level	172	428	1016	1279	1633	1776	1644	1825
Middle-level	238	703	1908	2335	2739	3196	3044	3082
Assistants	1191	2270	10027	10000	9813	9954	8380	7609

Table 152: Numbers of doctors, medical assistants and sick-beds per 10,000 head of population

	1960	1965	1974	1975
Doctors and medical assistants	1.4	5.1	11.1	12.1
Sick-beds	28	36	42	43

BIBLIOGRAPHY

Note: As well as works cited in the text, this Biblio-graphy contains materials that the authors have found to be of direct value in carrying out their work. It excludes a large number of studies in French, English and Vietnamese that are frequently cited (e.g. see the Bibliographies in Fforde (1982); Spoor (1985); Vickerman (1984)) but are not of great value. Those interested in carrying out further research should make every attempt to acquire a reading knowledge of the language, which is facilitated by its comparatively simple grammar and highly efficient Latin-based script. Such a know-ledge allows access to the abundant vernalucar materials which are to be found in various collections in the West. In Eng-land, those of the British Library are of special value, and include such things as provincial newspapers for certain periods in the early 1960s. A decent regional study of the DRV is sorely needed. It is important also for the researcher not to be distracted by the significant number of works that purport to be based upon 'inside' information that cannot be checked or reproduced: basic research on vernacular materials can be used effectively to understand what goes on in Vietnam.

Abbreviations:

NCKT - '**Nghien** **cuu** **kinh** **te**' ('Economic Research'): Journal of the Economics Institute, Hanoi.
NCLS - '**Nghien** **cuu** **lich** **su**' ('Historical Research'): Journal of the Historical Institute, Hanoi.

Note: Vietnamese authors are listed alphabetically by their first - family - name, and then by their last name.

M.M.Asvenev 1960 '**Demokraticheskaya** **Respublika** **Vyetnam**, **Ekono-mika** **i** **Vneshnyaya** **Torgovlya**' ('The Democratic Republic of

237

Vietnam, Economy and Foreign Trade'), Leningrad.

M.Bernal 1971 'North Vietnam and China - Reflections on a visit', New York Review of Books August 12.

P.Bernard 1934 'Le probleme economique indochinoise', Paris.

C.Bettelheim 1975 'The transition to socialist economy', London.

L.Bianco 1971 'Origins of the Chinese Revolution, 1915-1949', Stanford.

Georges Boudarel ed. 1983 'La bureaucratie au Vietnam', Paris.

F.Bray 1983 'Patterns of evolution in rice-growing societies', Journal of Peasant Studies October.

Bui Phung 1978 'Tu dien Viet-Anh' ('Vietnamese-English Dictionary'), Hanoi University Press.

Bui Cong Trung ed. 1960 'Kinh te Viet nam 1945-60' ('The Vietnamese economy 1945-60'), Hanoi.

W.E.Butler 1983 'Soviet Law', London.

G.Challiand 1969 'The peasants of North Vietnam', Harmondsworth.

E.Chassigneux 1912 'L'irrigation dans le delta du Tonkin' La Geographie.

N.C.Chen 1966 'Chinese economic statistics', Edinburgh.

J.Chesneaux 1961 'French historiography and the evolution of colonial Vietnam', in D.G.E.Hall ed. 'Historians of S.E.Asia', London.

J.Chesneaux 1966 'The Vietnamese nation', Sydney.

W.J.Conyngham 1982 'The modernisation of Soviet industrial management', Cambridge.

M.G.Cotter 1968 'Towards a social history of the Vietnamese Southwards movement', Journal of South East Asian History No.1.

J.Crawfurd 1830 'Journal of an embassy from the Governor-General of India to the courts of Siam and Cochinchina' 2nd ed., London.

R.D.Crotty 1966 'Irish agricultural production: its volume and structure', Cork University Press.

Dang van Ngu 1974 'Thuc hien nen nep quan ly moi o mot hop tac xa vung dong bang' ('Realising a new management system in a delta cooperative'), NCKT No.s 80, 81, 82 and 83. 1974 (A) is No.80; 1974 (B) is No.83.

Dang Phong 1970 'Kinh te thoi nguyen thuy o Viet Nam' ('The economy in primitive times in Vietnam'), Hanoi.

Dang Viet Thanh 1963 'Van de mam mong tu ban chu nghia duoi thoi phong kien o Viet Nam - gop y kien voi Nguyen Viet' ('The problem of the 'germs of capitalism' in feudal Vietnam - a comment on Nguyen Viet'), NCLS 34, 40.

Dao van Tap, ed. 1980 '35 nam kinh te Viet Nam 1945-80' ('35 years of the Vietnamese economy 1945-80'), Hanoi.

P.Devillers 1952 'Histoire du Vietnam de 1940 a 1952', Paris.

Dinh Thu Cuc 1977 'Qua trinh tuong buoc cung co va hoan thien quan he san xuat xa hoi chu nghia trong cac hop tac xa san xuat nong nghiep o mien bac nuoc ta' ('The process of step-by-step reinforcement and improvement of socialist production relations in the agricultural producer co-operatives of the north of our country'), NCLS No.175.

Doan Hai et al 1979 'To chuc va quan ly hop tac xa tieu cong nghiep thu cong nghiep' ('The organisation and management of artisanal and light industrial cooperatives'), Hanoi.

Doan Trong Truyen 1965 'Van de thuong nghiep va gia ca trong cuoc cach mang xa hoi chu nghia o mien Bac nuoc ta' ('The problem of trade and prices in the socialist revolution in the North of our country'), Hanoi.

W.J.Duiker 1976 'The rise of nationalism in Vietnam', Cornell University Press.

EFU (Economics and Finance University) 1962 'Ke hoach kinh te quoc dan' ('Planning the National Economy'), Hanoi.

D.W.Elliott 1976 'Revolutionary re-integration: a comparison of the foundations of post-liberation political systems in North Vietnam and China', Ph.D. Dissertation, Cornell.

D.W.Elliott 1982 'Training revolutionary successors in Viet-nam and China 1958-76: the role of education, science and technology in development', Comparative Communism No.'s 1 and 2.

M.Ellman 1979 'Socialist Planning', Cambridge University Press.

EPU (Economics and Planning University) n/d 'Giao trinh kinh te nong nghiep' ('Course in agricultural economics'), Hanoi.

EPU (Economics and Planning University) 1975 'Giao trinh kinh te cong nghiep' ('Course in industrial economics'), 4th Edition, Hanoi.

B.B.Fall 1956 'The Viet-minh regime', Institute of Pacific Relations, New York.

B.B.Fall 1960 'Le Viet-minh: la republique democratique du Vietnam', Paris.

B.B.Fall 1963 'The two Vietnams: a political and military analysis', New York.

A.J.Fforde 1982 'Problems of agricultural development in North Vietnam', Ph.D. Thesis, Cambridge.

A.J.Fforde 1983 'The historical background to agricultural collectivisation in North Vietnam: the changing role of 'corporate' economic power', Dept. of Economics, Birkbeck College, University of London, Discussion Paper No.148.

A.J.Fforde 1984 'Macro-economic adjustment and structural change in a low-income socialist developing economy - an analytical model', Dept. of Economics, Birkbeck College, University of London, Discussion Paper No.163.

A.J.Fforde 1985 'Law and Socialist Agricultural Development in Vietnam: the Statute for Agricultural Producer Coopera-tives', Review of Socialist Law No.10.

A.J.Fforde 1986 'The unimplementability of policy and the notion of Law in Vietnamese Communist thought', Southeast Asian Journal of Social Science No.1.

A.J.Fforde (forthcoming) 'The Agrarian Question in North Vietnam 1974-79: a study of cooperator resistance to State policy', New York.

A.George 1954 'Autonomie economique, cooperation internationale et changements de structure en Indochine', Paris.

J.Giffen 1981 'The allocation of investment in the Soviet Union: criteria for the efficiency of investment', Soviet Studies No.4.

Alec Gordon 1972 'Socialism and development in North Vietnam' SOAS Left Group.

Alec Gordon 1981 'North Vietnam's collectivisation campaigns: class struggle, production and the "middle-peasant" problem', Journal of Contemporary Asia No. 1.

P.Gourou 1936 'Les paysans du delta tonkinois', Paris.

S.Griffith-Jones 1981 'The role of finance in the transition to socialism', London.

G.C.Hickey 1982 'Free in the forest', London.

Ho Chi Minh 1977 'Selected Writings', Hanoi.

T.Hodgkin 1981 'Vietnam: the revolutionary path', London.

P.J.Honey 1961 'North Vietnam: Quarterly survey', China News Analysis No.401.

P.J.Honey 1963 'North Vietnam: Quarterly survey', China News Analysis No.460.

P.J.Honey 1961 'Modern Vietnamese historiography' in D.G.E.Hall ed. 'Historians of S.E.Asia' London.

P.J.Honey 1964 'North Vietnam: Quarterly survey', China News Analysis No.533

P.J.Honey 1969 'North Vietnam: Quarterly survey', China News Analysis No.760.

F.Houtart and G.Lemercier 1984 'Hai Van - life in a Vietnamese Commune', London.

Huynh Kim Khanh 1982 'Vietnamese Communism 1925-45', Ithaca.

JEC (Joint Economic Committee) 1973 'Soviet economy in a time of change', Washington.

JEC (Joint Economic Committee) 1979 'Soviet economic propects for the 1970s', Washington

M.Kalecki 1957 'The problem of financing economic development', Indian Economic Review No.3.

M.Kalecki 1972 'Problems of financing economic development in a mixed economy', in 'Essays on the economic growth of the socialist and the mixed economy', Cambridge.

J.Kenedi n/d 'Do it yourself', Pluto Press, London.

B.Kiernan 1985 'How Pol Pot came to power', London.

J.Kleinen 1982 'Regional development in Vietnam: an early Communist rising in Quang-Ngai province 1930-31', VZZA University of Amsterdam Working Paper No.5.

M.Kline 1980 'The loss of certainty', Oxford.

J.Kornai 1980 'Economics of shortage', two vols, Amsterdam.

J.Kornai 1982 'Growth, shortage and efficiency', Oxford.

J.Lacouture 1968 'Ho Chi Minh - a political biography',

transl. Peter Wiles, New York.

Lam Quang Huyen 1964 'Xung quanh van de xay dung vung lua trong diem o mien Bac nuoc ta' ('The problem of key rice production points in the North of our country'), NCKT No.24.

Leon Lavallee 1971 'Problemes economiques de la Republique Democratique de Vietnam', Paris.

Le Chau 1966 'Le Vietnam socialiste: une economie de transition, Paris.

Le Duan 1962 'Mot so van de co ban ve cong nghiep hoa XHCN' ('Some basic problems in socialist industrialisation'), Hanoi.

Le Duan 1974 'Giai doan moi cua cach mang va nhiem vu cong doan' ('The new stage of our revolution and the tasks of the trade unions'), in 'Selected Writings', q.v.

Le Duan 1977 'Selected writings', Hanoi.

Le van Hao 1962 'Introduction a l'ethnologie du dinh', Bulletin de la Societe des Etudes indochinoises No.1.

Le Thanh Khoi 1981 'Histoire du Vietnam des origines a 1858', Paris.

Le Thanh Nghi 1974 'Nhiem vu, phuong huong khoi phuc va phat trien kinh te hai nam, 74/75 va ke hoach Nha nuoc nam 1974' ('The tasks and direction of economic reconstruction and development for the two years 1974-75 and the State plan for 1974'), Hanoi.

Le Sy Thiep 1967 'Phat trien nganh co khi dia phuong Ha noi' ('The development of the Hanoi regional engineering branch'), NCKT No.40.

Le Vinh 1965 'Mot vai thanh tich cua 10 nam cong nghiep hoa XHCN' ('Some results from 10 years of industrialisation'), NCKT No.28.

R.Litthauer and N.Uphoff eds. 1972 'The air war in Indochina', Boston.

R.Lucas 1976 'Econometric policy evaluation: a critique', Monetary Economics 1 Supp.

Luu Quang Hoa 1967 'Ve van de quy mo cua hop tac xa san xuat nong nghiep hien nay' ('On the problem of the size of agricultural producer cooperatives at the present time'), NCKT No.37.

D.G.Marr 1971 'Vietnamese anti-colonialism 1885-1925', University of California Press.

D.G.Marr 1981 'Vietnamese tradition on trial 1920-1945', University of California Press.

E.Moise 1976 'Land reform and land reform errors in N. Vietnam', Pacific Affairs Spring.

E.Moise 1977 'Land reform in China and N. Vietnam - revolution at the village level', Ph.D. Dissertation, Michigan.

E.Moise 1983 'Land Reform in China and North Vietnam', University of California Press.

M.J.Murray 1980 'The development of capitalism in colonial Indochina (1870-1940)', University of California Press.

Paul Mus 1949 'The role of the village in Vietnamese politics', <u>Pacific</u> <u>Affairs</u> No.22.

Paul Mus 1950 'Vietnam: <u>sociologie</u> <u>d'une guerre</u>', Paris.

Ng Shui Meng 1974 '<u>The population of Indochina</u>', Singapore Institute of S.E. Asian Studies.

Ngo Vinh Long 1973 '<u>Before the Revolution</u>, Cambridge Mass.

Nguyen The Anh 1967 'Van de lua o Viet Nam trong ban the ky XIX' ('The rice problem in Vietnam during the 19th century'), <u>Su dia</u> No.6.

Nguyen The Anh 1971 '<u>Kinh te va xa hoi Viet Nam</u> duoi cac vua trieu <u>Nguyen</u>' ('<u>Vietnamese economy and society</u> under the <u>Nguyen</u>'), Saigon.

Nguyen Anh Bac 1985 '40 nam cai tao va xay dung kinh te de gianh doc lap dan toc va bao ve vung chac To quoc Viet nam xa hoi chu nghia' ('40 years of economic reform and construction for national independence and a firm defence of the socialist Vietnamese Fatherland'), NCKT No.5.

Nguyen Thanh Binh 1964 '<u>Mot so y kien ve phan phoi va tieu dung</u>' ('<u>Some opinions on distribution and consumption</u>'), Hanoi.

Nguyen Viet Chau, ed. 1963 '<u>Kinh te thuong nghiep Viet-nam</u>' ('<u>Vietnamese trade economics</u>'), Hanoi.

Nguyen Tu Chi n/d '<u>The traditional Viet village in Bac Bo: Its organisational structure and problems</u>', (Foreign Languages Publishing House) Hanoi.

Nguyen Huu Khang 1946 '<u>Le commune annamite. Etude historique, juridique et economique</u>', Paris.

Nguyen van Khoan 1930 'Essai sur le dinh et le culte du genie tutelaire des village au Tonkin', <u>Bulletin de l'Ecole francaise de l'extreme Orient</u> No.30.

Nguyen Xuan Lai 1977 (ed.) '<u>Problemes agricoles (5): la gestion des cooperatives</u>', Etudes Vietnamiennes No. 51, Hanoi.

Nguyen Huu Nghinh and Bui Huy Lo 1978 'May van de nghien cuu ruong dat cong trong cac lang xa nguoi Viet dau the ke 19' ('Some problems of research into communal land in Vietnamese villages of the early 19th century'), <u>Tap chi dan toc hoc</u> (<u>Ethnographic</u> Studies) No.2.

Nguyen Nien 1973 'Mot so van de phap ly trong quan ly tai chinh o xi nghiep cong nghiep quoc doanh hien nay' ('Some current legal problems in the management of State industrial enterprise finances'), <u>Luat Hoc</u> (<u>Legal</u> Studies) No.2.

Nguyen Nien 1974 'Quyen quan ly nghiep vu cua xi nghiep doi voi tai san nha nuoc trong tinh hinh cai tien quan ly xi nghiep cua ta hien nay' ('The enterprise's right of 'operational management' with regard to state assets during the current reforms of enterprise management'), <u>Luat Hoc</u> (<u>Legal</u> Studies) No.7.

Nguyen Chi Thanh 1969 '<u>Ve san xuat nong nghiep va hop tac hoa nong nghiep</u>' ('<u>On agricultural production and agricultural</u>

cooperativisation'), Hanoi.

Nguyen Tran Trong 1980 'Dang ta va viec dua nong nghiep tu san xuat nho len san xuat lon XHCN o nuoc ta' ('Our Party and the task of leading agriculture from small-scale production to large-scale socialist production'), NCKT No.113.

Nguyen Khac Vien 1974 'Histoire du Vietnam', Paris.

Nguyen Viet Chau 1963 'Mam mong tu ban chu nghia o Viet Nam thoi phong kien' ('The germs of capitalism in Vietnam'), NCLS 35 and 36.

Peter Nolan and Suzanne Paine, eds. 1986 (A) 'Re-thinking socialist economics', Oxford.

Peter Nolan and Suzanne Paine 1986 (B) 'Towards an appraisal of the impact of rural reform in China' Cambridge Journal of Economics No. 10.

I.Norlund 1986 'Social and economic studies on Vietnam: an overview' in ed. I.Norlund et al 'Rice societies: Asian problems and prospects', Scandinavian Institute of Asian Studies, Studies on Asian Topics No.10, London.

A.Nove 1977 'The Soviet Economic System', London.

A.Nove 1979 'Political Economy and Soviet Socialism', London.

A.L.A.Patti 1980 'Why Vietnam ?', University of California Press.

Pham Hung 1965 'Vi tri va nhiem vu cua thuong nghiep va gia ca trong cach mang xa hoi chu nghia o mien Bac nuoc ta' ('The role and function of trade and prices in the socialist revolution in the North of our country'), Hanoi.

Pham van Kinh 1971 'Vai y kien ve mot so van de khao co hoc trong quyen 'Kinh te thoi nguyen thuy o Viet Nam'' ('Some opinions on a number of archaelogical problems in the book 'The Vietnamese economy in primitive times''), NCLS 136.

Pham Dinh Tan 1962 'Gop phan nghien cuu 'Cong nghiep quoc doanh trong thoi ky khang chien'' ('A contribution to research into 'State industry in wartime''), Hanoi.

Pham Tran Thinh 1976 'Su dung hop ly nguon lao dong o hop tac xa Dai Thang' ('On the rational use of the labour supply in Dai Thang cooperative'), photo-copy of manuscript, Hanoi University.

Pham Thanh Vien, ed. 1962 'Ke hoach kinh te quoc dan' ('Planning the national economy'), Hanoi.

Phan Khanh 1981 'So thao lich su thuy loi Viet Nam' ('Outline history of water-control in Vietnam'), vol. 1, Hanoi.

P.G.Pickowicz 1981 'Marxist literary thought in China', University of California Press.

D.Pike 1978 'History of Vietnamese Communism 1925-76', Stanford.

D.Pike 1986 'PAVN: People's Army of Vietnam', London.

T.M.Podolski 1973 'Socialist banking and monetary experience: the experience of Poland', Cambridge University Press.

S.Popkin 1979 'The rational peasant: the political economy of rural society in Vietnam', University of California Press.

R.H. Portes 1984 'The theory and measurement of macroeconomic disequilibrium in centrally planned economies', Dept. of Economics, Birkbeck College, University of London, Discussion Paper No.161.

J.S. Prybyla 1966 'Soviet and Chinese aid to North Vietnam', China Quarterly No.27.

A.T. Rambo 1973 'A comparison of peasant social systems of Northern and Southern Vietnam: a study of ecological adaptation, social succession and cultural evolution', Ph.D. Thesis, Southern Illinois University at Carbondale.

'Revue Militaire d'information' 1957 'La guerre de l'Indochine', Paris.

Charles Robequain 1944 'The economic development of French Indochina', Oxford.

I.M. Sachs 1959 'Marxism in Vietnam', in F.N. Trager ed. 'Marxism in South East Asia: a study of four countries', Stanford University Press.

R.L. Sansom 1971 'The economics of insurgency in the Mekong Delta', Cambridge Mass.

J.C. Scott 1976 'The moral economy of the peasant', Yale University Press.

V. Sergeyevich 1965 'Finance and credit in the DRV', Moscow.

T. Shabad 1958 'Economic developments in N. Vietnam', Pacific Affairs March.

A. Shonfield 1965 'Modern capitalism: the changing balance of public and private power', Oxford.

R.B. Smith 1968 'Vietnam and the West', London.

R.B. Smith 1983 'An international history of the Vietnam war: vol. 1 - revolution vs containment 1955-61', London.

R.B. Smith 1985 'An international history of the Vietnam war: vol. 2 - The struggle for South East Asia 1961-65', London.

T.C. Smith 1959 'The agrarian origins of modern Japan', Stanford.

T. Smolsky 1937 'Les statistiques de la population indochinoise', Congres Internationale de la Population, Paris.

Max Spoor 1985 'The economy of North Viet Nam: the first ten years 1955-64 (a study of socialism in the Third World)', M.Phil. Thesis, Institute of Social Studies, The Hague.

J. Stalin 1952 'Economic problems of Socialism in the USSR', Moscow (also Pekin 1972).

Statistical Office (Tong cuc thong ke) 1977 'Tu dien thong ke' ('Statistical Dictionary'), Hanoi.

Statistical Office (Tong cuc thong ke) 1978 'Tinh hinh phat trien Kinh te va Van hoa mien bac xa hoi chu nghia Viet nam 1960-75' 'The Economic and cultural development of Socialist North Vietnam 1960-75', Hanoi.

P.M. Sweezy and C. Bettelhiem 1971 'On the transition to socialism', London.

Systems Analysis Study 1966 quoted in the Pentagon Papers,

Gavel Edition, Boston.

G.T.Tanham 1961 'Communist revolutionary warfare: the Vietminh in Indochina', New York.

K.Taylor 1974 'Review' of 'Lich su Viet Nam vol. 1', Journal of Asian Studies No.2.

K.Taylor 1976 'The birth of Vietnam: Sino-Vietnamese relations to the tenth century and the origins of Vietnamese nationhood', Ph.D. Dissertation, Michigan.

The Dat 1981 'Nen Nong nghiep Viet Nam tu sau Cach mang thang tam nam 1945' ('Vietnamese agriculture since the 1945 August Revolution'), Hanoi.

To Duy 1969 'Mot so van de ve luu thong phan phoi trong thoi ky xay dung chu nghia xa hoi va chong My cuu nuoc hien nay' ('Some problems in circulation and distribution during the period of socialist construction and the current anti-American struggle for national salvation'), Hanoi.

To Minh Trung 1963 'Van de mam mong tu ban chu nghia o Viet Nam' ('The problem of the germs of capitalism in Vietnam'), NCLS 37.

Tran Phuong ed. 1968 'Cach mang ruong dat o Viet nam' ('The land revolution in Vietnam'), Hanoi.

Tran Dinh Thien 1976 'May van de ve phan cong lao dong o hop tac xa Van Tien' ('Some problems of labour allocation in Van Tien cooperative'), NCKT 1976.

Tran van Tra 1982 'Ket thuc cuoc chien tranh 30 nam' ('The ending of a 30 year struggle'), Ho Chi Minh City.

Tran Nhu Trang 1972 'The transformatio of the peasantry in North Vietnam', Doctoral Dissertation, Pittsburg.

Tran Dang Van 1964 'Van de nhan khau khong san xuat nong nghiep o nuoc ta' ('Problems arising in our country from people not involved in agricultural production'), NCKT 21.

Truong Nhu Tang 1986 'Journal of a Vietcong', London.

R.F.Turner 1975 Vietnamese communism: its origins and development, Stanford.

TWD (Trung Uong Dang - Party Centre) 1963 'Nghi Quyet cua hoi nghi Trung uong lan thu 5 (7/61) ve van de phat trien nong nghiep trong ke hoach nam nam lan thu nhat (1961-65)' ('Resolution of the 5th Plenum (7/61) on the development of agriculture during the First Five Year Plan (1961-65)'), 2nd ed., Hanoi.

TWD (Trung Uong Dang - Party Centre) 1980 'Mot so van kien cua Trung uong Dang ve phat trien cong nghiep' ('Some documents of the Party Centre on industrial development'), Hanoi.

UKX (Uy ban Khoa hoc Xa hoi - Social Science Committee) 1971 'Lich su Viet nam tap 1' ('History of Vietnam vol.1'), Hanoi.

Van Tan 1970 'Tai sao o Viet Nam tu ban chu nghia khong ra doi trong long che do phong kien?' ('Why did capitalism not arise from feudalism in Vietnam?'), NCLS 130.

Van Tap 1960 'Thang loi hoa binh cua duong loi cai tao doi voi cong thuong nghiep tu ban chu nghia o mien bac Viet-nam' ('The peaceful victory of the reform of capitalist trade in north Vietnam'), in ed. Bui Cong Trung 1960.

VBS (Vu Bien Soan, Ban tuyen huan trung uong - Editoral Dept. of the Central Propaganda Dept.) 1978 and 1979 'Lich su Dang Cong san Viet Nam trich van kien Dang' ('History of the Vietnamese Communist Party: excerpts from Party documents'), vols 1 & 2 (1978) vol 3 (1979).

Andy Vickerman 1982 'Collectivisation in the Democratic Republic of Vietnam, 1960-66: a comment', Journal of Contemporary Asia No.4.

Andy Vickerman 1984 Agriculture in the DRV: the fate of the peasantry under "premature transition to socialism", Ph.D. Thesis, Cambridge.

Andy Vickerman 1985 'A note on the role of industry in Vietnam's development strategy', Journal of Contemporary Asia No.2.

M.Vickery 1984 'Cambodia 1975-82', Hemel Hempstead.

VSH (Vien Su Hoc - Historical Institute) 1975 'Viet Nam nhung su kien 1945-75' ('Vietnamese Dates 1945-75'), two vols, Hanoi.

Vo Nhan Tri 1985 'Vietnam: the Third Five Year Plan 1981-85 - performance and limits', Indochina Report No.4.

Vu Quoc Tuan and Dinh van Hoang 1962 'Ban ve nhip do phat trien kinh te quoc dan mien bac' ('Discussion of the speed of national economic development in the North'), Hanoi.

K.-E.Wadekin 1982 'Agrarian policies in Communist Europe', Dordrecht.

C.P.White 1979 'The peasants and the Party in the Vietnamese Revolution', in D.B.Miller, ed., 'Peasants and politics: grass roots reactions to change in Asia', London.

C.P.White 1981 'Agrarian Reform and National Liberation in the Vietnamese Revolution: 1920-1957', Ph.D. Thesis, Cornell.

C.P.White 1982 'Debates in Vietnamese development policy', IDS Discussion Paper No.171.

P.J.D.Wiles 1962 'The political economy of Communism', Oxford.

P.J.D.Wiles 1977 'Economic Institutions compared', Oxford.

A.B.Woodside 1970 'Decolonisation and agricultural reform in North Vietnam', Asian Survey August.

A.B.Woodside 1971 'Vietnam and the Chinese model', Cambridge, Mass.

A.B.Woodside 1976 'Community and Revolution in modern Vietnam', Boston

A.B.Woodside 1983 'The triumphs and failures of mass education in Vietnam', Pacific Affairs No.3.